And Then They Came For Me

And Then They Came For Me

The Lasantha Wickrematunge Story

Raine Wickrematunge

AuthorHouse™ UK Ltd.
1663 Liberty Drive
Bloomington, IN 47403 USA
www.authorhouse.co.uk
Phone: 0800.197.4150

© 2013 by Raine Wickrematunge. All rights reserved.

No part of this book may be reproduced, stored in a retrieval system, or transmitted by any means without the written permission of the author.

Published by AuthorHouse   05/09/2013

ISBN: 978-1-4817-8990-5 (sc)
ISBN: 978-1-4817-8991-2 (e)

Cover photo by Lalith Perera

This book is printed on acid-free paper.

Because of the dynamic nature of the Internet, any web addresses or links contained in this book may have changed since publication and may no longer be valid. The views expressed in this work are solely those of the author and do not necessarily reflect the views of the publisher, and the publisher hereby disclaims any responsibility for them.

Contents

Preface xiii
Prologue xv

Chapter 1	Early Signs	1
Chapter 2	Foray into Journalism	17
Chapter 3	Marriage, Fatherhood & Politics	29
Chapter 4	Who is Suranimala?	44
Chapter 5	The Sunday Leader	50
Chapter 6	Unleashing of the Goons	81
Chapter 7	Lasantha Outfoxes the Censor: 'Palaly not under attack'	105
Chapter 8	A President's Fury	122
Chapter 9	A Move to Arrest the Editor	137
Chapter 10	The Murder of Truth	151
Chapter 11	Aftermath	176
Chapter 12	The Murder Inquiry That Isn't	193

The Big Stories 200
Awards 207

"Cowards die many times before their deaths;
The valiant never taste of death but once."
—William Shakespeare in Julius Caesar

This book is dedicated to those gutsy men and women all over the world who have been harassed/abducted/tortured/murdered for daring to report the truth, and others who continue to do so with remarkable courage and spirit under the most trying circumstances.

Foreword

IT was in 2009 that I learned of the bravery of Lasantha Manilal Wickrematunge. It was also the year of Wickrematunge's assassination and the year that the International Press Institute honored the Sri Lankan journalist with its highest honor: IPI World Press Freedom Hero.

The memory of Lasantha, who was the editor of Sri Lanka's pioneering *Sunday Leader* newspaper, has been burned into the minds of his colleagues around the world not only for his commitment to exposing corruption and laying bare the truth behind the actions of Sri Lanka's government, but the circumstances surrounding his death.

As a good investigative journalist, Lasantha was smart and observant. He understood that there were those who wanted to see him dead. In fact, he anticipated it, going as far as to write a compelling editorial predicting his death.

In the editorial published in the *Sunday Leader* three days after his death, Lasantha wrote:

> "It is well known that I was on two occasions brutally assaulted, while on another my house was sprayed with machine-gun fire. Despite the government's sanctimonious assurances, there was never a serious police inquiry into the perpetrators of these attacks, and the attackers were never apprehended. In all these cases, I have reason to believe the attacks were inspired by the government. When finally I am killed, it will be the government that kills me."

In that poignant piece, Lasantha noted: "I hope my murder will not be seen as a defeat of freedom but an inspiration."

Indeed, inspiration is one of the motivations behind "And Then They Came for Me". This memoir will serve to inspire journalists old and new and, in particular, those who face challenges and pressures from those who would like to silence them.

Lasantha's irrepressible journalism drive embodied the fearless quest of the newspaper he edited, *The Sunday Leader,* to deliver impartial, critical information to the public it served: all Sri Lankans. In the chilling yet powerful editorial he wrote predicting his own assassination, he ended with this unwavering commitment:

> "If you remember nothing else, remember this: The Leader is there for you, be you Sinhalese, Tamil, Muslim, low-caste, homosexual,

dissident or disabled. Its staff will fight on, unbowed and unafraid, with the courage to which you have become accustomed. Do not take that commitment for granted. Let there be no doubt that whatever sacrifices we journalists make, they are not made for our own glory or enrichment: they are made for you. Whether you deserve their sacrifice is another matter. As for me, God knows I tried."

These words also underscore the extraordinary sense of selfless sacrifice that drives journalists across the world, on every continent, who look death in the face because of their work, and do not waver, do not bow, to the cynical ruthless attempts to silence them by those who fear the truth. Lasantha constituted a perfect example of a newspaper man who in his hour of gravest peril lost none of his courage and dignity, but met his end and paid the ultimate price for his devotion to journalism with his held head high, proverbially staring his killer or killers in the eye.

In the editorial, Lasantha paid tribute to the other brave journalists who share a similar plight, indicating that the killers of journalists will ultimately not triumph.

"That The Sunday Leader will continue fighting the good fight, too, is written. For I did not fight this fight alone. Many more of us have to be—and will be—killed before The Leader is laid to rest. I hope my assassination will be seen not as a defeat of freedom but an inspiration for those who survive to step up their efforts. Indeed, I hope that it will help galvanise forces that will usher in a new era of human liberty in our beloved motherland."

Who better to write this fitting tribute than Lasantha's ex-wife Raine Wickrematunge, a journalist in her own right? A wonderful writer, the book is filled with details and nuances of Lasantha's life. It is a book too long in the making and is a must-read for anyone aspiring to journalism or anyone disillusioned about having chosen this most noble of professions.

The International Press Institute and its hundreds of members around the world welcome the publication of this book. It is a fitting tribute to Lasantha's life and to the plight of journalists around the world who have fought for truth, for understanding, for the right of the people to know.

Alison Bethel McKenzie,
Executive Director, International Press Institute
April 2013

Preface

"Throughout the centuries there were men who took first steps down new roads, armed with nothing more than their own vision"—Ann Rand

SOON after Lasantha was killed in January 2009, people asked whether I was considering writing a book on his life. Indeed it was a remarkable life, an inspiring story that certainly needed to be told. However, at the time, shattered as I was, trying to make sense of what had happened, floundering around in an attempt to pick up the pieces and move on with our emotionally fragile children, the last thing I could think of was writing Lasantha's story. I couldn't even bring myself to read accounts of his death in the media or watch any of his old television programs. My daughter Ahimsa and I once fished out a tape from a trip we had made to Movie World in the Gold Coast some years back. As I was about to hit the 'play' button, we both froze; we became painfully aware that we simply couldn't bring ourselves to watch those recordings of Lasantha on that wonderful trip. It was too distressing.

In that troubled scenario, what strength would I have to revive personal memories, go through the painful process of retracing his steps and research his work? It was impossible.

It took almost three years for the wounds to begin to heal and enable me to take a detailed look back on my life with Lasantha. And sit down to write what was to become this book.

Most of what I have written about his childhood was derived first-hand from stories Lasantha himself told me. Some were related to me over the years by his mother Chandra. His sisters, brothers and friends filled-in information as well and I'm ever grateful to them. The rest of course consists of stories and anecdotes from our life together and his wide and varied experiences as a journalist.

As background to the narrative, in many instances I have provided details of the political and media climate which prevailed at the time and while hoping this doesn't detract too much from the story of Lasantha, I must emphasise that providing this background material was vital to the story.

I hope you enjoy the story of Lasantha, a man who knew no fear, a man who, armed with nothing more than a humble pen, tons of courage and a stoic resistance to the bullying and harassment meted out to the Sri Lankan media in general and himself in particular, strove to change for the better the society he lived in, to foster independent thinking and instil hope in a people for too long subjugated by those more powerful. A man who consistently called for accountability and transparency in our leaders while laying bare their many transgressions. A man who, within his newspaper pages, forged a battle against the oppressive jackboots of tyranny. His is indeed a remarkable tale of a pen-wielding Braveheart of our times, a modern day David who stood tall against the mighty goliaths.

It is the story of Lasantha Wickrematunge, a man who has inspired thousands. A man whose story needed to be told.

I take this opportunity to thank those good, decent people who our family has never had the opportunity to thank—the good Samaritans who came to Lasantha's aid when he lay grievously wounded and dying inside his car on that terrible day in 2009. To them he was a stranger, yet simple humanity overrode their own personal work commitments as they rushed him to hospital, holding him all the way and encouraging him to hang on.

Thank you also to the doctors who battled to save his life, the hospital staff, those who organised the funeral and to everyone who attended and helped in numerous ways during those darkest hours.

A big thank you also to every single person who helped me along the way as I worked through the manuscript of this book and to the publisher for making my dream of telling the world Lasantha's story, a reality.

Raine Wickrematunge
April 2013

Prologue

"I hope my assassination will not be seen as a defeat of freedom but an inspiration for those who survive to step up their efforts. Indeed, I hope that it will help galvanise forces that will usher in a new era of human liberty in our beloved motherland."—Lasantha Wickrematunge, Editor, The Sunday Leader.

THE morning of January 8, 2009

In the noisy rush-hour traffic on Attidiya Road in Colombo's seaside suburb of Mt. Lavinia, a silver Toyota Corolla wends its way south towards Ratmalana. At the best of times on Colombo's hot, dusty roads, traffic is thick and tempers thin and this Thursday morning too, everyone is caught up in the scramble of trying to make it to their individual destinations on time.

Behind the wheel of the Toyota, a man checks his rear view mirror every few seconds. Black-clad men on four motorcycles have been whizzing in and out of range for some time now and his office has called with the news that one of the bikes has trailed him from the minute he left his Nugegoda home.

The man, Lasantha Wickrematunge, is Editor of *The Sunday Leader* newspaper and a brilliant investigative journalist who has over a span of some 15 years, collected an arsenal of formidable enemies. A potent combination of courage, tenacity and skill has seen him expose some of the most groundbreaking stories of his time. Many have embarrassed and angered successive heads of state and other prominent individuals. Some have rocked the very foundations of powerful institutions. And the genius of his craft has set a very high benchmark for fellow journalists.

Today, there's urgency in his wheels. Thursday is a busy day at the office of his Sunday newspaper; it is the day when the main section begins to take shape and desk heads, reporters, sub-editors and page-layout artists trek in and out of his office reporting progress and receiving direction. It is also the day he hand-writes 'Inside Politics,' the long and exhaustive weekly column that has over the years amassed a reverential following. In addition to all this, he has an 11.30 meeting with the Leader of the Opposition.

The office, Leader Publications, is located at 24, Katukurunduwatte Road in Ratmalana, only a couple of kilometers away, and Wickrematunge is confident he still has a good chance of making it to the office safely.

He continues to drive, watchful and alert. Youthful for his 50 years, he is today dressed in black pants and white shirt, hair combed back—every inch the good-looking maverick. Right hand on the steering wheel, in his left hand he clutches his mobile phone into which he talks from time to time.

As the men hasten their pursuit and the hum of their engines revs into a menacing rumble, it dawns on him that this is no idle threat. He has been beaten and assaulted before, his home fired at, the presses set ablaze, but now the forces against him seem to have only murder on their minds.

Usually dismissive of warnings to be heedful by those concerned about his safety, it is only the steely determination of the men hot on his heels that prompts him to make the next call. It is to a friend who has close ties to the President of the country. Wickrematunge tells him of the ominous trail and the friend advises him to drive to the nearest police station.

Wickrematunge is a man who has not known fear. Never in all his 50 years has he cowered before intimidation or quaked in the face of dire threat. Now though, his heart beats fast; the claws of dread tighten their grip and foreboding casts a dark shadow. Is this then the day it all ends? Is this the day when his pen is finally stilled? When the relentless battle he has fought long and hard to expose the corrupt and give a voice to the oppressed, is laid to rest? Less than an hour earlier he had said goodbye to his 17-year-old daughter who had hugged him and cautioned him to be careful. Now, her words are echoing in his mind.

The traffic is thinning and as the car approaches Malagala Model Primary School, a bus that has been travelling ahead of him comes to a halt forcing Wickrematunge to slam his brakes. It gives the motorcyclists an opportunity to strike. They fire up their engines and surround the vehicle. Two men jump off one of the motorbikes and sprint towards the car. One of them strikes the windscreen with a weapon covered in newspaper and the other smashes the driver's side window. One of the men then lowers a concealed weapon through the window and attacks him brutally, inflicting a lethal injury to his right temple.

Bleeding profusely from the ear, the Editor, still clutching his phone, slumps onto the passenger seat as the assailants jump back on their bikes and speed away, merging into the mid-morning traffic.

Life is slowly ebbing away and the minutes that tick by seem like an eternity. He lies bleeding, moaning softly. The world is becoming a blur.

In the lifeblood that flows is written the story of indomitable human spirit, unwavering resolve, fearlessness and fortitude. Every crimson drop that falls tells the story of a good man, a visionary who would never give up his crusade for justice and equality. A man who, in his own words, 'walked tall and bowed to no man.'

While many had pandered to the powerful and wallowed in shameful servitude, he had fought the good battle long and hard, doggedly pursuing the cause of truth and justice. He had lived, breathed and was now, finally dying in the pursuit of the truth. Indeed he had said, "It has long been written that my life would be taken, and by whom. All that remains to be written is when."

As he had so articulately expressed in a chillingly prophetic editorial, they had finally come for him.

The Editorial

And Then They Came For Me

'NO other profession calls on its practitioners to lay down their lives for their art save the armed forces and, in Sri Lanka, journalism. In the course of the past few years, the independent media have increasingly come under attack. Electronic and print-media institutions have been burnt, bombed, sealed and coerced. Countless journalists have been harassed, threatened and killed. It has been my honour to belong to all those categories and now, especially the last.

I have been in the business of journalism a good long time. Indeed, 2009 will be *The Sunday Leader*'s 15th year. Many things have changed in Sri Lanka during that time, and it does not need me to tell you that the greater part of that change has been for the worse. We find ourselves in the midst of a civil war ruthlessly prosecuted by protagonists whose bloodlust knows no bounds. Terror, whether perpetrated by terrorists or the state, has become the order of the day. Indeed, murder has become the primary tool whereby the state seeks to control the organs of liberty. Today it is the journalists, tomorrow it will be the judges. For neither group have the risks ever been higher or the stakes lower.

Why then do we do it? I often wonder that. After all, I too am a father of three wonderful children. I too have responsibilities and obligations that transcend my profession, be it the law or journalism. Is it worth the risk? Many people tell me it is not. Friends tell me to revert to the bar, and goodness knows it offers a better and safer livelihood. Others, including political leaders on both sides, have at various times sought to induce me to take to politics, going so far as to offer me ministries of my choice. Diplomats, recognising the risk journalists face in Sri Lanka, have offered me safe passage and the right of residence in their countries. Whatever else I may have been stuck for, I have not been stuck for choice.

But there is a calling that is yet above high office, fame, lucre and security. It is the call of conscience.

The Sunday Leader has been a controversial newspaper because we say it like we see it: whether it be a spade, a thief or a murderer, we call it by that name. We do not hide behind euphemism. The investigative articles we print are supported by documentary evidence thanks to the public-spiritedness of citizens who at great risk to themselves pass on this material to us. We have exposed scandal after scandal, and never once in these 15 years has anyone proved us wrong or successfully prosecuted us.

The free media serve as a mirror in which the public can see itself sans mascara and styling gel. From us you learn the state of your nation, and especially its management by the people you elected to give your children a better future. Sometimes the image you see in that mirror is not a pleasant one. But while you may grumble in the privacy of your armchair, the journalists who hold the mirror up to you do so publicly and at great risk to themselves. That is our calling, and we do not shirk it.

Every newspaper has its angle, and we do not hide the fact that we have ours. Our commitment is to see Sri Lanka as a transparent, secular, liberal democracy. Think about those words, for they each has profound meaning. Transparent because government must be openly accountable to the people and never abuse their trust. Secular because in a multi-ethnic and multi-cultural society such as ours, secularism offers the only common ground by which we might all be united. Liberal because we recognise that all human beings are created different, and we need to accept others for what they are and not what we would like them to be. And democratic . . . well, if you need me to explain why that is important, you'd best stop buying this paper.

The Sunday Leader has never sought safety by unquestioningly articulating the majority view. Let's face it, that is the way to sell newspapers. On the contrary, as our opinion pieces over the years amply demonstrate, we often voice ideas that many people find distasteful. For example, we have consistently espoused the view that while separatist terrorism must be eradicated, it is more important to address the root causes of terrorism, and urged government to view Sri Lanka's ethnic strife in the context of history and not through the telescope of terrorism. We have also agitated against state terrorism in the so-called war against terror, and made no secret of our horror that Sri Lanka is the only country in the world routinely to bomb its own citizens. For these views we have been labelled traitors, and if this be treachery, we wear that label proudly.

Many people suspect that *The Sunday Leader* has a political agenda: it does not. If we appear more critical of the government than of the opposition it is only because we believe that—pray excuse cricketing argot—there is no point in bowling to the fielding side. Remember that for the few years of our existence in which the UNP was in office, we proved to be the biggest thorn in its flesh, exposing excess and corruption wherever it occurred. Indeed, the steady stream of embarrassing exposes´ we published may well have served to precipitate the downfall of that government.

Neither should our distaste for the war be interpreted to mean that we support the Tigers. The LTTE are among the most ruthless and bloodthirsty organisations ever to have infested the planet. There is no gainsaying that it must be eradicated. But to do so by violating the rights of Tamil citizens, bombing and shooting them mercilessly, is not only wrong but shames the Sinhalese, whose claim to be custodians of the *dhamma* is forever called into question by this savagery, much of which is unknown to the public because of censorship.

What is more, a military occupation of the country's North and East will require the Tamil people of those regions to live eternally as second-class citizens, deprived of all self respect. Do not imagine that you can placate them by showering "development" and "reconstruction" on them in the post-war era. The wounds of war will scar them forever, and you will also have an even more bitter and hateful Diaspora to contend with. A problem amenable to a political solution will thus become a festering wound that will yield strife for all eternity. If I seem angry and frustrated, it is only because most of my countrymen—and all of the government—cannot see this writing so plainly on the wall.

It is well known that I was on two occasions brutally assaulted, while on another my house was sprayed with machine-gun fire. Despite the government's sanctimonious assurances, there was never a serious police inquiry into the perpetrators of these attacks, and the attackers were never apprehended. In all these cases, I have reason to believe the attacks were inspired by the government. When finally I am killed, it will be the government that kills me.

The irony in this is that, unknown to most of the public, Mahinda and I have been friends for more than a quarter century. Indeed, I suspect that I am one of the few people remaining who routinely addresses him by his first name and uses the familiar Sinhala address *oya* when talking to him. Although I do not attend the meetings he periodically holds for newspaper editors, hardly a month passes when we do not meet, privately or with a few close friends present, late at night at President's House. There we swap yarns, discuss politics and joke about the good old days. A few remarks to him would therefore be in order here.

Mahinda, when you finally fought your way to the SLFP presidential nomination in 2005, nowhere were you welcomed more warmly than in this column. Indeed, we broke with a decade of tradition by referring to you throughout by your first name. So well known were your commitments to human rights and liberal values that we ushered you in like a breath of fresh air. Then, through an act of folly, you got yourself involved in the Helping Hambantota scandal. It was after a lot of soul-searching that we broke the story, at the same time urging you to return the money. By the time you did so several weeks later, a great blow had been struck to your reputation. It is one you are still trying to live down.

You have told me yourself that you were not greedy for the presidency. You did not have to hanker after it: it fell into your lap. You have told me that your sons are your greatest joy, and that you love spending time with them, leaving your brothers to operate the machinery of state. Now, it is clear to all who will see that that machinery has operated so well that my sons and daughter do not themselves have a father.

In the wake of my death I know you will make all the usual sanctimonious noises and call upon the police to hold a swift and thorough inquiry. But like all the inquiries you have ordered in the past, nothing will come of this one, too. For truth be told, we both know who will be behind my death, but dare not call his name. Not just my life, but yours too, depends on it.

Sadly, for all the dreams you had for our country in your younger days, in just three years you have reduced it to rubble. In the name of patriotism you have trampled on human rights, nurtured unbridled corruption and squandered public money like no other President before you. Indeed, your conduct has been like a small child suddenly let loose in a toyshop. That analogy is perhaps inapt because no child could have caused so much blood to be spilled on this land as you have, or trampled on the rights of its citizens as you do. Although you are now so drunk with power that you cannot see it, you will come to regret your sons having so rich an inheritance of blood. It can only bring tragedy. As for me, it is with a clear conscience that I go to meet my Maker. I wish, when your time finally comes, you could do the same. I wish.

As for me, I have the satisfaction of knowing that I walked tall and bowed to no man. And I have not travelled this journey alone. Fellow journalists in other branches of the media walked with me: most of them are now dead, imprisoned without trial or exiled in far-off lands. Others walk in the shadow of death that your Presidency has cast on the freedoms for which you once fought so hard. You will never be allowed to forget that my death took place under your watch. As anguished as I know you will be, I also know that you will have no choice but to protect my killers: you will see to it that the guilty one is never convicted. You have no choice. I feel sorry for you, and Shiranthi will have a long time to spend on her knees when next she goes for Confession for it is not just her owns sins which she must confess, but those of her extended family that keeps you in office.

As for the readers of *The Sunday Leader*, what can I say but Thank You for supporting our mission. We have espoused unpopular causes, stood up for those too feeble to stand up for themselves, locked horns with the high and mighty so swollen with power that they have forgotten their roots, exposed corruption and the waste of your hard-earned tax rupees, and made sure that whatever the propaganda of the day, you were allowed to hear a contrary view. For this I—and my family—have now paid the price that I have long known I will one day have to pay. I am—and have always been—ready for that. I have done nothing to prevent this outcome: no security, no precautions. I want my murderer to know that I am not a coward like he is, hiding behind human shields while condemning thousands of innocents to death. What am I among so many? It has long been written that my life would be taken, and by whom. All that remains to be written is when.

That *The Sunday Leader* will continue fighting the good fight, too, is written. For I did not fight this fight alone. Many more of us have to be—and will be—killed before *The Leader* is laid to rest. I hope my assassination will be seen not as a defeat of freedom but an inspiration for those who survive to step up their efforts. Indeed, I hope that it will help galvanise forces that will usher in a new era of human liberty in our beloved motherland. I also hope it will open the eyes of your President to the fact that however many are slaughtered in the name of patriotism, the human spirit will endure and flourish. Not all the Rajapakses combined can kill that.

People often ask me why I take such risks and tell me it is a matter of time before I am bumped off. Of course I know that: it is inevitable. But if we do not speak out now, there will be no one left to speak for those who cannot, whether they be ethnic minorities, the disadvantaged or the persecuted. An example that has inspired me throughout my career in journalism has been that of the German theologian, Martin *Niemöller*. In his youth he was an anti-Semite and an admirer of Hitler. As Nazism took hold in Germany, however, he saw Nazism for what it was: it was not just the Jews Hitler sought to extirpate, it was just about anyone with an alternate point of view. *Niemöller* spoke out, and for his trouble was incarcerated in the Sachsenhausen and Dachau concentration camps from 1937 to 1945, and very nearly executed. While incarcerated, *Niemöller* wrote a poem that, from the first time I read it in my teenage years, stuck hauntingly in my mind:

> *First they came for the Jews*
> > *and I did not speak out because I was not a Jew.*
> *Then they came for the Communists*
> > *and I did not speak out because I was not a Communist.*
> *Then they came for the trade unionists*
> > *and I did not speak out because I was not a trade unionist.*
> *Then they came for me*
> > *and there was no one left to speak out for me.*

If you remember nothing else, remember this: *The Leader* is there for you, be you Sinhalese, Tamil, Muslim, low-caste, homosexual, dissident or disabled. Its staff will fight on, unbowed and unafraid, with the courage to which you have become accustomed. Do not take that commitment for granted. Let there be no doubt that whatever sacrifices we journalists make, they are not made for our own glory or enrichment: they are made for you. Whether you deserve their sacrifice is another matter. As for me, God knows I tried.'

* * *

CHAPTER ONE
Early Signs

> *"There is always one moment in childhood when the door opens and lets the future in."*—Deepak Chopra, Physician, Spiritual Author/Speaker

WHEN the fiercely hot month of April dawns each year, great festive cheer engulfs the land of Lanka. As the harvesting season ends and preparations for the New Year begin in earnest, the seasonal song of the koel grows shrill and the air is filled with the fragrance of *mung-kevum* drenched in sweet treacle frying on outdoor hearths.

In 1958 Kotahena in the north of Colombo, the Wickrematunge household bustled with New Year anticipation. Mother Chandra had put her expertise with the needle into good use and sewn new, bright coloured outfits for her five children; the young ones couldn't wait for the celebrations to begin on the 13th. For this family however, the festive preparations coincided with another big event; they were about to have an addition to the family.

On April 5, as the first rays of light embraced the eastern skies, Chandra went into labour; it was surmised that perhaps the gruelling task of pounding raw, wet rice in the mortar to prepare the sweetmeat *athirasa* the previous evening had hastened the onset of labour. Chandra was admitted to De Soysa Hospital for Women in Borella where at precisely 14 minutes past nine that beautiful, blue-skied morning, a bawling baby boy was born.

Harris and Chandra took the tiny infant home and he became the darling of the family, a thing of curiosity and wonderment for the older children and their friends. He was named Lasantha Manilal Wickrematunge.

* * *

In the 1930s, the Wickrematunges were a fairly prominent family living in the bustlingly township of Kotahena in Colonial Ceylon's north Colombo region.

Weda Arachchige Wilson Wickrematunge had migrated northward from the southern coastal town of Galle, and by dint of sheer hard work and shrewd business sense, built up considerable wealth which he invested in small housing properties scattered across Kotahena, in the adjoining seaside suburb of Mutwal and in the hills of Nuwara Eliya. Wilson had married Rosalind Gertrude de Silva, daughter of a prominent Ayurvedic physician from Nuwara Eliya and the couple led a comfortable life with their large brood in one of the houses they owned on Wasala Road, Kotahena's burgeoning residential precinct.

Wilson's properties were all leased and rented out; he was what one would describe as a prosperous landlord. Yet, he was not careless with his wealth and impressed upon his family the many advantages of thrift and frugality.

Among Wilson and Rosalind's offspring was the energetic young go-getter Harischandra or Harris as he came to be known. The older of two boys among five girls, Harris, born in 1920, was a livewire with an unbridled passion for life. It was young Harris who would accompany his father when the older man set off on his regular tenant visits. Although Wilson owned a motor car, he would choose to travel by foot when he undertook these rent-collecting excursions and Harris tagged along the busy, dusty streets, trying in earnest to keep out of the harsh sun by staying within the shadow cast by the umbrella his father held aloft. When he grew up to be a young man, Harris was entrusted with the rent-collection task which bit of authority he enjoyed immensely.

When World War II broke out in 1939 and the anti-German coalition grew, young men from Ceylon began volunteering for service. Harris enlisted with the Ceylon Defense Force and was assigned to serve in Egypt as part of the Royal Army Service Corps. He however was terribly unimpressed with the many privations of war and the highly regimented army life. The pain of separation from creature comforts and loved ones was only softened by the close bonds and lasting friendships forged with other soldiers.

While still on the fringes of war, Harris, 20 years old at the time, received sad news from home. His father, still in his fifties, had passed away unexpectedly from a heart attack leaving the family reeling in shock. The strong matriarchal spirit in Rosalind rose to the fore and gathering her wits and every available resource, she steered the family through the dark and difficult times.

Back in Egypt after the funeral, Harris began suffering severe homesickness. He dispatched home regular missives detailing the many ordeals and hardships he was forced to endure. One day his anxious mother received news that her son had sustained an injury to his right arm in a horrific accident and was running a high fever. A distressed Rosalind wasted no time in making arrangements for her beloved son to be 'rescued' and shipped back to the safe shores of Ceylon.

Harris hero-worshipped his maternal uncle George Edmond de Silva[1], the tall, handsome, genial, people's man from Kandy who served as Minister of Health in the Donoughmore era and later as Minister of Fisheries and Industries in the first Parliament of Ceylon. Especially during elections, Harris would spend extended periods of time in his uncle's political fiefdom in the hills, learning from him the craft of politics that was to be his own calling one day. George's boundless service to the poor and his untiring championing of the cause of the peasantry, crushed under colonial might as they were, also served as great inspiration to the young Harris.

Considered an outsider by the haughty blue-bloods and snooty aristocrats who dominated the electorate, George had suffered numerous hurts and humiliations at the hands of his political adversaries during his early days in politics. Even before entering politics he had experienced the rabid discrimination of sections of Colonial Ceylon. When he entered the Kandy Bar as a lawyer, on his first day in court, the Dutch Burgher lawyers and several highbrow Kandyans who were not happy that an 'intruder' was sullying their sacred precinct, staged a protest walk-out. With just the British magistrate remaining in court, George went on to win his very first case.

It was to his eternal credit that George conquered racial and caste prejudice and forged ahead, establishing his name in history not only as a reformist and founding father of Independent Ceylon but as one of the greatest sons of Lanka in recognition of the invaluable services rendered to a nation.

George, affectionately referred to as 'Apey George' by his adoring constituents, later married Agnes Nell, daughter of the provincial engineer Paul Nell, a beautiful and gracious woman who, together with her husband, fought for independence, women's rights and reform on several other fronts.

* * *

It was while spending time with his uncle George in Kandy that Harris first laid eyes on Chandrawathie Dharmawardene, the only child of Albano Dharmawardene—a man of erudition and Principal of Pothupitiya Maha Vidyalaya, Wadduwa—and his wife Louisa. When Harris first beheld the pretty, fair and petite damsel as she wandered dreamily along the bund of the Kandy Lake with her chaperone in tow, he was mesmerised. It helped that Chandra was on friendly terms with some of George E. de Silva's family and the thoroughly-smitten Harris lost no time in wooing her with single-minded devotion.

Albano frowned upon this determined young man's advances towards his daughter and Harris realised he had to impress the prospective father-in-law if he was to have any chance of taking Chandra's hand in marriage. Learning that Albano was a Sinhala scholar, he enlisted the support of an acquaintance with a literary bent to pen a letter in high-flown Sinhala to Albano, introducing himself and indicating his interest in marrying Chandra. Harris then signed the letter and sent it off to Albano, who under the misconception this was Harris' writing, was duly impressed.

Harris' political connections must also have influenced Albano's decision to give his only child in marriage to this eager young man. After all, George, Harris' uncle, was one of the most loved and respected men in Kandy at the time.

In 1945, Harris and Chandra, 25 and 23 years old at the time, were married and set up home in Kandy. Two miscarriages later, in 1947 their first child was born and the doting parents named the beautiful little baby girl Savithri Kamini.

Not long after, the young family moved away from Kandy and returned to Colombo settling down in the Wickrematunge family turf of Kotahena.

Every morning Harris dressed up smartly and set off to work.

"Where do you work?" his naive wife would ask him.

"Home and Company," he would reply poker-faced before rushing out of the door.

It was much later that Chandra finally understood what he meant. He didn't have a job!

As time passed, Harris could not ignore the weight of responsibility that came with fatherhood; he pulled up his socks, sought employment and was hired by a private firm in Colombo. More babies began arriving in rapid succession; two years after daughter Savithri was born, Rukmani Malkanthi came along, followed by Lal Raj in 1950 and Anil Kumar in 1952.

Anil was a premature baby, a wee little thing that felt like a plucked bird in his mother's palm. The doctors at the maternity hospital didn't have any hope for the tyke and advised the parents the baby would not survive the night.

They however didn't reckon with the fierce protective streak in father Harris. He took the baby home swathed in a little blanket and nurtured it with the help of nothing more than a naked light bulb and an ink pipette to keep it warm and nourished. Under his loving care, the baby took a turn for the better and began to thrive.

After the fifth baby Kumudini Dushianthi was born in 1955, Chandra had her hands full. Her home was packed to the rafters and she wasn't inclined towards any more additions to the brood. When there was a nagging suspicion she might be pregnant again, friends suggested she take up the skipping rope. If she did indeed follow their advice, it proved that her sixth and last baby was made of sterner stuff; he was not about to go anywhere. And so on the warm Saturday morning of April 5, 1958, baby Lasantha Manilal Wickrematunge was born.

* * *

In the 60s and 70s when the Wickrematunge children were growing up, Kotahena was a predominantly Tamil-Catholic /Tamil-Hindu precinct with a large Sinhala Buddhist community and a sizeable Moslem, Colombo-Chetty and Burgher population.

The rich cultural and religious diversity of Kotahena and its environs was apparent in the many landmark sacred institutions spread throughout the region. It was home to several imposing churches, among them St. Lucia's, considered to be one of the oldest and largest Catholic churches in Sri Lanka. Then there was the famed Kochchikade Church where each day hundreds of troubled souls lighted candles and prayed for a miracle at the feet of Saint Anthony.

There were also the famous Buddhist temples and Hindu kovils held in great veneration by devotees from far and near. People flocked to the Marriamman Kovil hoping for some divine intervention at a time of personal crisis. Unmarried women placed a thread from their attire on the statue of the resident goddess and prayed for a suitable husband.

The Wickrematunges followed the Buddhist faith, with Harris keeping close contact with the monks of Deepaduttarama, one of Kotahena's premier Buddhist temples. In 1960 however, when the Schools Take-Over Act was passed and Harris feared his children's education at Catholic institutions was under threat, he entered the Catholic fold and was duly baptised.

Life was relaxed and slow-paced. Every neighbourhood was a small community of friends with all ethnicities bound together in close comradeship.

The children played hop-scotch on the streets and packs of schoolboys engaged in games of cricket and whistled at pretty girls that passed by.

Vendors traversed the maze of little streets signaling their arrival with a unique, long-drawn out cry. Hearing the vendors' call, the womenfolk ambled out of their homes, inspected the goods on offer and proceeded to haggle. There were the pingo[3] carriers with fish, and *thorombal kaarayas*[4] with trinkets and baubles, the knife-sharperners with their strident call "*Pihiya Muwaaath*," the bottle men—who paid a few coins in exchange for old newspapers and bottles—and others selling sticky sweets, vegetables and sugared buns.

Little Lasantha grew up absorbing the vibrance of Kotahena's social and cultural milieu. He was a happy and active child who showed signs of wit and charm from an early age. As a little boy however there was a total lack of stimulus in the form of playthings that a youngster yearns for; there were no toy soldiers or wind-up cars, in fact, not a single toy of any description ever came his way. He would watch furtively from behind the window curtains of the family's No. 180, Wasala Road home as the young boy across the road played with his toy cars and other delectable knick-knacks, wishing he could get his hands on such fascinating objects.

When sister Savithri began working at the Hulftsdorp branch of the Bank of Ceylon, she once managed to pull off the impossible; she persuaded her usually unyielding father to let her join her friends on a trip to Sharaz, one of the big shops in Colombo that sold toys, gift items and household goods. When Harris drove off to pick them up later, he took little Lasantha with him.

Inside the shop, Lasantha wandered about, staring in wonderment at the array of toys and other fascinating objects. He had never seen anything like this before! As the others busied themselves within the store, Lasantha ambled outside, gazing longingly for what seemed like an eternity at a toy cowboy gun and holster set in the shop window, wishing with all his little heart he could have it. Nose pasted to the glass, he stared in fascination until the others tumbled out of the shop and they all journeyed back home, the little chap's head still brimming with images of that exquisite toy.

* * *

In the 1950s Harris had taken to politics, starting off as a trade union leader with left wing inclinations. In the early 1960s he joined the United National Party (UNP) and in 1962, when Lasantha was just four, he was elected to the Colombo Municipal Council representing the Kotahena West Ward. His political career culminated with his appointment as Deputy Mayor of Colombo in 1965 under the mayor-ship of Vincent Perera.

A few years later, having suffered the vagaries of politics in those tumultuous times, Haris quit the UNP. He was however not ready to bid adieu to municipal governance just yet. In 1969 he contested the same Ward as an Independent candidate and despite the strong UNP presence in the Kotahena West Ward, was duly elected to office, proving beyond doubt the high esteem he was held in. Indeed Harris had been a hard-working member of the Municipal Council. During the 60s he had worked tirelessly for the people he represented, implementing a large number of welfare schemes and projects, some of which are enjoyed by grateful constituents to this day.

Harris had been instrumental in having a housing scheme consisting of 112 flats being built in Korteboam Street. He was also the main force behind community service projects such as the Kalimuttu Eye Clinic, the Kotahena evening dispensary service, the Bonjean Road reception hall, the Ayurvedic dispensary at Sri Gunananda Mawatha, public bath and convenience on Jampettah Street and the installation of various other public amenities. He had helped secure employment for hundreds of disadvantaged youth and organised poor relief for countless impoverished families. Recognising the needs of the large Tamil population in the Ward he represented, Harris single-handedly worked towards the implementation of the 'Tamil also' clause in the council administration.

In 1970 he went a step further in his political career, contesting the parliamentary election as an Independent candidate. Representing Colombo North, he was pitted against UNP political giant V. Sugathadasa. Despite not having a bulwark of powerful party machinery behind him, Harris polled 13, 783 votes—7,000 less than the UNP strongman—proving his vast popularity in Colombo North.

Later he was re-elected to the Colombo Municipal Council and until 1977 when the Council was dissolved, served the Colombo North electorate in general and the Kotahena West ward in particular.

He once said, "As one who acts according to the dictates of his conscience, I must say that the only guide to man is his conscience and the shield to his memory is the rectitude of sincerity of his actions. One may be heir to any other failing, but as long as he has these, he always marches in the ranks of honour."

During his days in politics and especially during his tenure as Deputy Mayor, Harris was a reporter's delight and enjoyed close friendships with several journalists, providing them with great news stories and even giving them access to confidential files. Some of these friendships continued for many years, even when Harris was well into the winter of his life.

* * *

The girls in the Wickrematunge household were sent to Good Shepherd Convent. Lasantha was admitted to St. Benedict's College, Kotahena's premier Catholic educational institution situated down leafy Mayfield Road where Harris himself had received his education. Lal and Anil who had previously been students at St. Thomas' College Prep in Kollupitiya, were also later re-admitted to St. Benedict's. Lasantha made many lasting friendships in junior school, one of the closest ties formed being with Shivanka Abeyratne, also from Kotahena.

Lasantha was small for his age and very, very lean. Because people thought he resembled a gecko, he was nicknamed 'Hoona' and the name stuck for life. Being the youngest, everyone including Harris and Chandra, also addressed him as 'Malli.'

As Lasantha grew into his teens, he played cricket and carom with the lads in the neighbourhood and engaged in boyish hi jinks and horseplay, but much of his exuberance and burgeoning spirit were kept on a tight leash by the ever-vigilant Harris who had become something of a fire-breathing dragon as far as both, his own, and the neighbourhood kids, were concerned.

Harris drove around the streets of Kotahena in his black Peugeot, cacophonous horn blaring, shooing errant kids home. When Lasantha, playing with his mates, heard that strident warning, he abandoned the game and rushed back home, jumping over fences and scooting through people's backyards. By the time his father got home, the little lad would be studiously poring over some book, deep in concentration.

From time to time, the school took the students away on various trips. Lasantha would beg his father to be allowed to join them but never once did Harris relent insisting that these trips were fraught with danger. It was a similar experience for Lasantha's siblings.

In school, the Wickrematunge boys played cricket and Lal and Lasantha in particular were well-regarded for their bowling prowess. Lasantha was an excellent left-arm spinner and in one glorious under-16 game he went on to take an impressive 8-wicket haul. Anil meanwhile had the gift of music in him, a talent he shared with all his sisters.

Even though Lasantha being the youngest, enjoyed a degree of favouritism at home, the exalted status of Family Pet was, for a long time, enjoyed by his sister Kumudini. Better known as 'Buncie' due to her excessive partiality to '*bunis*' or buns that the bread man would bring in a basket balanced on his head each afternoon, Buncie, due to a bout of ill-health and a series of accidents suffered as a child, had become firmly ensconced as Harris' undisputed pet. Nothing the pretty, wavy-haired Buncie with her milky skin and rosy cheeks did was ever wrong in her doting father's eyes.

Harris was very strict in his refusal to let the children go 'gallivanting.' Even in the case of the older boys Lal and Anil, permission to go out didn't come easy. After hours of begging their father to let them go out on some pre-planned jaunt, Harris would finally relent with the humiliating words, "If Buncie says yes, you can go." Buncie naturally used this position of influence to gain the upper-hand over her exasperated siblings.

Though the children were thus restrained, Harris enjoyed taking them along on many of his own excursions. Piling the brood into his car, he meandered about on his multiple errands and the children would spend hours in the sweltering car waiting for their father to return.

Harris was absorbed in his children's lives. He ensured they were always neatly and suitably attired and before they stepped out of the house, doused their heads liberally with coconut oil and took great pains in combing their hair neatly even as they fussed and grumbled.

Lasantha hated the fact that his father would drag him to the barber shop more often than necessary and then order the man to give the lad a very close shave. The kids in school would then tease the boy calling him 'Thatta Simee' (baldie) which he resented.

Years earlier, when Lasantha was still very young, an elderly Buddhist monk from the local temple had visited the Wickrematunges. From a distance Lasantha eyed the monk's shiny pate in great fascination. Unable to contain his curiosity any longer, he inched up to the priest and sticking his little arm out, stroked the bald head for a second or two and thus content, walked away, much to the acute embarrassment of the elders present.

Being closest in age, Buncie and Lasantha would get in to regular quarrels. When the altercations reached parental ears, Harris would invariably be partial to his daughter. Once after a fierce brawl that saw Buncie run to dad with complaints, Lasantha received a sound caning. Later, as he huddled in bed whimpering from the ache of the thrashing and the pain of a slighted ego, Harris slipped in to the room with some soothing ointment and tenderly rubbed it on his writhing son's bruises. Lasantha was naughty and often got into trouble, but he was also the youngest, and despite all the impish antics, 'Malli' was loved by all.

Perhaps due to the intense parental control he experienced, Lasantha developed a rebellious streak. He was never cruel, but took great delight in teasing and mild bullying in a bid to gain control over any situation. When his victims ran off to complain to their parents, fathers would arrive in a huff to confront the pint-sized pest. Lasantha would then stick his lean little chest forward and shout, "What, you bugger, do you want a fight?" thus challenging *them* for a fight! He seemed to fear nobody but Harris.

School was not a very pleasant experience for Lasantha. Some would beg to differ and say Lasantha was not a very good experience for the school. His skills in the sports ground didn't translate in to classroom brilliance. In fact, he was quite hopeless. During much of his school career at St. Benedict's College, he didn't have ownership of a single book nor did he take down any notes; the teachers at the respected institution had all but given up on the rascal.

Once however, Lasantha, around 12 at the time, feared that his lack of performance in school would be relayed to his father and he dreaded the dire consequences. An important Sinhala test was coming up and the teacher, a diminutive man who wore the traditional Ariya Sinhala attire, was hinting that the test marks would be sent home for the scrutiny of parents.

The next day in class Lasantha's well-coached friends approached the teacher with contrived concern. They told him they were anxious as Lasantha had come to school armed with a knife that day. Lasantha meanwhile placed himself in vantage position in full view of the teacher and calmly and casually took out a small knife from his pocket and began filing his nails, throwing dark and ominous glances at the master from time to time. What impact this had on the master is uncertain but neither the Sinhala test nor the weapon of intimidation resulted in any major distress for the little scamp.

After elder brother Lal finished his A/Levels, he went back to St. Benedict's for a while, this time as a mathematics master, and for a few months functioned as class master in Lasantha's form. One day Lal happened to give the class a maths problem to solve. After he had collected the papers, Lal worked out the problem on the blackboard; he then took the papers home to be marked.

At home, Lal left the papers in a file in his room and went out for his cricket training. It was time for Lasantha to strike. Stealthily, he crept into the room and shuffled through the papers. He knew he had got the answer wrong because Lal had worked it out on the blackboard at the end of the lesson. Retrieving his paper and that of his good buddy Haniffa—another young scamp—he rubbed out the wrong answers and re-did the right one on both papers. He then slipped the two papers back into the file and went about his business.

Marking the papers later that night, Lal noticed that while the entire class had got the wrong answer, strangely, his brother and his friend Haniffa had got the maths problem right. He smelled a rat but decided he wouldn't say anything. The next day he went to class and much to the disappointment of the two young rascals waiting expectantly to hear praise for good work, he announced that the test had been cancelled!

During this same time, one day, Lasantha was pulled up by one Brother Alexander for disturbing the class. After having chided the boy, Brother Alexander told him he would end up in hell if he continued to behave this way.

"I will gladly go to hell," little Lasantha chirped.

"What does that mean?" a surprised Brother Alexander asked. "Explain my boy."

"Well if I go to heaven, Brother Director will be there. You also might be there. But if I go to hell, I will be with James Dean and Marilyn Monroe!"

The class burst into raucous laughter and Brother Alexander chided the sinful boy. Later, running into Lal in the corridor, he gave him an earful of young Lasantha's latest shenanigans. Lal feigned shock horror but inwardly he was chuckling. That little brother of his may not have impressive academic achievements but he was certainly good with the witty comebacks, he told himself.

Sometimes when Lasantha had been particularly naughty at home, Chandra would put him out of the house. Instead of crying and banging on the door, Lasantha would march up and down the street shouting, *"Menna, Harrisge putha eliyata daala!!"* (Look, Harris's son has been thrown out!) The embarrassment was too much for Chandra and she would hurriedly open the front door and as amused neighbours watched, drag her errant son in.

But sometimes it was Lasantha who left the house in a huff on his own will. When he had had a particularly serious difference of opinion with his mother or one of his sisters, he would pack up a parcel of clothes and walk out of the house announcing that he was running away. His mother and sisters would peep through the window and see him crouching behind the mailbox not far away. He would wait there hoping someone would come out of the house looking for him so he could go back home with his pride intact. But nobody would come for him and after moping for some time he would silently and sheepishly creep back in.

Sometimes, after a fight with one of the siblings, he would throw a little tantrum and threaten to jump over the balcony wall. One day, tired of his constant threats, brother Lal grabbed him and held the squirming lad out of the window and ordered, "Ok, go ahead and jump!" Lasantha immediately began screaming blue murder begging to be hauled back to safety.

When he was dispatched for elocution classes to Daphne Lord School of Speech and Drama, Lasantha gleefully engaged in pestering the other students. Instead of handing out punishments, the wise lady Daphne came up with another solution to the problem—she told the young rascal, who also had a charming side to his personality—that he was to be the class monitor in charge of all the others in the room. That ploy worked and the classroom continued like clockwork from then on as Lasantha, thrilled with this bit of authority, desisted from teasing the others. It seemed, from an early age, he was showing signs of thriving in a leadership role.

Sometimes however devious means were resorted to in a bid to gain such leadership. The cricket-crazy lads in the neighbourhood had banded together and formed a cricket club. Thirteen-year-old Lasantha desperately wanted to be captain but the rest of the boys had other plans. One day Lasantha arrived at the cricketing venue bristling with excitement. In a conspiratorial tone he whispered to the boys that he had managed to get some cigarettes and anyone who wanted a smoke could have a go. One by one the boys followed him to the back of a shed and drew on a few puffs. When they had all had a turn, Lasantha casually informed his bunch of spluttering and coughing friends that unless he was appointed captain, their smoking misdemeanor would reach parental ears. The boys were livid but had no option but to comply.

Despite this bit of devilry, Lasantha never smoked a cigarette himself; he never tried one even for a lark. He despised the smell and taste of tobacco just as he did alcohol. But an event occurred one day that tested the limits of his sworn abstinence. This happened when Lasantha, around 16 at the time, had a disagreement with Buncie and the fight ended with Buncie snapping in two a music record he had borrowed from a friend. Lasantha was furious and got in to a huge argument with both his sister and mother. Hurt and angry, he stormed out of the house.

By this time Lal had moved out and lived with his wife in a house not too far away from the family home. Lasantha marched towards his brother's house and finding the front door unlocked, walked in and surveyed the sitting room. In a cabinet he could see several bottles of liquor standing in a neat row. He walked up to it and extricated a bottle of arrack. He then proceeded to gulp down its contents, his face contorted with revulsion.

It didn't take too long for the arrack to have an effect and Lasantha found himself swaying about and feeling very light-headed. He walked in to the bathroom and eyed himself in the mirror. *"Kaatath baya ne yako,"* ("I'm not scared of anyone") he slurred at his reflection. Then he stumbled out of the house and on to the streets. He began staggering towards home dodging vehicles and shouting at no one in particular. Passers-by were aghast at this rowdy spectacle; it was Harris' son they whispered in shock.

When he reached home, Lasantha was still hollering in choice Sinhala. Neighbours—mostly young girls and their scandalised mothers—began peeping through their curtains. Catching sight of them the young man yelled out, "Spying on others as usual!" and all heads vanished in a trice. Lasantha's mother heard the commotion and squirming in embarrassment, dragged her son inside. Lasantha collapsed on the bed and passed out. When he woke up several hours later, a replica of the record his sister had broken, sat on the dresser.

This was the young man's first and last experience with alcohol. To his dying day, he never again touched a drop.

With the years, Lasantha was developing into quite the comic artiste, teasing everyone and coming up with funny lines. One day, hearing voices outside, Chandra looked through the window and saw Lasantha walking down the road with a pack of girls. Opening the front door she asked him what he was doing to which he shot back as quick as pat, "I'm canvassing girls for your sewing classes!"

Lasantha was most often able to turn any adverse situation into one of advantage. One day he got into a fight with sister Buncie who in a fit of rage, ripped a 100 rupee note that belonged to her. Lasantha pounced on it in a trice, picked up the pieces, glued them together and with a delighted 'thanks!' left with it.

Another time, needing some money, he asked Lal's wife Shiromi whether she would lend him some. Shiromi, ever-ready for a laugh, told him she would give him the money if he walked up and down the street dressed up as a girl. Scamp though he was, Shiromi did not believe Lasantha would do it but later that day she watched in open-mouthed shock as he walked down the street in dress, wig, high-heels and make-up. Lasantha had certainly earned that money!

* * *

When Lasantha was 10, his eldest sister Savithri was given in marriage to a well-presented young man by the name of Raja Ratnapuli. Before the marriage, he would visit Savithri and whenever one of the younger children passed by, he would tell them he had brought them a chocolate. "Partner," he would call out as Lasantha skulked past, "there's a chocolate for you." Hearing this, Buncie would immediately make her appearance upon which Raja would tell her that there was a slab of chocolates waiting for her. As soon as Raja left the house, there would be a mighty tug-o-war for the chocolate, each one claiming it was theirs.

When Savithri and Raja were married on March 4, 1968, father Harris, then Deputy Mayor, ensured that he put up a grand show for the nuptials. Among the very large gathering at the Samudra Hotel were the top political figures of the day.

Despite the distinguished gathering, Lasantha and Buncie only had goggle-eyes for the array of sumptuous food that the waiters kept bringing on large silver platters. After filling up on an assortment of sweets and savouries, the duo then crept into the kitchen and binged on ice cream to their hearts content. By the end of the wedding, brother and sister were doubled up in pain with terrible stomach cramps. The wedding celebrations ended with Harris making a late-night visit to the family doctor with the whimpering gormandisers in tow.

Sometime after their marriage, Savithri and Raja moved to Scotland. The next year Anil moved to England. In December 1971, Rukmani married Lakshman Navaratne, a young man hailing from the illustrious Navaratne cricketing family. At the time, with a Sri Lanka Freedom Party (SLFP) government in power and rationing and limitations in place, there was a ceiling imposed on the number of invitees to a hotel function and the couple married at the bride's home in Kotahena and a modest reception followed.

In 1975, when Lasantha was 17, he moved to England with his mother and sister Buncie. Lasantha entered a school in North London to study for his Year 10 Ordinary Levels (O/Levels).

Studying alongside his predominantly English peers, for the first time in his life Lasantha began to experience faint feelings of alienation and difference. Despite his lackluster academic past he now resolved to prove a point that he was as good, if not better, than the rest of his class. He began studying in earnest, applying himself with great perseverance to passing his O/Levels which came as a surprise to his family who had never seen a studious bone in the boy before. He was fortunate that he seemed to have a photographic memory; he only needed to read something once and he could recall almost all of it later. When examination time came along, he sat for it confidently and passed with distinctions and credits. Next, he began studying for his Year 12 Advanced Levels (A/Levels).

A few months after his arrival Lasantha had moved to a flat at 67 Anson Road in Tufnell Park, London with his brother Anil and their good friend, musician Conrad Gooneratne. Anil was acquainted with one Mr. Qureshi, a gentleman of Asian origin who was the floor manager in charge of all the restaurants and bars on the ground floor of Strand House Corner. This was a busy complex comprising bars, restaurants, pubs and dance and dine halls on the corner of Northumberland Avenue and Strand.

Anil himself had worked in a restaurant there during his college holidays in the summer of 1974 before he had left for Scotland. Qureshi had told Anil he could come back and work there anytime, which offer Anil took up when he returned from Scotland the following year.

Sometime after Lasantha arrived in London, Anil once again sought his friend Qureshi's help in securing a job opportunity for Lasantha. The young man was duly interviewed but Qureshi was worried because Lasantha, tiny-framed and lean, was just 17 and looked even younger.

Qureshi informed Anil it would be a risk to employ Lasantha because it was obvious to anyone he was still a boy. He added that he would only take the risk if Lasantha would claim he was already 18 if questioned. Lasantha started work at a Wimpy Bar in the Strand House Corner waiting on tables and washing plates. The need to divulge his age never arose.

The manager took to Lasantha right away. He found the youngster a diligent and conscientious worker with an admirable work ethic.

The head chef at the Wimpy Bar at the time was a man from Mauritius. He was well-read and kept abreast of politics and current affairs and enjoyed discussing and sharing his knowledge with Lasantha. In addition he supplied Lasantha regularly with rice and prawn curry and other delicious tidbits which only he had access to as the head cook. Back home in the flat Lasantha took great delight in regaling Anil and Conrad with tales of the delicacies he feasted on, making them drool with envy.

Lasantha was now working and studying like he had never done before. He worked the night shift on Fridays and the day shift on Saturdays and Sundays. During school holidays he worked six days a week. It was not an easy life.

Then one day he returned home tired after a hard night's work and feeling somewhat peckish—perhaps it was head chef's day off—he decided to fry some potato chips. He put the chip pan on the gas fire and while waiting for the oil to heat up, nodded off on the sofa, totally exhausted. Suddenly he woke up to find the flat engulfed in smoke. Flames from the pan were rising high, almost scorching the ceiling. In total panic, he stood rooted to the spot for a few seconds, then thinking fast, he threw a damp cloth around the handle of the burning pan, grabbed it and rushed out of the flat. By thinking fast he had averted a major disaster.

When his eldest sister who was by now living in Middlesbrough with her husband, visited, she was moved by Lasantha's situation. "This little fellow can't go on working like this," she said and took him away to live with them in Middlesbrough. Lasantha joined Stockton-Billingham Technical College and threw himself in to his A/Levels in great earnestness.

Lasantha kept in touch with his friends back home in Kotahena through long letters full of descriptions of life in England. His friends could see a growing sense of activism and social and political awareness in the youngster's communications.

It wasn't just his mind that was improving rapidly; Lasantha also began working out regularly, pumping iron for good measure, and was delighted when all the hard work began paying off.

It was while studying for his A/Levels that Lasantha and Catherine Hardwicke—daughter of one of the college masters—who had developed a friendship over stodgy fish and chips and political discussions, took a shine to each other. Catherine was taken with the young man's social consciousness and political opinions and his good humor and cheekiness. She was probably impressed with his recently acquired Afro hairstyle as well. Before any romance could blossom however, Mr. Hardwicke buttonholed the young lad in the school corridor one day. The latter feared he was in for a sound telling off. Instead, the master flashed a knowing smirk and asked in a conspiratorial whisper, "So when are you going to ask my daughter out?"

Lasantha never looked at Catherine the same way again and the romance fizzled before it began.

When brother Anil completed his studies in London, he moved to West Germany to marry his fiancée Beate who he had met while Beate and a friend were holidaying in London. Lasantha meanwhile applied to the London School of Economics and was accepted, but before he could enter, overseas student fees were increased and Lasantha was forced to abandon the idea of studying at the prestigious institution.

By then, he was yearning for home and not long after, he, his mother and sister Buncie, returned to Sri Lanka.

---

[1] George and Agnes's second son Frederick (Fred) became known as the 'Lion of the Kandy Bar' and went on to become Chancellor of the University of Peradeniya, Mayor of Kandy and Ambassador to France and Switzerland. His son Desmond de Silva is a highly respected Queen's Counsel in England who married a direct descendant of Queen Victoria. Desmond was knighted in 2007. Fred's sister Minette de Silva was the first woman trained as an architect in Sri Lanka and the first woman from South Asia to be elected as a member of the Royal Institute of British Architects.

[2] According to the 1981 census, Colombo North population by religion: Buddhist—33,924, Hindu—20,921, Muslim—15,671, Catholic—33,646, Other Christian—2,227, Other—97

[3] Two baskets hung on the two ends of a long pole balanced on one shoulder

[4] Men selling bangles and other trinkets in a large basket balanced on the head

CHAPTER TWO
Foray into Journalism

> *"Burke said there were Three Estates in Parliament; but, in the Reporters' gallery yonder, there sat a Fourth Estate more important far than they all."*—Thomas Carlyle, writer, essayist, historian.

WHEN Lasantha left for England in 1975 he was little more than a lean, gangling, slip of a boy. Upon his return less than four years later, his friends and neighbours at Bloemendhal Lane and Wasala Road couldn't believe what they were seeing. Instead of the little 'Hoona' with close-cropped hair and lean limbs, here was this fuzzy-haired youngster flaunting muscle in a Prussian-blue singlet.

His friend Darrel Fernandopulle for one says he will never forget the day Lasantha returned from England.

"He reminded me of Leo Sayer with his afro hair. He tried to fake a heavy British accent and talk to me, but I wouldn't bite."

No sooner than he was back at home in Kotahena, Lasantha got down to the business of happily re-establishing his childhood and teenage friendships, spending time larking around with the boys. His mother re-commenced her sewing business and began conducting dress-making classes for young girls from the neighbourhood. Lasantha, high-spirited as ever and an irrepressible joker and a charmer, thoroughly enjoyed teasing his mother and her students. Sometimes he would burst into the room singing a tune to a fabricated song 'Chandra oh Chandra,' and the girls would giggle at the cheeky young man's comic antics.

When the neighbourhood boys and girls organised house parties, 'Lasa' would strut around to the blaring sounds of the Bee Gees doing his John Travolta imitation, complete with velvet jacket and broad collar. Everyone thought he was a scream.

During this time, having being fed quite an extensive diet of Bollywood movies while in London, Lasantha also fancied himself a Rajesh Khanna look-alike. Khanna was the handsome matinee idol of the day.

Life was carefree for the young London-returnee and his father noted with some concern that he should find his son some part-time work to keep him occupied. One of the early jobs he found for the restless young man was as a management trainee in a beach resort in Hikkaduwa. A week there and Lasantha decided this life wasn't for him. He ran away from the hotel one night and arrived at the family doorstep, much to the disapproval of his father.

In his heart, Harris held two fervent wishes. The first was that one of his children would study to become a lawyer. The other was that one of them would one day pursue a political career, and perhaps do one better than him and go that extra step into parliament. Lasantha, fresh after his Advanced Levels, seemed ripe for the legal picking and Harris set about having him admitted as an external student of the University of Colombo Law Faculty.

Just as he had done in England, Lasantha once again applied himself unreservedly to his academic pursuits. Some nights though, several of the friends who formed the Bloemendhal-Wasala rat-pack[1] would meet up in one of their homes for joint study sessions despite the fact that they were all pursuing different study paths—law, accountancy, engineering, travel, marketing and banking. After an hour of poring over their books, out came the pack of playing cards and the boys would throw themselves into a rambunctious game of 304.

Despite this occasional deviation Lasantha passed his tests and with time, found he had a great deal of free time in between exams.

One day, Harris, ever on the lookout for some part-time employment for 'Malli,' brought home a copy of the *SUN* newspaper and pointed to an advertisement. It was an in-house ad calling for trainee reporters and sub-editors.

"This might be good for you," he remarked, pointing out that the newspaper office, located as it was on Hulftsdorp Hill, wasn't too far away from home either.

Harris then proceeded to type out an application on his trusty Remington and, instead of posting it to the Independent Newspapers office, took it to No. 5, Gunasena Mawatha and handed it in personally. That act on the part of a determined father was the beginning of a completely new chapter in Lasantha's life, unleashing as it were, the full force of the remarkable destiny that lay before him.

At this time, I was already working at Independent Newspapers which published the English language *SUN* and *WEEKEND,* Sinhala language *Dawasa* and *Riviresa,* Tamil language *Dinapathi* and *Chinthamani* and a few other periodicals. I had joined the company soon after my Advanced Levels and was a sub-editor on the daily *SUN*'s Sunday edition, the *WEEKEND*. I also conducted the women's and children's pages and wrote feature stories under the by-line Raine Amarasinghe.

Independent Newspapers, under the ownership of the Gunasena family, was enjoying a fresh and vibrant second lease of life. The company had re-opened in 1977 after having been shut down by the government of

Sirima Bandaranaike in 1974. With the SUN Group presses chugging back to life after a three-year hibernation, the management had begun recruiting young blood to man several editorial slots.

The Editor of the *SUN* was the dashing Rex de Silva whose creative talent took the paper to great heights. He had trained a considerable number of young people, mostly school leavers, to work as reporters and sub-editors. For them, the *SUN* offices were a home away from home for they spent much of their day here at No.5, Gunasena Mawatha in Hulftsdorp.

Among my colleagues during the early days were Dinoo Muthukrishna, Lakshman Gunasekera, Palitha Samarajiva, Arjuna Ranawana, Faizal Samat, Kshama Ranasinghe, Jumar Preena, Thushantha Wijesinghe, (who introduced me to the SUN office), Hiranthi Wijesinha, Nireka Weeratunga and veterans such as Eustace Wijetunga and Kenneth Amerasekera on the news desk and Anil Atapattu, Zaneeta Careem, M. L. M. Haniffa, Nirmalli Hapugoda and Kumudini Hettiarachchi on the subs desk. Several others joined soon after. Lalith Allahakoon, Maryanne Perera, Lasanda Kurukulasooriya, Jennifer Henricus, Rohan Gunaratna and Minoli de Soysa joined the news desk while Ranee Mohomed, Stephen Prins, Lyn Ockersz, Shamala Selvaratnam, Manohari Pillai, Renuka Masilamony, Lasantha de Alwis, Sharmini Dias Nagahawatte, Fathima Akbar, Nayomini Ratnayake and a few others entered the sub-desk. Iqbal Athas was Deputy Editor of the SUN, Sinha Ratnatunga Deputy Editor of the WEEKEND, Ranil Weerasinghe News Editor, Louis Benedict the Chief Sub-Editor and Lawrence Heyn the Sports Editor. A small group of energetic lads headed by Lawry Machado made up the sports desk. Lasantha, a couple of years older to me, joined Independent Newspapers in July1981, just as I was completing two years there.

It was a typical working day for me as I sauntered in to the office around 10 in the morning having invariably worked late the previous night. I passed through the visitor's waiting area where a young chap was sitting casually, waiting to be called in for his first day on the job. As I passed by, he glanced up and for a brief moment we studied each other. To this day I remember the defiant look in his eyes. Neither of us knew at that moment how our destinies would intertwine and herald the beginning of a remarkable series of events. I realised though that this must be one of the new chaps Rex had interviewed as potential sub-editors.

Within half an hour Rex came up to my desk followed by two young men. He introduced them as Damodaran Sivalingam and Lasantha Wickrematunge. Rex told me they were new recruits to the subs desk and wanted me to train them in the art of sub-editing.

During some preliminary small talk with the two, Lasantha and I discovered we had mutual friends from Kotahena and realised we had both been at the same home-coming party a few weeks earlier, he as a friend of the groom and I as a friend of the bride. He had been with his band of Kotahena buddies and I with my girlfriends from Nugegoda. We remembered each other at that point and much to my surprise, Lasantha went on to describe what I had worn to the party.

Taking the boys under my wing, I delivered a long lecture on the functions involved in sub-editing which I myself had learnt from Dinoo Muthukrishna and then in a sink-or-swim process when she left for Australia soon after. I explained the use of editing symbols, giving headlines, strap-lines and sub heads, fitting an article into an allotted space, the process involved in illustrating articles, doing a layout on a dummy, overseeing the page-making process and proofreading. After dinning into them the finer points of editing for the best part of an hour, I took them on a tour of the office. The first stop was the library upstairs. The Dawasa/Sun Group had one of the most comprehensive libraries among newspaper offices and as sub-editors we made several trips to the library each day in search of pictures to illustrate articles.

Next, I took the boys downstairs to where all the 'grease' action took place—the dark room, the block department (where pictures were transposed onto metal plates and mounted on solid lead blocks) and finally the 'Stone' or Works Department.

At the time, the *SUN* and its sister papers were operating on the hot metal system and the Works was where all the heavy-duty page-making took place. The Works comprised three sections for the English, Sinhala and Tamil newspapers. Noisy Linotype machines clattered away as *beedi*-smoking operators typed in the articles which then came out as a series of lead slugs on a long tray. Page makers, Ranasinghe—forever a smile on his pock-marked face, betel-chewing Jayasoma, fiery-tempered Jayakody and several others—transferred these slugs onto metal casts the size of a newspaper page together with picture 'blocks' and headlines, meticulously following the dummy sent to them by the sub-editors. The Ludlow machine operator busied himself churning out headlines which came out piping hot.

We sub-editors spent a great deal of time in the Works Department's noisy, frantic, stuffy atmosphere, overseeing the page makers as they worked at a feverish pace. Our elbows were always blackened with grease as we peered over the metal pages, cutting and chopping articles as necessary, changing lay-out and editing on the run.

I don't recall much of those early days of training Lasantha and Damo. I mostly remember Lasantha clowning around and teasing me while Damo sat there shaking with uncontrollable laughter. I was not one bit amused at the antics of this new kid on the block and told him off on several occasions but that didn't put him off a bit. On Sundays I would go through the newspaper at home, circling any typos on the pages that Lasantha had overseen. I would take these pages to the office on Monday morning and brandish these in his face, pulling him up for missing a typographical error.

Lasantha must have seen through my veneer of toughness as he had told a family member, I later learnt, that he had met the most unspoilt girl with the softest heart in the world!

Damo who wrote a tribute article in *The Nation* newspaper many years later, seems to remember much more than I do. He wrote, "I first met Lasantha when we started our working life on the same day at the WEEKEND Newspaper sub-desk as trainee journalists. We were trained by no other than Raine, his wife-to-be, though she did not know that just then. I think it was love at first sight for Lasantha as he plotted away to win her heart almost immediately. We became good friends right from the beginning as I became his '*golaya*' in promoting his advances much to the annoyance of Raine who often said, 'I am not interested in you.' I guess all of you know she had to eat her own words. I remember them as a happy and devoted couple. This story tells you a lot about Lasantha. He always knew what he wanted in life and pursued it with all his heart."

Lasantha quickly made friends with many of the young people both on the sub desk and the news desk.

Several weeks after the two boys had joined, Editor Rex was on a mission to find a couple of subs willing to relocate to the news desk. One by one, he asked all the men on the desk whether they wished to move on to reporting. When it came to Lasantha's turn, he was quite insistent that he preferred to stay right where he was—opposite me! Damodaran however thought he would give news reporting a shot and agreed to move. A few months later he left Independent Newspapers.

Sometime later, Lasantha told me of his interest in law studies. He said he was already an external student at the Colombo University's law faculty working towards a law degree and was hoping to join Law College to obtain his attorneys-at-law.

Lasantha convinced me that I too should apply for the Law College entrance exam and set about organising the paperwork. We were required to sit for two tests, a language paper and a general knowledge paper, one of which had to be done in Sinhala and the other in English. Since the Sinhala language paper was known to be quite tough, we decided to sit for the English language exam and do the general knowledge test in Sinhala; it turned out to be a good choice because both of us passed the entrance exam without a day's preparation.

Before we entered Law College however, at the SUN offices, changes were being effected. Despite his initial refusal to move across to the other side of the office, due to a sudden need to beef-up the reporting ranks, Lasantha was despatched to the news desk. Here, he thrived, finding a passion and an amazing knack he never knew he possessed for news-gathering. Lasantha was assigned the police and courts beats and in a short space of time he was bringing in some good leads. It was during this time that Lasantha cultivated a contact in the form of Ranil Wickremesinghe, then a young minister in the J. R. Jayewardene cabinet.

Lasantha had a huge sense of humour and his loud laughter would reverberate throughout the office. At the time, some of the old-hands had left, and the news and sub desks were made up of such reporters and sub-editors as Chris Dharmakirti, Tyronne Devotta, Jack Herft, Aruna Kulatunga, Malkanthi Leitan, Mary Anne Noyahr, Roshan Karunatilleke, Kumari Dayananda, Melanie John, Sakuntala Navaratnam, Delrene Wijeratne, Anoma Tillekaratne, Larry Campbell and a host of other young girls and boys. Asoka Rajapakse, Victor Benjamin, T. B. Rahaman, Siva Ilankesan, Dirk Tissera and Trevine Rodrigo had joined the sports desk. The photographers' desk was made up of such veterans as Bertie Mendis, Dunstan Wickremaratne, Henry Rodrigo, Lakshman Gunathilake and newcomers such as Thilak Seneviratne, Padmasiri Gamage, Pushpakumara Mathugama, Gemunu Wellage and Ranjith Perera. Dayananda was the talented chief of the artists' department.

Sometimes office seemed like a social gathering for a bunch of revellers rather than a newspaper organisation. Especially at the sub-desk, we girls had more flexibility with our time. Some of us would send off our dummy pages to the Stone to be cast by the page makers and jump in to an office vehicle going towards Pettah or Fort. A favourite haunt was the busy hub of Chatham Street and we would stop by at Pagoda for a quick snack and a giggle—there was no resisting those cream buns, éclairs, Chinese rolls and iced coffee! Most birthdays in the office were celebrated with pineapple gateaux or that divine Pagoda chocolate cake.

Of course it wasn't all play and no work. We slogged and sweated, and most days, especially Fridays, many of us worked late into the night. Any social life on a Friday night was out of the question; for seven years I scorched the midnight oil every Friday, most nights getting away from work well past 1 o'clock. Early the next morning I would be back at work to finish off the news pages.

During lunch time each day, many of us would gather in the modest lunch room and everyone eagerly waited for Lasantha's lunchbox to be opened; his mother packed some tasty morsels for him and we girls would get bits to savour. One day as we sat for lunch, Lasantha opened his lunch box and grinned to himself. When we asked him what he was smiling about, he said, "I only have plain rice today. I had a fight with Chandra (his mother) this morning and she seems to have punished me." Of course all of us in the room laughed our heads off and proceeded to share with him whatever we had in our lunches.

* * *

At the time, the UNP government under the hawkish J. R. Jayewardene was in office having been elected in a landslide victory in 1977. Jayewardene's government enjoyed a five-sixths majority in parliament and introduced massive constitutional and economic reform. The government was bestowed with unprecedented authority to create new legislation and introduce amendments to existing ones. As Jayewardene himself once famously quipped, "The only thing I can't do is change a man into a woman or a woman into a man." His powers however were sometimes used to serve the government's own questionable ends.

An election was due in 1983 and the UNP were desperate to continue with this powerful state of affairs. However, Jayewardene's own new constitution promulgated in September 1978 which introduced the Proportional Representation (PR) system (as opposed to the previous first-past-the-post system) was an obstacle to their ambitions. The PR system would never confer upon the UNP that same majority in parliament. Jayewardene and the government decided the only avenue open to them was to extend the life of the current parliament. To do this, they had to avoid an election and instead, hold a national referendum. Voters would be asked simply whether or not they wished to extend the life of parliament through a fourth amendment[2] to the constitution. Voters would be required to place their ballots against the lamp symbol for a 'yes' or the pot symbol for a 'no.'

Before extending the life of parliament however, Jayewardene, who had by then earned the nickname 'The Old Fox,' had to ensure for himself a further term at the helm as President. Having clipped the wings of his political opponent Sirima Bandaranaike through a special presidential commission that had found her guilty of misuse of power, Jayewardene announced a presidential election set for October 20, 1982.

With Mrs. Bandaranaike unable to contest the election as the Sri Lanka Freedom Party's (SLFP) Presidential Candidate, the mantle fell on SLFP veteran Hector Kobbekaduwa.

At the time, actor turned politician Vijaya Kumaratunga was making great strides in the political scene. Both, due to his popularity as a film star and the seeming sincerity in his desire to pursue a peaceful resolution to the ethnic crisis, the tall, handsome and charismatic Vijaya was admired both by the Sinhalese and the Tamils. His visits to Jaffna in the North together with his wife—Mrs. Bandaranaike's daughter Chandrika—would see him being mobbed by an appreciative Tamil populace.

When the government called the presidential election, Vijaya spearheaded Kobbekaduwa's election campaign, travelling the length and breadth of the country with Kobbekaduwa. At the SUN office, Lasantha was assigned to cover the SLFP presidential election and he forged a close rapport with Vijaya.

J. R. Jayewardene went on to win the election garnering 52.91 percent of the vote while Kobbekaduwa received 39.07 percent. Jayewardene then made the next crafty move in his political chess game. He informed the country via a TV and radio bulletin that a band of 'Naxalite'[3] rabble-rousers within the SLFP were planning to assassinate him and wrest control of the country. The President said these unsettling developments had necessitated the extension of the life of parliament via a referendum. This was also crucial, he said, for the completion of massive development projects the government had initiated.

According to what transpired later, in the run-up to the presidential election, Vijaya Kumaratunga is alleged to have uttered some words to the effect of ". . . there will be a trail of blood leading to Ward Place." (referring to No. 66, Ward Place, President Jayewardene's private residence). Vijaya denied this; what he had in fact said was that after their election victory, mobs would try to attack President's House (and Jayewardene) and they should avoid any spilling of blood.

Vijaya Kumaratunga and several other party loyalists were arrested on the trumped-up charges of being 'Naxalites' and thrown in Welikada prison. As someone who had closely associated with Kumaratunga during the polls, Lasantha was interrogated by the CID for eight hours but they could not come up with any evidence to frame charges.

The *SUN* newspaper management immediately summoned Lasantha and grilled him about his affiliations with the jailed Vijaya. Was he also a Naxalite? he was asked. I wonder whether even the SUN management really knew what a 'Naxalite' was; nevertheless, it was declared that Lasantha was to be suspended forthwith. The moment the words about the suspension were out, Lasantha retorted, "In that case, I'm quitting this newspaper," and stomped out of the room.

Within moments he arrived downstairs in a tizzy to see me and announced he was leaving Independent Newspapers. I was aghast. That night he arrived at my home in Nugegoda and explained in detail what had transpired at the meeting with the management.

The very next day he was hired by Vijitha Yapa, Editor of *The Island* and *The Sunday Island* newspapers. It was here at *The Island* newsrooms that Lasantha fully unleashed his reporting brilliance.

The young Upali Group was owned by the debonair Upali Wijewardena who had married Mrs. Sirima Bandaranaike's niece, Lakmini. Although Wijewardena was also closely related to the President, the *Island* journalists seemingly enjoyed more independence than their *SUN* counterparts and Lasantha was able to write without much proprietary pressure. It certainly would not have been very pleasant for the *SUN* management to see their rival paper score one-up on them almost on a daily basis with exclusive stories under blaring headlines and Lasantha Wickrematunge's prominent by-line.

Lasantha was making great strides as a journalist and was well on the way to becoming one of the best newsmen in the country. His, soon became a name that peers and readers came to envy and admire.

As one of his *Island* colleagues was to later recount, "Lasantha would work his butt off in pursuit of a good news story. As a young reporter at *The Island* I was, quite frankly, jealous of his success; but then I figured it out—and decided to learn from him. It seemed people couldn't resist talking to him for some magical reason, but that wasn't quite the case.

"Like every good journalist, Lasantha worked without regard to the clock. (and unlike them, stayed sober while he did so!) Always a charmer, he nevertheless cultivated his sources carefully, diligently, patiently. If people talked to him, it was because of his tireless effort. He ignored no source.

"Consequently, when he investigated a scandal, it wasn't surprising that he uncovered its every detail, however trivial. That was the strength of his work: he convinced you not just by making extravagant accusations against the powerful, but by the weight of the detail of his reporting. At his best, Lasantha convinced you that there couldn't be another side to the story."

Gamini Weerakoon, Deputy Editor of *The Island* recalled, "In the 80s there were few rough diamonds around and I was surprised to be introduced to a young man who had left the *SUN* newspaper for *The Island* . . . . He looked too young to be among ruffians, some of them veterans with 20 to 30 years experience who dominated the news desk and the sub-editors' desks and I had my doubts whether he would last long. However, I was soon to realise that he was a serendipitous find for the newspaper.

"While the veterans roamed the streets, bars and bragged about their brawls and nocturnal adventures, Lasantha quietly got about his job and when it was deadline for printing, almost invariably he produced the lead story."

Despite his busy, deadline-driven schedule on *The Island* news desk, Lasantha would be mindful of the fact that I was working late on Fridays at the *SUN* office. He would drive to Gunasena Mawatha on these nights with a sumptuous dinner parcel—usually a pack of crispy hoppers with several curries or a few packets of *biriyani*—which I would share with the others working late with me.

* * *

On December 22, 1982, despite campaigns by various political parties and civil rights groups who saw the referendum as a dictatorial move by J. R. Jayewardene and a threat to parliamentary democracy, the referendum was held under a state of emergency. In an election that saw unprecedented thuggery and intimidation, the Lamp symbolising an 'yes' to the extension of the life of the current parliament emerged victorious over the 'Pot.'

On July 25, 1983, just weeks before the new extended six year term of parliament was to commence, the race riots broke out, leaving a trail of misery and despair and a permanent scar on Sri Lanka's image.

That Monday morning as I caught the bus from Nugegoda to travel to the office in Hulftsdorp, I overheard the concerned mumblings of passengers discussing the funeral of the 13 soldiers who had died in an LTTE (Liberation Tigers of Tamil Eelam) ambush in Thirunelvely in the North. At that point however there were no signs of the violent events unfolding. By the time the bus neared the Lake House junction, everyone on board sensed that something was amiss. People were running helter-skelter. The bus driver brought the boneshaker to a halt and announced to the passengers that he wasn't continuing with the journey because the people on the street—now swollen to stampede proportions—made it impossible to move an inch further. The passengers, anxious and perplexed, all spilled out of the bus. There were a few kilometres more to my office but I had no choice, I had to walk, and walk I did. As I neared the main Pettah bus terminal, it seemed like I was walking into a wall of people. They were moving forward in waves. I was the only person walking in the other direction, going against the tide as it were.

As I got closer to M. D. Gunasena Mawatha where the office was located, it became almost impossible to keep going; mobs of marauding hooligans had taken over the streets, Shops owned by Tamils were burning, vehicles were smouldering and a thick cloud of black smoke made it almost impossible to see a few feet ahead of me. It was a horrific scene but I plodded on until I got to the safety of the office.

Only a few people had managed to get to work that day and we were all in shock. I remember Sinhala journalists inviting their Tamil colleagues to move in with them until the danger subsided. I desperately tried to contact friends who had not turned up at work.

That evening everyone packed in to the office vehicle to go back to their respective homes; there were about a dozen of us in the van travelling to various locations all over Colombo and its suburbs and I was the last to be dropped off. At one point, as I sat alone at the back of the hi-ace van, a mob burst in to the vehicle brandishing cudgels and knives. They seemed to be on an adrenaline high and wanted to hitch a ride in our van. I sat there stone-faced opposite them, trying to act casual, but my heart was racing.

An intermittent curfew was in force the next few days. By Friday however things seemed to settle and the curfew was lifted. An office colleague Roshan Karunatilleke dropped by and I suggested to her that we should pay a visit to Louis Benedict, our chief sub-editor. We decided to take a bus to Ratmalana. Everything seemed calm that day with few people on the streets. We managed to get to Louis' house, spent some time with him and then started heading back home. There were hardly any buses on the road and after waiting for what seemed like an eternity, finally, one heading for Nugegoda came rattling by and we hopped on gratefully. That was when all hell broke loose. Suddenly the streets were teeming with rampaging mobs armed with clubs and knives, screaming, shouting and generally "looking for *kotiyas*." (Tigers). Apparently, rumour had spread like wildfire that a posse of Tigers had infiltrated Colombo and incensed mobs were running riot. The carnage of that day will remain Sri Lanka's eternal shame.

It was later that we learnt, the mob violence was not the result of a spontaneous Sinhala reaction to the killing of the soldiers in the North. They were organised groups of thugs and the talk on the streets was that the insidious hand of a government minister or more, was behind the riots although this was never verified. The Tamil community also felt let down by the fact that several days of bloodletting had passed before the President of the country addressed the nation.

India meanwhile was breathing fire and the Sri Lankan government engaged in convoluted machinations and hasty damage-control measures. They also found a convenient scapegoat in the Marxist-Leninist Janatha Vimukthi Peramuna (JVP), the Communist Party (CP) and the Nava Sama Samaja Party (NSSP) to blame the riots on. Although the CP and NSSP leaders were subsequently released, the ban on the JVP continued. The group went underground and made their presence felt several years later following the Indo-Lanka peace pact.

Lasantha's house in Kotahena meanwhile had turned in to a refuge for their Tamil friends and neighbours. Lasantha had several friends from the Tamil and Colombo-Chetty communities and he, in particular went looking for his friend Darrel Fernandopulle. When he knocked on the door of the address he had been given, Darrel anxiously peeped through the fence and this image of his dear friend standing there with fear in his eyes, stuck in Lasantha's mind and made a deep impression on him.

Meanwhile, because they had opened their home to distressed friends, a group of thugs one night set Harris' beloved car ablaze and the Volkswagen he had imported from Germany was left a burnt-out shell. Harris was both furious and devastated but he was also determined to prove a point to the miscreants. He had the car repaired, primped and polished back to its original condition and then drove all around Colombo North tooting the horn for good measure. After thus rubbing it in the noses of the villains, he disposed of the car.

In 1984 I was nominated by the SUN to attend the Harry Brittain Memorial Workshop organised by the Commonwealth Press Union. I flew to London on May 12 that year and spent three months together with nine other journalists from Commonwealth countries, travelling through England, Scotland and Wales. During that time, a lovelorn Lasantha penned dozens of long and ardent letters in his terrible fowl-scratch, keeping me informed of the goings-on in Colombo and in his life.

---

[1] The group of friends comprised Shivanka Abeyratne, Darrel Fernandopulle, Kumar Sabaratnam, Kumar Johnpulle, Valentine Fernando and a few others.

[2] "(e) unless sooner dissolved, the First Parliament shall continue until August 4, 1989, and no longer, and shall thereupon stand dissolved, and the provisions of Article 70 (5) (b) shall, mutatis mutandis, apply."

[3] The term originated in India to describe radical militant Communist groups.

CHAPTER THREE
Marriage, Fatherhood & Politics

> *"Were it left to me to decide whether we should have a government without newspapers, or newspapers without a government, I should not hesitate a moment to prefer the latter."*
> —Thomas Jefferson, third US President.

1987-1990 was a particularly violent and disruptive period in the history of Sri Lanka.

In 1987 when President Junius Richard Jayewardene announced the impending signing of the Peace Accord with India, giving way to a system of provincial councils and depositing the Indian Peace Keeping Force (IPKF) on Sri Lanka's shores, sections of the Sinhala majority saw this as a monumental betrayal. The general perception was that, couched in the smiling baby-face of Rajiv Gandhi was the belligerent fist of India, forcing a hastily-conceived Peace Accord down Sri Lanka's throat. The agreement sought to devolve more autonomy to the provinces and temporarily merge the North and East, creating a northeast provincial council.

The main opposition party, the SLFP, protested long and hard. Civil unrest and riots instigated by the leftist Janatha Vimukthi Peramuna (JVP) who viewed the Accord as an expression of Indian imperialism, followed. Mobs created havoc on the streets; state property was set ablaze.

The Prime Minister of India arrived in Sri Lanka to sign the Accord with President Jayewardene on July 29,1987, 'acknowledging the imperative need of resolving the ethnic problem of Sri Lanka, and the consequent violence, and for the safety, well being, and prosperity of people belonging to all communities in Sri Lanka.'

After the signing of the Accord which took place under a curfew, a press conference was held which was later aired on television. It was here that viewers first got a glimpse of a small statured young man in the front rows, one leg thrown over the other—casual sandals in full view—giving the Prime Minister of India and the President of Sri Lanka a tough time with a volley of hard-hitting questions. It was evident that the President was getting annoyed with the reporter's questions and members of his cabinet present at the press conference were riled.

The young man was *The Island* newspaper's Deputy News Editor Lasantha Wickrematunge. His questions, in particular, revolved round the proposed merger of the Northern and Eastern provinces, and the Muslims of the East who could potentially be rendered a minority within a minority.

Lasantha went on to ask Rajiv Gandhi whether his anti-Lanka stance had now changed as he had once accused Sri Lanka of lacking the guts to solve the ethnic problem but was now signing an accord with the same leadership. The Indian Prime Minister replied that he now saw Jayewardene as someone with great courage and statesmanship.

Having established his niche primarily as a political reporter, Lasantha was assigned by his editors to report on many of the major political stories of the day. He had covered much of British Prime Minister Margaret Thatcher's visit to Sri Lanka in April1985 and been sent by *The Island* to cover the first South Asian Association for Regional Cooperation (SAARC) summit in Dhaka, Bangladesh in December 1985 and the second SAARC summit in Bangalore, India, in November 1986. He was also, almost on a daily basis, breaking stand-out political stories.

I had returned to Sri Lanka in January 1987 having worked as a sub-editor on *The Hong Kong Standard* for a year. A week after my return to Sri Lanka I joined *The Sunday Times*, Lasantha having 'put a word in for me' with his former boss Vijitha Yapa who had joined the Wijeya Group as the founding Editor of *The Sunday Times*. In a tribute article after Lasantha's death, Yapa recalled how I was recruited to *The Sunday Times* staff.

"My next encounter with Lasantha was when I was Editor of *The Sunday Times*. He said there was a talented journalist named Raine who had just returned after a stint with *The Hong Kong Standard*. I employed her and it was months later I discovered Raine was his girlfriend," he wrote.

While I was in Hong Kong, Lasantha had been impatient to get on with our marriage plans, urging me to return home instead of staying on to complete a year there. He wrote that his parents Chandra and Harris had visited my folks at our Gamsabhawa Junction, Nugegoda residence and discussed plans for the nuptials. Harris had also indicated his interest in getting both our horoscopes matched and obtained a copy of my natal chart from my mother.

A few days later Lasantha wrote that the astrologer had remarked Lasantha and I had been partners in many lifetimes before and that my stars indicated I would bring luck to the man I married! Whatever dangers that would present in later years, he had said, Lasantha would always be protected due to some planetary influence in my horoscope.

Lasantha also wrote that his sister Buncie was due to get married in March '87—co-incidentally to a boy from Gamsabhawa Junction where I myself came from—and he was hopeful we could be married around the same time. His sisters in Canada and brother in Germany were hoping to be in Sri Lanka at that time and it would be wonderful, Lasantha wrote, if they were present at both weddings. Harris had suggested a double wedding and Lasantha wrote to ask whether I would be agreeable. True to my easygoing nature I agreed; Buncie's new in-laws however were superstitious about double weddings and that idea was soon jettisoned. Lasantha's parents were then keen that we get married within a few days of Buncie's wedding. It was thus that we were married at Hotel Ceylon Intercontinental on Wednesday, March 11, two days after his sister had wed.

On the morning of the wedding, a florist delivered a beautiful bouquet of red roses from Lasantha, a tradition he continued every wedding anniversary thereafter. Despite this and other somewhat grandiose displays of affection, Lasantha was a simple guy at heart. He didn't believe in limos and flashy cars; instead he drove his own humble white Renault to the hotel that evening together with his bestman Darrel Fernandopulle.

All our friends from the *SUN*, *The Island* and *The Sunday Times* were among the 250 guests. The witnesses to the marriage were Leader of the Opposition Anura Bandaranaike and Youth Affairs Minister Ranil Wickremesinghe, former classmates who were on different sides of the political divide. There was none of the solemnity that is customary during such a momentous occasion. Instead, Ranil, Anura and Lasantha guffawed as they bantered with each other while the registrar tried to ignore the merry chatter and concentrate on his job.

Many had assumed Mrs. Sirima Bandaranaike, the world's first woman prime minister, would be one of the witnesses instead of her son, and in fact when Lasantha handed over the wedding invitation to the grand old lady, she asked half-jokingly, "How come I'm not signing at the wedding?" Embarrassed, Lasantha replied that her son was going to be one of the witnesses.

Lasantha had been happy to let me plan most aspects of the wedding. He didn't demur when I told him he had to wear a mangosteen-maroon bow and cummerbund with a suit of an ivory shade to complement my bridal sari and the attire of the retinue.

But Mrs. Bandaranaike didn't think much of the cummerbund and asked a red-faced Lasantha, "What is this thing you are wearing?"

"It's called a cummerbund or something Madam," Lasantha blushed.

After the reception was over, covered in confetti, we drove off in Lasantha's Renault which had been thoroughly decorated—or desecrated—by family and friends. There were balloons and other objects stuck on the car and slogans scrawled all over in lipstick among which was one that declared, "Hoona has his day!"

We drove to Lasantha's friend Shivanka's home in Kotahena where we got rid of all the fluff and then drove back to the hotel. Once we entered the hotel room, there were muffled sounds of giggling coming from somewhere. We examined the room and discovered Lasantha's sisters and mine, hiding behind the heavy curtains!

On the same day as our wedding, Lasantha learnt he had passed his final year law college exams and soon after, took his oaths as an attorney-at-law. The much respected Judge of the Supreme Court, Justice P. Ramanathan, a friend of father Harris, gifted Lasantha the lawyer's cloak. Within the year, Lasantha began working as a junior in the chambers of criminal lawyer Ranjit Abeysuriya, one of the most highly regarded professionals in the field.

Two days after the wedding Lasantha flew to England to follow a Thompson Foundation training course for which he had been recommended by *The Island*. He was not happy about the timing and neither was I. He wanted me to join him, so a friend stepped in and arranged accommodation for me in a flat owned by one Gamit Amerasekera in London's Gloucester Road and a month later I flew to join Lasantha.

My Editor Vijitha Yapa was not one bit impressed about me leaving my job of three months to dash half-way across the globe to be with my new husband. "So, if he goes to Mozambique the next time, are you going to be rushing off to Mozambique too?" he vented.

Lasantha and I were too happy to get our spirits dampened. We enjoyed all the sights of London, posed for pictures with pigeons on our shoulders at Trafalgar Square and took cruises down the River Thames. He was eager to show me places where he had lived and worked during his time in London in the 70s and we jumped into the Tube and explored these and other fascinating places.

Back in Sri Lanka in May 1987, we moved into the pretty, sunlit condominium that Harris had built for us adjoining the main house on Wasala Road, Kotahena. White-washed and streaming with light, many visitors commented it had a great energy and felt like a 'lucky' house.

Like any new bride, I tried my hand at cooking and discovered to my delight that whipping up all manner of culinary experiments could be great fun. Lasantha was the guinea pig but he ate whatever I cooked with many appreciative comments. Most nights he would be seated in the bedroom upstairs totally immersed in the Carrington-Colby family dramas on *Dynasty*—and I would carry his dinner plate to him, a plate that had no obvious concern for cholesterol—and he would generously compliment me and my cooking as we tucked in happily.

* * *

The re-emergence of the JVP in the late 80s was creating chaos all across the nation. The leader of the JVP was Rohana Wijeweera who had cut his Marxist teeth as a student in Russia in the early sixties. With a sizeable following comprising mainly disgruntled workers and students, the group had staged a violent uprising in the early 70s. Brutally crushed during that attempt at destabilising the government and grabbing power, the group went underground after being proscribed by the government of Sirima Bandaranaike. They later entered the democratic path but, following the 1983 ethnic riots, the party was once again proscribed by President J. R. Jayewardene.

Even while operating as an underground outfit during 1987-1990, the JVP were far more organised and powerful than they had ever been and held the country to ransom by unleashing unprecedented violence and intimidation. Denouncing the ruling United National Party's 'colossal treachery' in selling-out Sri Lanka with the connivance of India through a peace accord, the JVP went on a killing spree, shooting down politicians, government officials, police officers, school principals, government media personnel, estate superintendents and anyone who dared disobey their *hartal*[1] orders. It was an era when the T-56 ruled supreme.

One of the victims of JVP terror was actor-turned-politician Vijaya Kumaratunga who paid with his life on February 16, 1988 for extending his support to the Indo-Lanka Accord. Several popular media persons lost their lives during this blood-soaked period in Sri Lanka's history. Among them were talented lyricist and state television anchor Premakeerthi de Alwis (July 31, 1989), news reader Sagarika Gomes (13 September 1989), Chairman of Independent Television Network (ITN) Thevis Guruge (23 July 1989) and popular writer, dramatist and human rights activist Richard de Zoysa (18 February 1990).

The JVP's splinter group, the Deshapremi Janatha Viyaparaya, devised a 'chit' system run by invisible operatives and signed by Keerthi Wijayabahu (Alias of JVP Military Wing Leader Saman Piyasiri Fernando) who issued various directives by means of these chits. They ordered the people to remain in their homes after a certain hour on any given day. Shops and other establishments including hospitals were ordered shut at their whim. More than a few shop owners who dared disobey were brutally murdered. Schools and universities were closed down as the country lay suspended on a razor edge of terror.

In retaliation, government forces unleashed their own unofficial para-military groups and killing became the order of the day. Bodies of JVP suspects were burnt on tyres on roads as a deterrent to others. In some areas, severed heads were placed prominently on parapet walls with placards declaring them either murderous insurgents or despicable traitors, depending on which side of the political spectrum they belonged to. But even the State's massive anti-JVP onslaught under a tough-as-nails Defence Minister Ranjan Wijeratne it seemed, could flounder any minute.

The JVP's undoing however was not too long coming.

Smelling murderous victory, they had issued yet another directive that unless all police personnel resigned forthwith from the force, their families would be wiped out. They did just that with the family of Deputy Inspector General (DIG) Premadasa Udugampola who—his mother included—were savagely massacred. When it seemed like all was lost, government forces and the vigilante groups unleashed a ruthless, blood-soaked retaliation, hounding out suspects from every hiding place and safe-house.

The vigilantes targetted not just active JVPers but their immediate families as well. Many young people with even a hint of an association with the dreaded revolutionary group disappeared overseas fearful of becoming victims of the government's massive crackdown. No one wanted to end up on a tyre.

On September 2, 1988, we had gone to my parent's home to wish my father on his birthday when a call came through to Lasantha on my parents' house phone. The caller, a top government minister, informed him that Attorney-at-Law Wijedasa Liyanarachchi had died that day while in police custody. Liyanarachchi had been arrested by the Counter Subversion Unit of Tangalle on August 25, 1988 and detained at the Tangalle police station. He had later been brought to the Counter Terrorism Unit in Sapugaskanda in Colombo.

Liyanarachchi had managed to pull the wool over everyone's eyes. He had been a quiet, unassuming sort working alongside Lasantha and other juniors in Ranjit Abeysuriya's chambers. In fact he had once even visited our home. What his colleagues didn't know was that Liyanarachchi was allegedly a member of the dreaded JVP. It was a shock to everyone when the story came out but Lasantha had been fond of Liyanarachchi and he was saddened by the news.

The final cherry on top for the government was the discovery of the hidden den of Rohana Wijeweera in November 1989. Politburo members and other officials of the JVP including Political/Military Secretary Upatissa Gamanayake and Saman Piyasiri Fernando were subsequently smoked out and went to their deaths. Only one member of the JVP politburo—Somawansa Amerasinghe—escaped death by fleeing to safer shores.

It was in this grim backdrop, during the JVP's killing heyday and the government's bloody backlash that Lasantha first got in to active politics.

His association with the main opposition party and close relationships with Sirima Bandaranaike, her son Anura and other party stalwarts, resulted in him being offered to contest the Colombo North seat in the 1989 general elections.

Before that however, a presidential election had been called for December 19, 1988. The SLFP's presidential candidate, Mrs. Sirima Bandaranaike—her civic rights restored—launched her election campaign from the family bastion of Horagolla. Lasantha was a big part of that campaign trail, travelling the length and breadth of Sri Lanka with Mrs. Bandaranaike and her party workers.

Lasantha was away from home for long periods of time during the campaign but he called daily and whenever we talked, he was bubbling with optimism and excitement. He felt that, if crowd reactions all over the country were the barometer, Mrs. Bandaranaike had a very good chance of winning the election.

"They love her," he enthused, "Everywhere we go people mob her. The signs are very good."

Mrs. Bandaranaike had a less than stellar track record on certain fronts. During her time at the helm from 1970-1977—much of it under emergency rule—the Trotskyite-Communist influence of alliance partners and her own Socialist policies had seen the country experience a bleak period of rationing of essentials, scarcity and queues. The government's well-intentioned policy of encouraging local agriculture and banning all imports did not bear the desired results; instead, it forced the people to suffer harsh privations. Memories of these hard times were still fresh in people's minds, but many had had enough of the UNP, besieged by allegations of intimidation and corruption, as well.

On a personal note, Lasantha was hugely enamored with the firm but kindly nature of the 73-year-old Bandaranaike who he said treated everyone on the campaign trail with the utmost hospitality, good cheer and motherly concern.

During this time, another event occurred which because of its very secret nature, remains unknown to many, even to this day.

In the run-up to the presidential election, a few top-notch SLFP members including Anura Bandaranaike and Anuruddha Ratwatte together with Kumar Ponnambalam (who was on Mrs. Bandaranaike's bandwagon during that election), and Lasantha, embarked on a secret mission to meet representatives of the Liberation Tigers of Tamil Eelam (LTTE) in the Wanni jungles.

By its very nature, the mission was wrought with danger and the trip had not been an easy one. The SLFP wanted it to be kept top secret with not a whisper of it getting back to the government. Hence, no one, not even the Indian Peace Keeping Force (IPKF) deployed in the North and East, were aware of the mission. The group met an LTTE cadre in Vavuniya who led them deep in to the jungles and into the hideout of an LTTE divisional head where the forthcoming election and the LTTE's position with regards to it, were discussed.

After the discussions and a delicious meal of rice, sweet potato and wild game, the visitors from Colombo left, once again driving through deep jungle terrain, now dark and eerie. Somewhere along the way heading for Vavuniya town, their vehicle was stopped by an IPKF patrol and the soldiers proceeded to grill the occupants. When they were told Anura Bandaranaike, son of presidential candidate Sirima Bandaranaike, was one of the passengers in the vehicle, one IPKF officer banged his palm on his forehead in sheer frustration that such a dangerous mission had taken place without their knowledge.

The relief I felt when Lasantha returned home safely from that trip was indescribable.

The presidential election was held amidst unprecedented violence. In the three months leading to the election, more than 400 UNP organisers, office-bearers and supporters were murdered by JVP operatives. Hundreds of others were attacked.

Despite the SLFP's tremendous campaign efforts and positive feedback from the people at large, Ranasinghe Premadasa of the UNP defeated Sirima Bandaranaike in that election. Premadasa's promise of a poverty alleviation scheme was a smart vote-grabber but the fact that the election had been one of the most violent in the history of Sri Lankan elections—and the voter turn-out was a paltry 55.3 percent—contributed to the SLFP's defeat.

Mrs. Bandaranaike however was not going to concede defeat without a fight. She and her party were of the firm opinion that intimidation, non-compliance with provisions of the Presidential Elections Act and the government's failure to conduct a free and fair election had cost her party the election. She filed an election petition in the Supreme Court citing President Premadasa and Elections Commissioner Chandananda de Silva as respondents, challenging the outcome of the election. This petition was to drag on for more than two years before it was finally dismissed in 1992.

After the presidential election, the government announced that parliamentary elections would be held on February 15, 1989. When on December 20, 1988 parliament was dissolved, Lasantha handed in his nominations as a candidate for the electorate of Colombo North.

Lasantha and I had talked at length about him getting in to politics and the implications it would have on our lives. In fact, while I was in Hong

Kong in 1986, he had written in one of his letters to me, "Last week Mrs. B and Anura called me and said they wanted me to be the SLFP candidate for Colombo North at the next parliament elections. They wanted me to start organising the electorate immediately. I said I will take over from December. They said to let my father organise it for me till December. They are very keen on me."

At the time, politics had become the refuge of scoundrels and dabbling in politics was a dangerous game. Especially in 1989 when the JVP, government forces and para-militaries were collectively turning Sri Lanka into a killing fields, running for election was a frightening prospect. Adding to the diffidence was the fact that I was expecting our first child. But politics was almost like a virus in Lasantha's blood and encouraged by father Harris, he was rearing to go. He felt he needed a platform even more confrontational than the newspaper columns from which to attack UNP policies. I was not going to stand in his way. Thus, Lasantha resigned from the Upali Group and threw himself into the political minefield.

In the grim backdrop of JVP terror, candidates from every party contesting the elections were issued with arms and ammunition to protect themselves. One day Lasantha came home carrying a Smith and Wesson 9 mm revolver that had been issued to him. At first I recoiled in horror at the sight of it. It was not something we relished having in our home but the violent times we lived in had rendered it a 'reluctant accessory.'

Every day we read or heard horrendous tales of 'the dreaded knock on the door' where people were taken away from their homes in the dead of night and their bodies discovered the following day, often bearing signs of brutal torture. There were many nights I lay in bed in fear wondering if there would be a knock on the door, gaining little comfort from the weapon that lay beneath the bed. The worst part of all this was that we couldn't be certain of the source of a potential attack. It could be the JVP because Lasantha was contesting the elections, some state-sponsored goon or a member of some vigilante group. It could even be someone with an axe to grind, exploiting the savage bloodletting and lawless situation to commit murder. One could never be certain. I am grateful to this day that we never had the need to use the revolver which was returned some time after the conclusion of the parliamentary elections.

Lasantha, his family, friends and supporters jumped in to the election campaign in earnest. His father, having as a politician in the 60s and 70s, experienced the highs, the lows and the downright unsavoury side of politics, was a seasoned master at the game and was a great strength to Lasantha. But the fact remained that Colombo North was traditionally a UNP seat and under the proportional representation system, Lasantha was not only competing with the UNP stalwarts but several of the SLFP leading lights as well. There was at least one of them however that extended their support; SLFP's Kotte veteran Jinadasa Niyathapala promised he would call upon his supporters to give Lasantha a preference vote.

Five month pregnant, I accompanied Lasantha on his campaigns and watched with great pride his speeches on public platforms. He was not as eloquent in his Sinhala as other breast-beating, jabberwocker politicians but he did manage to pull off some good lines that elicited thunderous cheers.

Lasantha's main campaign thrust was geared at highlighting glaring corruption in the governing party's ranks and promising a cleaner, fairer future. His electorate had a strong multi-ethnic flavour and Lasantha promised equality for all. It wasn't easy convincing the Tamil population in Colombo North to vote for a SLFP candidate. However, father Harris' reputation as a hard worker with a genial nature and an admirable work ethic, helped win over significant numbers.

Lasantha's election propaganda material and posters also highlighted the fact that he was an educated, fresh face who spelled hope for the Colombo North electorate. The catch-phrase on his propaganda material read "*Kaatath hithawath, kaageth hithawatha, Lasantha*" (Friendly towards all, everyone's friend, Lasantha)

Haleem Ishak, SLFP Member of Parliament for Colombo Central, endorsing Lasantha's candidacy said, ". . . . He is the youngest son of Mr. Harris Wickrematunge whose name is a household word in Colombo North. Harris Wickrematunge is a dedicated social worker who still serves people at grassroots level without any distinction. At a time when the country is torn by ethnic strife, I am confident that Lasantha who is a highly disciplined young man will serve all people irrespective of race, caste or religion and help in the process of national reconciliation."

Anura Bandaranaike, who before parliament was dissolved, had been Leader of the Opposition and Vice President of the SLFP said, ". . . when he offers himself as your representative in parliament he has just two or three immediate objectives before applying himself to other issues. He demands the elimination of corruption and employment for all without exception. In eliminating corruption he does not seek vengeance but insists that the corrupt repay to society the money they have amassed . . . he seeks to generate employment not by creating a powerful class of crony capitalists employing only a few thousands but by creating thousands of small and medium businessmen employing millions . . ."

During the run-up to the election, Lasantha's mother Chandra's sewing room was converted in to campaign headquarters where dozens of us would gather each day to stuff envelopes, call up voters and make tea and coffee for the men who worked day and night with Lasantha on the campaign trail. Huge posters of Lasantha were plastered on city walls, a sea of flags and streamers in bright blue—the SLFP colour—adorned the road leading to our house and little pocket calendars were printed for distribution with his picture and candidate number on the reverse.

Although our spirits were high and we were optimistic, I felt that winning this election in the face of titanic UNP muscle wasn't going to be easy. As I slept that night before the elections, I had a prophetic dream. I dreamt that while Lasantha and I stood watching in horror, the blue Volkswagen, Harris' pride and joy which had done a great deal of running during the election campaign, began gradually sinking and was slowly swallowed up by the earth. On Lasantha's face was an expression of acute distress. I knew then that Lasantha, and most probably the SLFP too, would lose the election. I however didn't air my fears to anyone.

The next morning, all of us went to the polling booth and placed a cross against the hand symbol of the Sri Lanka Freedom Party and then cast our votes for Number 19.

As the votes were being counted and the results aired on radio and TV that night, it became clear that the UNP was emerging victorious. There were accusations that rigging and intimidation had cost the SLFP the election. Lasantha himself did not get the required number of votes to gain a place in parliament although for a newcomer in the political scene contesting a traditional UNP seat, his performance was regarded as impressive.

The next day he and I were at home discussing the elections when the telephone rang. Mrs. Bandaranaike, by now Leader of the Opposition, was at the other end.

After exchanging pleasantries, Mrs. Bandaranaike came straight to the point.

"Lasantha, I'd like you to be my Private Secretary, would you be interested in taking up this offer?" she asked.

Lasantha thanked Mrs. Bandaranaike and told her he would call her back with his decision in five minutes. He put the receiver down and told me about the offer. "What do you think?" he asked.

I told him it would be a wonderful opportunity for him to work closely with the Opposition Leader and be part and parcel of the team that charted opposition policy and stood up to the might of the UNP government. Lasantha agreed. After the election defeat he had been somewhat crestfallen but this offer threw him back into the action as it were. He called his leader back to accept the offer and with his appointment as Private Secretary to the

Leader of the Opposition, his life, and mine by default, suddenly assumed whirlwind proportions.

Lasantha was now working three jobs; he was a junior to leading criminal lawyer Ranjit Abeysuriya, Private Secretary to the Leader of the Opposition and he had begun writing a political column in *The Sunday Times* under the pseudonym Suranimala.

I was writing and sub-editing for *The Sunday Times* and we were expecting our first baby in June. I worked at Wijeya Newspapers until the day I was due to enter hospital.

* * *

At Hospital Services down Havelock Road, some of the young female attendants were quite clever at predicting the sex of the baby by looking at the shape of the mother's belly; they were certain I was going to have a boy.

Just as they said, on June 24, 1989, a bawling baby boy was born. It happened to be one of those days when a JVP *hartal* order had been issued and most establishments were closed and the public transport system paralysed. There was hardly anybody on the streets and all the talk in the hospital among the nurses and attendants was of the *hartal*.

The baby, delivered by Professor G. Samaranayake, was a wee thing with long fingers and an elfin face. When Lasantha first held the baby in the maternity hospital, tears streamed down his face. But he thought the baby's slightly elongated head due to a lengthy labour, was adorably funny and he promptly nicknamed the infant 'Siribiris' after the long-headed cartoon character in a Sinhala comic strip.

We named the baby Avinash Sinha Ganesh; the last being the fulfillment of a vow I had made to the beloved elephant-headed God.

Back in the condominium with the new baby, life was not easy. All my family lived in Nugegoda and here in Kotahena, I didn't have any of them at hand for ready assistance. Lasantha's family except his father, were all away in Canada. Harris's blaring horn didn't help with the baby's sleeping patterns either. I was cooking, cleaning, taking care of a new baby and helping Lasantha in his court work by typing out the lengthy submissions on a rackety typewriter. The baby woke up several times in the night and didn't go back to sleep easily even after a feed. I was, like most new mothers, suffering from severe sleep deprivation.

Lasantha was wonderful with the baby. He fed him and changed nappies and woke up several times during the night when he cried. I would urge him to go back to bed because invariably the next day he would have an early start either in court or parliament but he would delight in walking up and down the room with the baby in his arms crooning and singing lullabies.

Avinash never slept during the day and I was constantly tired. It so happened that one afternoon I had put all the plastic feeding bottles and their attachments into the pan and left it to boil on the kitchen stove. The baby had miraculously fallen asleep and I lay down and closed my eyes for a moment. Suddenly I started up to the strong smell of burning. I had been so sleep deprived that I had dozed off in an instant without intending to. I peered out of the window to check whether a neighbour was burning rubbish but that didn't seem to be the case. I then walked downstairs and was assailed by the smell of roasting coming from the direction of the kitchen. With a tremendous shock I realised that I had forgotten the pan with the bottles on the stove and fearfully tip-toed into the kitchen to survey the damage. Thick smoke was billowing out of the pan; I peeped in—it was empty! All three feeding bottles and their attachments had melted and there was absolutely nothing left!

I began to panic. When you are a new mother, every little hitch sends you into a tailspin. What if the baby woke up and cried for a feed, I asked myself. Luckily, in a few minutes Lasantha returned home from work and hearing of the drama, rushed to the shops in Kotahena town to get a new feeding bottle. It was a cheap glass bottle unlike the fancy Mothercare ones I had received from my sister in Australia, but I was happy, and so was little Avinash who never noticed the difference! Lasantha meanwhile showed great empathy and related how as an 18-year old, exhausted after work, he had almost set the London flat on fire when he fell asleep while trying to fry chips.

I was feeling more and more homesick for my folks in Nugegoda. More than once I brought up the subject of moving closer to my parents and sisters. To my surprise, Lasantha agreed. After all his years of visiting Nugegoda, he had come to enjoy the suburb and was happy to relocate. Harris didn't fuss either. I think he himself was entertaining an idea of moving there sometime in the future. In a few months we sold the condominium and rented out a place in Nanda Mawatha, Nugegoda.

The property came with two houses on two different garden levels. We occupied the upper level residence while my sister Desiree who had recently married, occupied the house at the lower level.

The result of this was that Lasantha now had a partner in Desiree's husband to play scrabble during all hours of the day and night. I had all but given up playing scrabble with him because he hated to lose and would sometimes invent words, or so I thought. Once, stuck with the letter Q, he thought long and hard but couldn't come up with a word. Finally, he placed his letters to form a four-letter word beginning with Q. I jumped up and protested saying I had never heard such a word and insisted he was inventing it. "Check the dictionary," he said confidently. I did, but I still could not find the word.

"Actually it's a very rude word," he grinned. "You are such a sweet, unspoilt girl that you have probably never heard it."

I had nothing to say to that one!

During this time Lasantha also started playing squash at a Colombo venue with my brother-in-law and was enjoying it tremendously. This bit of recreational sporting activity continued until he slipped on the floor of the squash court one evening and fractured the bone in his left arm. He was required to wear his arm in a sling for several weeks during which time I played nursemaid, showering, dressing and attending to all his other needs. A few weeks prior Lasantha had written an article which was in effect a scathing attack on four members of Mrs. Bandaranaike's parliamentary group. Some people joked that it must have been their collective curses that put Lasantha's writing hand out of action for a few weeks. This handicap of course didn't put the brakes on his column. He dictated and I typed out the column for a while until his arm was in working order again.

On Valentine's Day in 1991, our second child, a baby girl, was born. She arrived with a shock of tight curls and a knowing stare. My mother commented it looked like she had been to the salon and had her hair set before arriving! I remember a beaming Lasantha telling everyone who came to St. Michael's Hospital, "Raine has given me the best Valentine's Day gift ever."

We named the baby Ahimsa Samadhi Ganesha.

Lasantha proved to be a doting dad who put his children on a pedestal but I was not happy about them being spoilt with too many toys and treats. I felt he was over-compensating for what he had himself missed out on, as a child.

Those years at the Nanda Mawatha home when the two children were little, passed by happily. Memories abound of the many children's parties held at that home, the entertaining we did and just the simple joy of watching the children grow. The main ingredients in our lives at the time were laughter and joy. The only times I put my foot down was when Lasantha indulged the kids in their every whim. Still, he would tell our friends that I never nagged him and would proudly regale all and sundry about my cooking which in his biased eyes were 'gastronomical marvels.'

But there were occasions when, biased or not, there was no evading the obvious truth. We had invited Ranjit Abesuriya, his gracious wife and their two sons and daughter to dinner one night and I had decided to try my hand at turning out a North Indian feast. With recipe book by my side I managed to get most of the dishes right but try as I might the *naan* bread refused to behave like *naan* bread. When everyone sat around the table and began tucking in, it was quite obvious that the *naan* was rock-hard. I was embarrassed and began offering my excuses. Lasantha thought he would put an end to my misery with a joke and declared, "I'm sorry but you will have to hit the *naan* on the gate-post first!" Fortunately everyone saw the funny side of it, laughed heartily and proceeded to enjoy the rest of the fare on the table.

When Ahimsa was still a few months old, we moved from Nanda Mawatha to the house in Kandewatte Terrace. This house was built by Lasantha's sister Buncie and her husband but before the house was completed, they were passed for migration to Canada. Buncie asked Lasantha and me to live there instead and this became our home and the house where Lasantha lived until his dying day.

---

[1] A word originating in India denoting civil disobedience and stoppage of work. In Sri Lanka, a JVP-enforced *hartal* was an 'order' that all work should come to a halt which impacted on the transport system, hospitals, schools and other establishments.

CHAPTER FOUR
Who is Suranimala?

> *"Put it before them briefly so they will read it, clearly so they will appreciate it, picturesquely so they will remember it and, above all, accurately so they will be guided by its light."*
> —Joseph Pulitzer, American lawyer, journalist and publisher.

IT was soon after Lasantha's unsuccessful bid to enter parliament in 1989 that the idea of a political column in *The Sunday Times* was first discussed. The Editor of the *Times* was Vijitha Yapa, a self-made man and founding Editor of three English language newspapers in Sri Lanka. It was Yapa who had as Editor of *The Island* in 1982 snapped up the young Lasantha when the latter walked out of Independent Newspapers in a huff.

After the initial discussions, Lasantha was asked to come up with a catchy pseudonym. I remember the two of us sitting in bed in our sunny condominium, putting our heads together and tossing names about.

I can't say we were all that innovative. At the time, the trend among many English newspaper columnists was to use pen names inspired by Sri Lankan or world history. There was the *WEEKEND*'s 'Migara' in the late 70s and early 80s. However, although Migara was a name that appeared in the Sinhala historical tomes, writer Sinha Ratnatunga chose it because it was his middle name.

Then there was the Kautilya column in *The Sunday Island* written by Mervyn de Silva. Kautilya was a name from Indian history, Kautilya being the learned minister of King Chandragupta Maurya.

After brainstorming for a little while, I suggested 'Suranimala,' one of 10 giant swashbucklers in the army of the second century BC monarch, Dutugemunu. Regarded with great veneration by the Sinhala people for uniting a fractured nation and particularly by the Buddhists for his grand efforts in the propagation of Buddhism, Dutugemunu waged war with the help of his giants, the second strongest of who was the mighty Suranimala.

It was his wizardry with the sword that made Suranimala of yore a celebrated warrior. The basis of my suggestion of the name Suranimala was that since the pen is considered to be mightier than the sword, Lasantha, with his feats with the pen, would equal or surpass the exploits of the great warrior.

Lasantha was taken up with the name and the reasoning behind it. He conveyed it to Yapa who also liked the choice of pseudonym. The maiden column was to make an appearance the following Sunday and Lasantha began tapping all his political connections for information. With his law background, political work and years of reporting, his list of contacts by this time had grown into an impressive little black book. Many of them were people who had a close ear on the corridors of power or those who traipsed the corridors themselves.

Since Lasantha's handwriting was considered an unintelligible scribble and no typesetter was expected to decipher it, once he had written the piece—amounting to about 30 A4 sheets—I typed out the entire article on our typewriter. Later when I was in hospital having our first baby, Yapa's wife Lalana took over the task of typing out the copy.

The very first Suranimala column appeared in *The Sunday Times* of April 16, 1989 during the Sinhala and Tamil New Year holiday season, under the headline 'Main star in drama refuses to perform.' The story, with a great deal of inside information, revolved round the JVP's unwillingness to play ball with the government and the main opposition party who were attempting a reconciliation of sorts with the radical party.

As one condition of writing the column was an assurance of complete anonymity, Lasantha didn't take the article to *The Sunday Times* office. Technological marvels such as e-mail were not available at the time; articles had to be either handwritten or typewritten and taken to the relevant office to be sent for typesetting. But Lasantha didn't want to be seen anywhere near the Wijeya Newspapers office with the article. Even though I was working on *The Sunday Times* at Wijeya, Lasantha didn't want even me taking the article to the office in case we were found out. Instead he would take the article to Yapa's house in Classen Place in Havelock Town every Thursday evening. This way, no one found out who the author of the column was.

Only the Publisher Ranjit Wijewardena, Editor Yapa, Lasantha and I knew the identity of Suranimala. Some of the desk heads were annoyed about being kept in the dark; one of them went so far as to visit the typesetting department and ask to see the original copy in a bid to ascertain whether he could identify the writing. But since it was typed, he was unsuccessful in his efforts.

Very early in its publication, the column began generating huge public interest and became a talking point in political and media circles. 'Who is Suranimala?' became a matter of hot conjecture not only at society events but in the corridors of power as well. The column stirred interest because of the writer's in-depth knowledge of internal matters of state and his no-holds barred writing.

Written in unpretentious, simple language, the column provided fly-on-the-wall style details of backroom maneuverings and high-level, closed door confabs. Most often the article would reproduce word-to-word the verbal exchanges that occurred at Cabinet meetings. And one phrase Suranimala used liberally in his columns—'be that as it may'—became his stamp of identity.

But Lasantha wasn't merely an eager-beaver reporter reproducing an array of delectable anecdotes from the political spectrum. He had a keenly analytical mind, a deep knowledge and legal understanding of matters of state and a good grasp of the political milieu and its machinations. He had contacts all over—in governance, in opposition, the legal fraternity, the private sector, the defence forces, the diplomatic circles—who were more than willing to share information with him. All this was clearly evident in his writings.

Because the identity of the writer was kept hidden, the secrecy itself gave rise to intense speculation. We were once at an embassy cocktail party and I was chatting to some journalists when one of them, from our very own newspaper, began to deride the column's use of a clichéd phrase. "What kind of writing is that?" he scoffed. "The article said so and so 'graced the occasion' . . . who writes like that?"

I kept a straight face and made a mental note that no one should 'grace an occasion' in the column anymore!

Lake House journalist Ajith Samaranayake who had a supreme and very creative command of the English language and displayed this in his articles, and his wife, my friend Mano (Manohari), were also present. Mano kept asking me whether I knew who Suranimala was and I replied that I wasn't certain. Ajith then said, "Whoever it is, he certainly has a great deal of inside knowledge." Just then Lasantha sauntered towards us.

"They are all wondering who Suranimala is . . . do you have any idea?" I asked him with a twinkle in my eye.

Without batting an eyelid, Lasantha looked at another journalist who was standing in our group and in his usual loud, jovial manner, slapped him on the back and bellowed, "Hey . . . don't act all innocent . . . I heard you are Suranimala!"

The man squirmed and muttered something in his defense. Everyone laughed because they knew Lasantha was joking but they still didn't suspect it was Lasantha himself who was the author of the column.

At the time President Premadasa was at the height of his unpopularity; engaged in running battles with certain members of his Cabinet, he didn't trust anyone and his style of governance was abrasive to say the least.

Vijitha Yapa in an article about the birth of Suranimala said, "Once he wrote of the President's proposals on devolution which had been sent out confidentially. Lasantha discovered the President had used four different colours of ink on the copies so he could trace the 'leak' if there was one. Lasantha, or Suranimala, deliberately mentioned the colour of the ink used in the file copy which led to a major crisis in the Presidential Secretariat. The President's secretary telephoned me in a flurry wanting to know who the source of information is. I refused to divulge any information even though the caller said it was a request from the President himself."

During this time the government was still engaged in its ferocious battles with the Marxist JVP. Defence Minister Ranjan Wijeratne, spearheading the anti-JVP onslaught, was determined to leave no stone unturned in his efforts to crush the radicals. The Suranimala column was giving detailed information on the government's crackdown on the JVP and Wijeratne was getting increasingly irked by the stories being published. He went to great lengths to discover the identity of the writer and once successful, he telephoned the Chairman of the newspaper. Having vented spleen about what his paper was publishing, Wijeratne ranted, "I know who Suranimala is . . . it is Mrs. Bandaranaike's private secretary . . . if he's not careful he could get into all sorts of trouble!!"

This bit of news was duly conveyed to Lasantha via the Editor. In customary style Lasantha brushed it aside as a peril of the profession. Not so his father Harris who got wind of the situation and sensing danger, began pushing his son to leave the country for a while with his family.

It was at this time that Lasantha's disenchantment with the SLFP began. He felt that when he was in difficulty, Mrs. Bandaranaike had not stepped up with any concrete help or advice expected of a leader. When, pushed by his father, he broached the subject of a very real threat to his life, Mrs. Bandaranaike merely said, "Why don't you ask your friend Ranil for help?"

Ranil at the time was a Minister in the government.

On February 18, 1990, when another popular and talented media personality, Richard de Zoysa, was ruthlessly murdered and his body washed ashore, father Harris' push became shove. Requests were made to the Australian High Commission who arranged for holiday visas forthwith and in April 1990, Lasantha, myself and our 10 month old baby left for Melbourne.

In Melbourne we stayed with my sister Fern and her family, Lasantha taking a break from the frenzied pace of his political commitments, legal work, the newspaper column and the violent events in Sri Lanka, to enjoy the many delights of Australia. Video footage shows a clowning Lasantha dancing in the park with his baby son on his shoulders, playing cricket, chasing me around rose bushes mimicking Bollywood film song-sequences and generally having a rollicking good time.

While we were in Melbourne, Australia went to the polls and Lasantha and I were both fascinated and hugely impressed with the peaceful manner in which the election was conducted. It was such a huge contrast to Sri Lanka's violent, blood-soaked affairs. That week, together with Jennifer Barthelot, ex-*Sunday Times* staffer now domiciled in Australia, I wrote a piece for *The Sunday Times* on the Australian federal elections in which the incumbent Labor Party's Bob Hawke defeated the Liberals' Andrew Peacock.

Lasantha's father Harris meanwhile was busy in Sri Lanka. He was not happy with his son's grumblings about wanting to return home and get back to his legal work, his politics and his writing. Using old political connections from his Deputy Mayor days, Harris organised a meeting with President Premadasa. When he met the President at the latter's private residence Sucharitha in Hulftsdorp, Harris aired his fears for Lasantha's life. According to what he related to us later, during the discussions the President had, referring to Lasantha said, "Yes, I remember him. Isn't he the little fellow that used to come with you in the car?" Thereafter the President told Harris he would ensure his son was safe.

Having received this assurance from the President, Harris conveyed the news to us and we booked our return flight to Colombo. We had been in Melbourne for little less than two months. Once back, Lasantha happily picked up his pen from where he had stopped. Suranimala was back.

During this time, because I was taking care of our first-born, I had resigned from *The Sunday Times* but wrote a column titled '*Behind The Headlines*' focusing each week on a current newsmaker.

Not long after our return home, *The Sunday Times* got into the government's bad books once again, not least due to Suranimala and his writings. As Yapa wrote of this in his tribute to Lasantha, "The Premadasa era brought many things to a head. The President wanted Sirisena Cooray (Cabinet Minister and the President's close confidante) to help him form the Cabinet which Mr. Cooray declined by saying he did not want to be blamed for cutting other people's necks and took off in a helicopter to Devinuwara to be with Mahinda Wijesekera . . . . Mr. Cooray knew that President Premadasa wanted to cut the powers of Lalith and Gamini. The publishing of this item infuriated Premadasa who felt we were trying to convey to the world that there was a rift between him and Mr. Cooray. The publisher and I were attacked from public platforms . . . .

"Lasantha's column was embarrassing to the Premadasa government. They applied pressure. The independence of an Editor was more vital than stopping columns and I bid goodbye to mainstream journalism in Sri Lanka."

The exit of Vijitha Yapa was quite a shock to everyone in the *Times* Editorial. He had been a firm and exacting boss who demanded the best from everyone and many of us had been at the receiving end of his biting sarcasm; I personally know that my page lay-out skills improved by leaps and bounds under his thorough scrutiny. Thus it was Yapa who had built up the *Times* to what it was and the journalists were sad to see him go. At the time nobody was quite certain as to what had pushed him to resign. I remember asking him this and his reply was, "It's better to leave when people ask 'why' rather than 'why not?'"

Sinha Ratnatunga succeeded Yapa. I had worked for seven years from 1979-1986 with him at Independent Newspapers when he was Deputy Editor of the *WEEKEND*. As a sub-editor on the *WEEKEND*, I had, all those years, subbed and proofread his 'Migara' column every Saturday afternoon. Upon taking over as Editor of *The Sunday Times* in 1990 he called me up at home and urged me to re-join the *Times*. I couldn't, I protested, I had a baby to take care of. Sinha persisted. The Features Editor was leaving he said—to join Mr. Yapa's new public relations company (and later a chain of hugely successful bookstores)—and *The Sunday Times* needed a new Features Editor.

Having discussed the offer with Lasantha, and having acquired the services of family faithful Menika to take care of Avinash, I re-joined *The Sunday Times* as its next Features Editor.

For another three years, until we left in April 1994 to start *The Sunday Leader*, Lasantha and I continued at the *Times*, he, a freelancer writing the Suranimala column and occasionally standing in for the news editor when he was away and I handling the features desk as Features Editor. By then everyone in the office knew he was the man behind 'Suranimala.' Lasantha was now free to submit copy in his own handwriting much to the dismay of the typesetters who struggled to decipher the unintelligible scrawl. Luckily for them, they could come running to me whenever they needed a 'de-code.'

"If anyone can read his handwriting it has to be you," they would tell me.

For 14 years after we left the *Times*, Lasantha continued to write the political column under the pseudonym Suranimala in his beloved *Leader* newspaper. The last, titled 'Cabinet defies Supreme Court as LTTE spoils Killinochchi party' was published in the *Leader* on January 4, 2008, four days before he was killed.

CHAPTER FIVE
The Sunday Leader

> *"Each time a person stands up for an ideal, or acts to improve the lot of others, or strikes out against injustice, he sends forth a tiny ripple of hope, and crossing each other from a million different centres of energy and daring, these ripples build a current that can sweep down the mightiest walls of oppression and resistance."—Robert* Kennedy, former US Attorney General.

ONE day in January 1994, Lasantha's brother Lal arrived at our home bursting with the exciting news about a tentative idea to launch a new newspaper.

Lal worked for Multi-Packs, a company that printed Sinhala cartoon periodicals among other things and he and Haris Hulugalle, Chairman of Multi-Packs, were considering starting a national, English language newspaper.

Lasantha was seen as an essential element in the venture, both from the editorial and business aspects. His journalistic credentials were formidable—as a newsman he was one of the best the country had produced. From a business standpoint, his vast pool of wide and varied contacts would be an invaluable asset to a new company. Lasantha however was adamant about one thing. He would come on board, he said, only if he was afforded full editorial autonomy with no pen-wielding boss breathing down his neck. No stifling of his pen nor that of other journalists working on the newspaper would be tolerated, he insisted. That assurance given, Lasantha and I threw ourselves into the planning of the project with Lal and Haris and slowly the formative bones of Leader Publications began taking shape. A director board was formed and the new management scouted around for a printing press and office premises.

Initially, the aim was to publish a Sunday paper which would be called *The Sunday Leader*. Down the road they would consider starting a Sinhala edition, and later, if everything went well, even a mid-week.

Lasantha and I were to be involved in all the initial planning of the format of the newspaper and be responsible for recruiting staff, steering the editorial department and the newspaper's content.

I was not thrilled about moving out of *The Sunday Times* which, after seven years, had become a second home to me. I realised however that leaving was inevitable and that the time had come to bid farewell to all my colleagues at Wijeya Newspapers.

While I was at the tail-end of my days at the *Times* and news about the *Leader* had leaked, the *Times*' resident astrologer/translator G. Athukorale came to my desk one day with a funny snippet. He said, a member of the Wijeya Group management who he refused to name, had asked him if he could predict whether or not the *Leader* would become a success.

"So what did you tell him?" I asked, curious to know of our own fate!

"I told him this new newspaper would become very popular because it's written in both Raine and Lasantha's stars," Athukorale replied.

On April 5, 1994, Lasantha's 36th birthday, we said our fond goodbyes to the *Times* staff, all of who came down to the entrance steps on Nawam Mawatha, to see us off. Earlier in the week they had given us a memorable farewell at a resort hotel in Negombo.

As Lasantha and I drove from the *Times* building to Ward Place where our new offices were located, there were mixed feelings. There was some diffidence and yet, a spirit of great adventure and excitement bubbled.

The Ward Place office looked like somebody's old home. Even a hasty paint job, a few pot plants and Lal's wife Marie's creative touch, didn't quite elevate it to the standards of corporate respectability. The garden—complete with clumps of grass, sand and straggling weeds—was a favourite haunt of stray dogs, one of which was adopted later as part of the *Leader* family and christened 'Steffie.'

Inside, the main front area was designated for both the subs and news desks while most desk heads were to share small rooms with their deputies. It wasn't the ideal newspaper office but it wasn't the pits either and the cosiness itself lent it a charming, homely feel.

Right from day one—together with Lal and Haris Hulugalle—Lasantha and I rolled up our sleeves and got down to the business of developing the format and design of the newspaper. We worked out the different sections, their sizes with regards to number of pages and sectional titles. We pored over typography, column widths and layout and we experimented with mastheads, logos and taglines. Haris's daughter Shani was an asset with her knowledge of computer technology and her design and lay-out skills. Dummies of each section were prepared and an artist commissioned to create banners and logos. We brainstormed for a catchy slogan, one that encapsulated the essence of the newspaper and the ideals it would champion. Lasantha suggested 'Unbowed and Unafraid' which everyone agreed was an excellent motto.

Although the pages were to be produced in the manual cut-and-paste style on paste-up boards, the plan was to experiment with desktop publishing using PageMaker software to design and produce Page One. When this was successfully achieved, several other pages were thereafter produced on the computer.

In that first week at the office there was just Lasantha, myself, an office helper, driver and a couple of production staffers who had been sourced from Multi-Packs, the parent company. A couple of weeks later Rukshana, a young trainee reporter, a few typesetters and paste-up artists, joined the ranks. The office was equipped with two Apple Mac computers, a Macintosh Quadra and an A3 printer.

At the outset, Lasantha wanted me to take on the role of Features Editor continuing what I had done at the *Times*. I however yearned for a break from titles. I preferred to work behind the scenes as a sort of Girl Friday—write, edit, do lay-out and pen a column or two—without the weight of a title hanging around my neck. While applying for media accreditation cards however, it appeared applicants were required to provide their designations and I had none. Defence Analyst Iqbal Athas who had joined the *Leader* ranks as Deputy Editor, hurriedly conjured the title 'Features Consultant' and that remained my designation throughout my *Leader* life.

At the time, several other English-language Sunday papers were on the market, and some of them, aware of Lasantha's journalistic skills, were sprucing up their act in preparation for this latest rival, revealing lots of colour and glitz. If we were to survive, we had to be different; we needed to give our readers something they had never experienced before. The answer lay with Lasantha and his news-gathering genius and his potential as a great investigative writer.

A few English newspapers in the years past had run investigative pieces from time to time, mostly delving into departmental bureaucracy, ongoing social justice issues or minor ministerial misdemeanors. During the UNP government's massive development schemes in the early 80s, articles had appeared in the press highlighting various contentious issues and minor controversies surrounding such projects. A couple of anti-government Sinhala tabloids in later years, especially during the Premadasa era, had exposed scandals from time to time but unfortunately, due to the public perception of tabloids, such stories were sometimes relegated to the realm of sensationalist journalism.

Except for the occasional exposure, no English newspaper in our times had boldly and consistently published stories that would rock the very foundations of state, the defence establishment, the judiciary or any other powerful institution. Readers were not accustomed to reading in-depth investigations backed by extensive evidence of a head of state's serious transgressions, ministerial corruption, crooked arms deals, irregular tender procedures, corporate criminality or state-underworld links.

These were stories that the people of Sri Lanka had a right to know but had thus far not been privy to. That kind of no-holds barred investigations after painstaking and meticulous research was an unknown commodity to a people who were either only offered the highly manipulated official line in the state-run newspapers, the fluff and colour in other publications or stories that barely scratched the surface in still others.

This state of affairs however was about to change with the arrival of *The Sunday Leader* and the daring brand of investigative journalism that Lasantha was poised to introduce. He was, in a sense, ready to revolutionise the media, for few before him had possessed the potent combination of skill, spunk and a vast reservoir of sources that would enable him to write the stories that he did, and the courage and license in the form of managerial non-interference, to publish them.

* * *

With the launch date approaching, several desk heads—news editor, features editor, sports editor, chief sub editor—and other staff, were recruited to the Editorial. All of us went about our tasks at a frantic pace in preparation for the first issue due to come out on June 19, 1994. Despite having collected a bank of articles and several pages completed in advance, with a few days to go, there was still so much more to be done. The number of typesetters and paste-up persons was limited; they had to be stretched out to cover the TV Guide, the *Now!* Entertainment tabloid, the *Review* features section, any advertising supplements and the main section which included the news pages, news features, investigations, business pages and sports.

Then there were other major issues cropping up. The printing press, a 26-year-old Goss Suburban which had been purchased from Kansas, USA, several months previously and shipped in dismantled form and assembled again like a giant jigsaw puzzle, had hit a snag. Despite all the efforts of the technicians it seemed like the press would not be operating in time for our first issue. Lasantha was beside himself with worry. All our advertising campaigns had specified a launch date and it was inconceivable that the paper didn't come out on that day. The only option was to out-source the printing at a huge cost.

On the Thursday before the launch, Lasantha wrote his Suranimala column which had been 'transported' from *The Sunday Times*. There had been discussions at the *Times* management as to whether the copyright of a writer's pseudonym lay with the writer or the newspaper; a senior member of the Editorial had pointed out that a pseudonym belonged to the writer and that he/she could use the same pseudonym elsewhere.

Everyone worked late into the night in the final run-up to D-day. By around 9.30 on Friday night, barely keeping to our printing deadline, the last page was put to bed. We had completed a 58-page edition comprising four sections. On our cover page we also announced a competition where readers could win a Datamini personal computer, a Singer radio/cassette player, a Mellanex dinner set, a Singer waffle iron, gas cooker and music CDs.

For two months Lasantha and I together with the rest of the Editorial staff had laboured for this day. Two weeks earlier the highly confidential plan to issue a TV guide with the newspaper had leaked through an advertising agency and a week before the *Leader* came out into the market, we heard that *The Sunday Times* had pounced on our idea and was issuing a TV guide the following Sunday. I was sorely disappointed and prevailed upon Lal and Lasantha to advance the launch date of *The Sunday Leader* to Sunday, June 12, instead of the 19th as planned. Logistics didn't allow that, and we had to see our rival come out on June 12 and beat us by a whisker with a very colourful extra.

Our first issue had been completed and sent off to the printer. Voila! In our minds, everything else would happen like clockwork—the paper would be printed and hang prominently in the shops come early Sunday morning. We didn't realise what a gargantuan task lay ahead for Lal whose printing and distribution ordeal had only just begun.

In his words, 'The print problem was overcome by hiring out the printing, though at a huge cost. The distribution turned out to be a nightmare. No one expected the time it took to transport the printed pages from the printshop. Not a single sheet was allowed to be moved out unless full payment was received by the printer. Then the pages had to be gathered and bundled in correct quantities to be distributed. The night before the first issue hit the stands was chaotic. Everything was way behind schedule. My brother Lasantha was frantic.

"I tried my best to persuade him that everything was under control. By 4 am I made a frantic dash to the factory. Large sections of Colombo were yet to be served and the distribution system or what it was supposed to be had gone haywire. I realised too late that the periodical system of delivery had a two day lead time and the staff was not used to a newspaper distribution system.

"Mustering whoever was available, sections were put together and some of us with cars took over delivery. Around 6.00 am, still in my shorts and rubber slippers, I delivered 600 copies to an agent opposite the Narahenpita labour secretariat. There was a long queue patiently waiting for the newspaper. The agent however was not of the same disposition. "I say," he addressed me with a stern look. "If this is the way you handle the first issue you will not be able to sustain this. You tell your boss that I will speak to him about this."

And it was in this state of affairs that we kept plodding along. With editorial content we were making our mark; with each passing week we were gaining readers; as a finished product however the newspaper's quality left much to be desired. The 'state-of-the-art printing' that had been promised in our advertising campaigns was non-existent. The cutting-edge technology was nowhere in sight unless one took the single Macintosh Quadra into account! The finish of the paper was shoddy, the colour separations were un-cordinated and some pages came with unsightly smudges.

Fortunately the high quality of our content overrode the poor quality of the finished product. The Suranimala political column which had acquired a large following in *The Sunday Times* with its many exclusive revelations and insightful analysis was at the beginning, our main draw card. The news too was fresh and more often than not, the lead stories were scoops. The columns were daring and the stories bold. As Lasantha began featuring in-depth investigations exposing those in high places, many began viewing the new paper as a trail-blazer which dared to call a spade a spade. Respect grew and circulation figures surged.

Lasantha and I, together with a wonderfully supportive and talented group of fellow journalists and production staff, worked 10-12 hour days, sometimes longer. Our two young children whinged and complained and got up to a lot of mischief. At home with the maids most of the time, they came up with novel ways to keep themselves entertained. One night we went home tired after a hard day's slog to find that the two young mischief-makers had managed to set alight their collection of soft toys. Brother and sister who had not expected such a huge conflagration were running up and down in a mighty dither, throwing cups of water on the poor crisping cats and burning bunnies.

In those early times there were grim days when Lasantha and I seriously wondered whether the paper would survive the strains and pressures it had to endure. Chairman Hulugalle meant well but he was unpredictable and temperamental. One day he would breathe cold, and the next he would snort hot, angry fumes and tear pages off the paste-up boards. Despite having promised not to interfere in matters editorial after his initial involvement during the planning stages, Haris wanted his continued say in certain aspects such as layout and format. Lal was caught in between Haris's spoilt child tantrums and Lasantha's threats to throw in the towel.

Another minor dispute arose with regard to hiring the services of former *Sunday Observer* cartoonist S. C. Opatha. Hulugalle wanted him in but Lasantha was horrified. Opatha, he insisted, had, during his long stint at the government-controlled Lake House group, gone too far in his political vilification of the opposition, in particular the Bandaranaikes and the Kumaratungas. Lasantha didn't want Opatha anywhere near the *Leader* office. Hulugalle insisted and finally Lasantha gave in reluctantly. Opatha came in for an interview and was hired. With time, Lasantha took to Opatha and the latter became a well-liked fixture at the office continuing until his death several years later.

At the office, I would start the week organising and putting together content for the *Now!* Magazine. I came up with new story ideas, assigned reporters, edited copy, sat with the lay-out artist at the computer putting pages together and finally proofread everything. By Tuesday evening I would start on the TV guide and on Wednesday, sub-edited some pages of *Review*, the features section. Then came laying out and proofreading advertising supplements followed by subbing some main section pages. In addition I was penning two columns, doing the parliamentary round-up and writing feature stories.

Lasantha and I put in so much back-breaking work in those early days that one desk-head was to quip, "If it ever came to a crunch, Lasantha and Raine can easily run this paper by themselves."

That was a huge exaggeration but in a sense it encapsulated the simplified version of how the rest of the staff viewed us—Lasantha brought in the news, Raine put it together. In addition, the young ones saw us as 'mum' and 'dad'—Lasantha, the dependable, hard-working, clever, outspoken Editor who had the time to joke around the office, tease the girls and boys and stand by them through thick and thin, and I, the one who the girls came running to for everything from boyfriend problems to getting that first para right.

It was hard, that first year. I remember all I wanted at that stage was to complete our first year in circulation. I was terrified the *Leader* would be just a three-month wonder; a flash in the pan.

Lasantha and I decided one day that perhaps we should appeal to the gods for help. We made the trip to an old Buddhist temple near Siripura, Talawatugoda and prayed to the deities asking that they cast their divine benevolence on the *Leader* and help us pass the one-year mark. We were confident that if we notched a year, the worst of the teething problems would be settled and we had a good shot at making a success of this.

The monk at the temple gave us some oil that had been blessed with repeated chanting of *Budu Guna*[1] and advised us to light a lamp for a week in the office premises. We had to ensure that the flame never died out during that week. The responsibility of that fell on Sandanam, our dear, old-faithful who had been a long-standing Wickrematunge family loyalist from Kotahena and had been hired as an office-helper at *The Leader*. Sandanam hastily constructed a makeshift enclosure for the lamp and ensured it was kept alight at all times that week.

The flicker of hope continued to burn but there was no shortage of the challenges that came thick and fast.

Lal, as the managing director, handled all matters business with the support of Financial Director Sivakanthi Kumar. He had a heap of his own headaches to contend with as it dawned on him that running a national newspaper was not quite the same as printing entertainment periodicals. National newspapers in Sri Lanka were by and large owned and run either by the government or powerful business tycoons with solid financial backing. *The Sunday Leader* however had been started with no significant capital investment. Lal had put in all his life's savings which didn't amount to much while Multi-Packs provided some backing. There were no big bank loans that had been taken out. Funds for the printing machine had been received from a well-wisher with the understanding that it would be re-paid down the road. In a financial sense we were on shaky ground. However, we all had collectively undertaken—with naiveté, bravado, or both—to deliver an elephant, and we were not about to give up with a rodent's squeak of defeat. If it took blood, sweat and tears to produce a top-class newspaper, we were going to do it. And *The Sunday Leader* literally exacted all three, and in no small measure either.

Advertising was not easy to come by either. The Advertising Manager when we began was World Cup star cricketer Asanka Gurusinghe. With 'Gura' away playing cricket overseas much of the time, it fell on the shoulders of his deputy—quietly confident Sanjeeva Wettewe—and his team of able reps, to do the needful. Government advertising which made up roughly 40 percent of a newspaper's advertising did not come our way as a result of the Leader's confrontational stance. In the private sector, some business houses that were canvassed were wary of giving us advertising lest they were branded as *Leader* allies and earned the wrath of the government.

More steadily than slowly, the small but determined and persistent advertising team built up a rapport with ad agencies and big businesses. The young reps met up with ad agency bosses and corporate executives, establishing camaraderie and vital business links. In those early days, much of the advertising that came through was purely due to the goodwill thus created or through Lal and Lasantha's personal friendships.

The advertising team also came up with various strategies to bring in advertising such as weekly specialised supplements and vantage positioning at no extra cost. Their efforts helped stop the wolf from clawing at the *Leader* door. Each time Sanjeewa came up to the Editorial, Lasantha would ask him how much revenue they had managed to haul in that week. It was a day-to-day existence and we were grateful to those who, at the risk of their businesses being affected by backing what was perceived as an anti-government newspaper, continued to support us with their advertising.

With time, as the demographics of our readership became clearer and the Leader began settling into a definite niche, more companies began advertising with us because they felt the *Leader* reached their business' targeted up-market and upper-middle class consumers in particular. Advertising agencies came to regard the *Leader* as a dynamic media partner and encouraged their clients to advertise with us.

Despite the single-storey office building itself being old and somewhat decrepit, it was placed in a prime location in Colombo's elite Ward Place and demanded a huge rental outlay. There were colossal production and transport costs, staff salaries and the day to day running expenses of the newspaper. All this had to be covered by what trickled in as advertising and later, as sales revenue.

Due to its virtual hand-to-mouth existence, Leader Publications did not carry stocks of newsprint nor did it have any stockpile inventory. Newsprint was purchased at the last minute each time as cash was scarce. In the early days some essentials such as furniture and computers were obtained on barter in exchange for advertising.

Internal issues notwithstanding, Lasantha at the helm as Editor-In-Chief, was turning the *Leader* into a much sought after, if somewhat controversial, newspaper. With his investigative journalism, credibility grew and soon, the public was riding the wave with us, egging and encouraging us on. In a sense, the *Leader* was jolting its readers out of their defeatist acceptance of mediocrity and corruption and opening their eyes to the fact that a public-spirited newspaper could indeed drive much-needed change. *The Sunday Leader* was emerging as the standard-bearer of journalistic excellence.

Lasantha's investigations tied him down to hours of painstaking research. He used up dozens of notebooks as he scribbled away while on the phone to his countless contacts. He taped exhaustive interviews with those who provided details for some exposure or the other. And then, he sat and put it all together making up a stunning investigative piece.

Lasantha was extremely thorough in his information-gathering and when he worked on some big investigation, apart from his main source, he talked to as many other contacts as possible, cross-checking facts and gleaning even the most trivial of information to embellish his narrative which gave it added credence. If a story had an international link, he would contact every relevant foreign source—both individuals and institutions—collecting information, documents and photographs with the diligence and zeal of a private investigator.

He was also completely fearless in 'naming and shaming the devil' whoever it was and whatever office he or she held. He was driven by the principle of the public's right to know and the knowledge that a good newspaper was not just an agent of change but the upholder of democracy itself.

Lasantha realised early on that he had set the bar very high and readers expected big, ground-breaking stories from *The Sunday Leader* each week. It was time-consuming and stressful but for Lasantha, digging up stories and writing them was also intoxicating. He was running high on adrenaline. Because of his legal training he was able to immediately recognise the implications of a story and had the necessary skill to retain the crux and appeal of the narrative while still keeping it within the perimeters of libel and defamation.

Lasantha's bold revelations earned him such respect that there were times when complete strangers would come in to the office just to shake his hand and tell him what a great job he was doing. In a sense, readers were stunned that there was this man bold enough to take on presidents and governments, to name powerful miscreants and present the facts like no one had ever done before. It empowered people by giving them knowledge and rendered hope for change where there had been none before.

At the beginning however, some critics were quick to tag Lasantha a partisan journalist who was dishing out the dirt on the newly appointed Prime Minister Chandrika Kumaratunga and her government because of his close friendship with the Opposition Leader Gamini Dissanayake. In fact right to the very end of his days Lasantha was viewed as being partial to the UNP. Yet, during the UNP government's short stint in power, the newspaper took many ministers to task and revealed corruption in high places. Despite the perception of him being a 'UNP journalist' Lasantha maintained his integrity and was hugely admired and respected.

Lasantha was a journalist and a brilliant one at that, but he was also a political animal wading knee-deep in murky political waters. He and *The Sunday Leader* were in a sense what gave the opposition the courage and the drive, in many instances, to take the government head-on.

Lasantha's relationship with Gamini Dissanayake, the Opposition Leader at the time *The Sunday Leader* began, could at best be termed a chequered one. During Lasantha's early days in journalism he had not enamored himself to the powerful—and some would say, arrogant—Minister in the J. R. Jayewardene cabinet. Gamini was a friend of India and had extended his whole-hearted support to the Indo-Lanka agreement signed in 1987. He did not like the stories, with their strong anti-government flavour, that Lasantha was writing in *The Island* newspaper at the time and had made no secret of his dislike for the young journalist.

The former Deputy Editor of *The Island* newspaper Gamini Weerakoon recounted an episode involving Lasantha and Gamini that occurred when Lasantha was still a young reporter.

"One of the few incidents I recall was when he was to interview the then powerful UNP Minister Gamini Dissanayake on a Mahaweli project.[2] Gamini did not like probing questions and a verbal row had flared up. Lasantha, not intimidated by ministerial rank, pressed on with his questions. An angry Dissanayake was then on my line saying: 'This fellow is asking me impertinent questions and I am not going to answer him.' Lasantha shouted into the phone: 'He is dodging the vital question!'

"I felt proud of him but clearly he was exceeding his limits. I persuaded Dissanayake to give the phone to Lasantha and explained to him that at an interview with the Minister, he (Lasantha) was the guest and could not force the Minister to answer him. An indignant Lasantha came back to office muttering, not too happy about my stand."

Gamini Dissanayake had been one of the favoured young bucks in the J. R. Jayewardene government together with Lalith Athulathmudali and Ranil Wickremesinghe, each harbouring their own personal ambitions. The fact that Lasantha enjoyed a friendship with the latter two must also have made him suspect in the eyes of Gamini. In fact, Lalith Athulathmudali, at the time Minister of National Security, was one of the first guests to arrive at our wedding in 1987 while Ranil Wickremesinghe and Anura Bandaranaike acted as our witnesses. Gamini was not on the guest list.

By 1994, much of this had changed. Gamini had by this time metamorphosed into something of a master political strategist and perhaps as a result of the conflicts he faced within his own party, matured tremendously both as a man and a politician. He and Lasantha formed a close relationship which grew into a personal friendship.

In 1991 Gamini, Lalith, G. M. Premachandra and nine other dissidents had been expelled from the UNP following a failed impeachment motion to oust President Premadasa. At the time the dissidents formed the Democratic United National Front (DUNF), the spectre of fear and unease in the country had been almost palpable. President Ranasinghe Premadasa's governing style, especially towards the end of his days, had generated a fear psychosis so intense that the country was gripped by near-mass paranoia. People no longer felt safe discussing politics on a bus or any other public place. They refrained from engaging in political gossip on the telephone for fear the bogeyman was listening in.

It was in this backdrop that we would sometimes receive a hurried telephone call from Gamini and he would arrive at our home shortly thereafter to discuss some latest development or the other. At other times, Lasantha and he would be huddled in animated conversation inside Gamini's car which would be parked outside our gate.

On April 23, 1993 when Lalith Athulathmudali was gunned down in Colombo while making a political address, the country, and the young DUNF, was plunged into a whirlpool of sorrow and despair. At a press conference held at his home, a visibly upset Dissanayake vowed to continue with the DUNF's work. In the week that followed it seemed as if the country's collective contempt was focused on President Premadasa and the air was literally thick with doom and gloom. When a week later the President was assassinated by a suicide bomber, Prime Minister D. B. Wijetunga was sworn in as President and the breakaways re-joined the UNP. The DUNF split with Lalith's widow Srimani forming the Democratic United National Lalith Front. (DUNLF)

On August 16, 1994 the country went to the polls. The UNP's main opponent was the new People's Alliance—comprising the SLFP and six other political parties—led by Chandrika Kumaratunga, daughter of Sirima Bandaranaike.

The UNP's track record from 1977-1994 had hardly been lily white. In fact, despite opening up the economy and initiating a number of massive development and welfare programs, much of their 17-years of governance had been deplorable and the image of the UNP branded into the people's minds was that of a high-handed, corruption-ridden regime. The powerful executive presidency introduced through J. R. Jayewardene's 1978 constitution was unpopular and this was exacerbated by the final *'bheeshanaya'* or terror-infused years of President Ranasinghe Premadasa. Premadasa had started out with the best intentions of alleviating poverty and easing the sufferings of the *'nethi beris'* (the 'have-nots') but these laudable efforts had been overshadowed by the unhealthy effects of a paranoid personality.

The people of Sri Lanka had had enough of the UNP and were thirsting for a change. They were even willing to forget the years of privation suffered in the 1970s under a Sirima Bandaranaike government. Daughter Chandrika held great promise, and the country, buoyed by a new spirit of hope, swung in favour of the People's Alliance (PA).

That night, *The Sunday Leader* editorial staff were on 'election duty' at ETV television studios as part of an election result telecast collaboration between the newspaper and the television station. Although as the results kept coming in, it seemed like the PA was going to sweep the boards, Lasantha analysed the results quite early in the night predicting that no single party or alliance would obtain an absolute majority.

He was right. In the end, the PA, with 105 seats as opposed to the UNP's 94, formed an alliance with the Muslim Congress. A sole MP from the Up-Country People's Front also extended his support giving them a simple majority of 113 in parliament.

Chandrika was sworn in as Prime Minister on August 19 while D. B. Wijetunga remained President. Although they represented two rival political parties, the new Prime Minister and her government found co-habitation with the fatherly and mild-mannered Wijetunga relatively smooth-sailing.

President Wijetunga announced he would not be running for President in the presidential election due to be held in November. After engaging in a brief battle of numbers with Ranil Wickremesinghe, Gamini emerged as the leader of the UNP and was nominated as the UNP's presidential candidate.

Despite the PA's new-broom popularity, Gamini—seen as a man with a vision for the 21st century—stood out as a formidable contender to Chandrika. While accepting that the UNP should take some responsibility for the country's problems, Gamini said, "I would be unconvincing if after 24 years in the frenetic world of politics I were to say that I lacked ambition. Ambition is a noble virtue when used constructively and creatively. It is an inner energy that provides the driving force for success.

"I do not seek the Presidency just for its glory, glamour or power. I have seen the emptiness in the lives of too many Presidents and Prime Ministers who chose that path but failed to place a stamp of moral authority on their office.

"I seek the Presidency to bring about change and to provide a new kind of leadership that will alter our political landscape and climate, produce genuine consensus among our political parties, initiate much needed political reform and move our country towards a new kind of politics—the politics of principle."

It was during this presidential campaign that, on October 24, 1994, Gamini was killed in a LTTE suicide bomb attack while on a political stage in Grandpass, Colombo. Chandrika Kumaratunga went on to win the election, defeating UNP candidate Srima Dissanayake, wife of the slain Gamini, who the party had fielded as a candidate following Gamini's assassination.

For a long time, Lasantha mourned the death of his friend. For years afterward, whenever there was some new development in the political scene, he, like thousands of Gamini-loyalists, would extol the late leader's political sagacity and analyse how "Gamini would have handled it."

Meanwhile, due to this close association that had developed with Gamini, relations with his old friend Ranil Wickremesinghe had soured. More than once, when we ran into Ranil at some function or the other, there was awkwardness or a snide remark or two made in passing.

Once, we were at a reception hosted by Managing Director of Express Newspapers M.G. Wenceslaus. Ranil and Lasantha studiously ignored each other, even as they stood next to each other dishing out chicken korma from the buffet. Leaving the reception later that night, Lasantha and I got in to the elevator when moments later Ranil stepped in. He seemed to be in a jovial mood but ignoring Lasantha, he addressed me. "I enjoy your Lobby column," he declared with a wide smile, "That is the only thing worth reading in your newspaper!"

When we got off the elevator and walked towards our car, Lasantha was shaking with laughter. "That was a broad hint at me," he said.

When Lasantha received news that Ranil, a confirmed bachelor for many years, was engaged to be married that year to Maithree Wickremasinge, a lecturer at Kelaniya University, he was eager to get his hands on a picture of the bride-to-be but the groom was tight-lipped about his fiancée and the impending marriage. As luck would have it, one of the young Leader reporters chirped that she had a picture of Maithree taken at a girl guide event at Musaeus College, her old school and that of Maithree. The next day she arrived at office armed with a picture of a very young Maithree and Lasantha splashed it on page one scoring an exclusive for the newspaper.

When Ranil assumed the leadership of the UNP and was appointed Leader of the Opposition following Gamini's assassination, I did an interview with him at his Cambridge Terrace office and the article appeared on November 20, 1994. Sometime later, the strained relationship between Lasantha and Ranil was mended.

* * *

At the *Leader*, Lasantha gave free reign to other journalists and columnists who had their own views or didn't quite see eye-to-eye with him on national or political issues. Just as much as he valued his independence as a writer, he afforded it to all others and many of these journalists wrote freely without the shackles of an in-house censor.

When Lasantha had worked on certain other newspapers, he had at times suffered the fetters of proprietorial censoring. Many were the times he had griped about 'vital bits of information' being chopped off his political column. Now, there was no leash; no one to rein him in, and this meant that while Lasantha was able to write freely with no 'big boss' brandishing the dreaded red pencil, he did not apply any self-censorship either. Due to this, he sometimes went to extreme lengths to prove a point which I thought was not always wise.

Lasantha's views on self-censorship were articulated by him years later when the media he stressed, should make maximum use of the fact that (at that particular time) there was no official censorship prevailing. He reiterated that the real problem was self censorship entrenched in the media as a survival tool. Self-censorship he said was more harmful than state oppression 'for it destroyed the spirit within the media community more than the forces from outside.'

Although I supported Lasantha one hundred percent in his work, on a few occasions I wondered about the public humiliation the subjects of some of his exposures had to endure. We would then wind ourselves around the thin line between the public's right to know Vs. the individual's right to privacy. I sometimes felt that certain revelations intruded on privacy but Lasantha was firm in his opinion that when one assumed public office, his or her actions were wide open to scrutiny, especially those actions which had a bearing on their obligations to the people and the office they held. The very few times he relented and held back or edited a story was when I reminded him the person he was writing about had young children who had to go to school the next day and face certain embarrassment.

"Ok then," he would say reluctantly. "Just this once."

Lasantha however often stressed that when he presented certain facts it was not for public titillation or to chase a sensationalist headline. He once said, "The *Leader* has always refused to publish even the sauciest of stories it has encountered that deal with the private lives of people. These are no concern of ours and they ought not be the concern of our readers. We have continuously strived to ensure that stories that may be construed as 'gossip' get into print if, and only if, they are in the public interest."

Once Lasantha was doing a series of articles on Anura Bandaranaike, the President's brother and for a while Speaker of the House. The articles focused on Bandaranaike's extravagance, monies spent on overseas trips and the proposed building of a palatial Speaker's official residence near parliament.

I was sitting at the computer with the lay-out artist planning the structure of the page, giving headlines, captions, editing and proofreading when Lasantha rushed in to the room, excitedly waving a sheaf of pictures. These were meant for illustrating the article and showed a big, burly Bandaranaike soaking in a friend's mini pool. The photographs did not portray the man in a complimentary light. I was not happy about the pictures that would embarrass Bandaranaike and prevailed upon Lasantha to refrain from using them.

Lasantha however thought they were 'classic' and in his usual jovial manner proceeded to suggest rib-tickling captions for each photograph. I walked off from the computer at that point telling him if he was using those pictures he could get someone else to do the page. Lasantha found it all quite hilarious. Finally we compromised and used the least embarrassing of the images.

Anura was enraged and took every opportunity to tear Lasantha and *The Sunday Leader* to pieces whenever the opportunity arose. This was the same Anura who had been our friend and especially Lasantha's close confidante for many years, moreso during the time he was locked in battle with his sister the President.

I remember one instance when Anura came home for lunch; Menika prepared a delicious spread but at the last moment I couldn't find the one presentable rice ladle and was running hither and thither looking for it, turning out kitchen drawers and emptying out pan cupboards. Lasantha, jumping at a chance to tease and embarrass, guffawed and disclosed my plight to our visitor who pacified me saying an ordinary spoon would do very well.

Another time we were at Anura's residence having dinner when a friend of his began to gush about how Lasantha and I resembled each other and how well-suited we were. "I have never met a couple as well-matched as the two of you," she enthused to which Anura snapped, "Stop it . . . . don't put a jinx on them!"

For all his stentorian ranting and indignant rasping in parliament, Anura had a soft side to him; he adored his friends, entertained well, went to the extent of giving his visitors warm bear hugs as they left, and was all-in-all, a jovial sort.

Once as lobby correspondent, I had written a piece mainly focusing on Anura titled 'Speaker Speaks Up.' Two days later I received a letter in the mail from him on Speaker of Parliament letterhead. It said,

"I have read with interest your article titled 'Speaker Speaks Up' in yesterday's Sunday Leader.

"I am writing to convey my appreciation of most of your observations, articulately expressed with great candor and objectivity. Be that as it may, I was somewhat amused to note that some of the added comments <u>were not entirely yours!</u>"

Anura was hinting, with the underlined emphasis of Lasantha's trademark phrase 'be that as it may,' that Lasantha had made some additions to the article, perhaps the few references that were not entirely complimentary to him.

This however wasn't an accurate assumption on Anura's part because although Lasantha had indeed read the article before it went to print, he had not added anything to it.

* * *

During the early years of *The Sunday Leader*, the war in the north and east between the Sri Lankan Army and the Tamil rebels raged with great ferocity. When the ogre of war began devouring an ever-increasing number of lives on both sides of the divide and the country continued to be torn apart by violence, Lasantha began to lean more towards a negotiated settlement to the ethnic conflict rather than a military one. During his early years in journalism, even into his years as Editor of *The Sunday Leader*, Lasantha had been a passionate Sinhala patriot and a great believer in preserving the unitary status of Sri Lanka through the war effort. The change in his stance towards a negotiated settlement was gradual. I believe it was borne more out of disgust at what he saw; the manner in which the war was being used as a political tool and the great suffering of the people as a whole. He also found distasteful the overt chauvinism demonstrated by certain media groups. And as he persistently continued to present his long-term vision for Sri Lanka, many began to see this as a betrayal of the Sinhalese, believing his support lay firmly with the terrorists fighting for a separate homeland. Such accusations ignited his stubborn streak pushing him further into presenting his line of thinking.

As Lasantha himself wrote in the newspaper's 10th anniversary supplement, "Inasmuch as *The Sunday Leader* strives to be a general family newspaper, we are alive to the perception that it is purchased largely for its political content and fearless independence. We are not good at winning friends and have, no doubt, made loads of enemies. Quite apart from politicians and those dependent on them for their bread and butter, our outspoken support of secularism and pluralism has won us the ire of bigots of many flavours."

During this time Lasantha was still practising law and sometimes he would appear in cases with his friend Kumar Ponnambalam. A story that retired Supreme Court Judge, Justice C. V. Wigneswaran wrote in a tribute to Lasantha, sheds some light on Lasantha's changing views and his thinking on the ethnic issue.

Justice Wigneswaran wrote of a time when Kumar Ponnambalam handled a case during a time when he, the judge, was receiving a promotion and needed to expedite unfinished cases. In an effort to cut down on the time-consuming translations by the interpreter, the judge asked Kumar if he would cross-examine the witness in Sinhala which Kumar did with the judge interrupting with clarifying questions in Sinhala. This spectacle of two Tamil-rights champions conducting proceedings in Sinhala attracted several young lawyers who would come in to witness the proceedings.

Justice Wigneswaran wrote,

> "Kumar and Lasantha, on the last day walked into my chambers and wished me good luck with the anticipated promotion. While we chatted, Lasantha said, 'Sir, it was refreshing to see two Tamils conducting a High Court case in Sinhala!' I retorted, 'More Tamils would have followed suit without any reservations if only their basic right to the Tamil language in the Northern and Eastern Provinces had been recognised by law in 1956!'
>
> "It was what Lasantha said next which prompted me to write this piece.
>
> "Lasantha was forthright. 'Sir, I have always felt that since the Tamil speaking people, both Tamils and Muslims, have been for centuries the majority in the Northern and Eastern Provinces, they should have made Tamil the official language of those two provinces and Sinhala the official language of the other seven provinces or given parity of status to both languages!'
>
> "I was taken aback. Lasantha in fact was prepared to concede to the Sri Lankan Tamil speaking people more than what the aborted Bandaranaike-Chelvanayagam Pact had envisaged! Agreeing with him wholeheartedly, I told him I had started studying Sinhala under a teacher at Royal who later became a university vice chancellor but that I stopped studying Sinhala when S.W.R.D. Bandaranaike introduced the Sinhala Only Act.
>
> "Again Lasantha said something very rational, though unexpected by me. 'It is not the language Sir that matters! It is how you feel about the situation!' I couldn't agree more.
>
> "We Tamils who had been equals with all other communities up to 1956 suddenly found ourselves relegated to a subordinate position due to lack of recognition of our mother tongue even in areas where we were the majority," I said. Kumar too nodded his head. I told

Lasantha, 'You seem to have been indoctrinated by Kumar!' Kumar hurriedly interjected, 'No Sir! It is the other way round. My Junior is more radical in his views and I learn from him!' We all laughed."

* * *

In the early years of the newspaper, apart from his many stunning exposures, Lasantha commandeered several experts in specific fields to write columns for the newspaper. One of those he met and asked to do a column was accountant and anti-corruption activist Nihal Amerasekera who began a series of articles on privatisation, corruption and graft, writing under the pseudonym Bismarck. Earlier, Amerasekera had figured in a series of investigative pieces Lasantha had done on the settlement of the Hilton hotel project but when Lasantha subsequently met him and invited him to do a column for the paper, Amerasekera accepted and began writing the exhaustive and in-depth weekly article.

D. B. S. Jeyaraj, with his vast and almost unparalleled knowledge of the LTTE and Tamil politics who had been a colleague and friend of Lasantha during his *Island* days, was also invited to write, and he began a regular column in *The Sunday Leader*.

Another writer was the late media personality Ravi John. He and wife Rashmi were friends of ours and Ravi began doing an excellent personality column for the paper which was very well received.

A column that was hugely popular was 'Matilda'—a hilarious, extremely witty and brilliantly entertaining piece that lampooned the powers that be. The writer, a friend of Lasantha whose identity was never revealed, referred to the Editor throughout his column as 'Shorty.' That, Lasantha thought all this was hilarious, demonstrated the fact that he never took himself too seriously and was able to laugh at himself.

Also popular in those early days, especially with the young ones, was Dear Sharon—the agony aunt column I conducted in the *Now!* Magazine. There were weeks when I would receive 25 or more letters, mostly from lovelorn youngsters, hoping for some empathic words and practical advice from Sharon that would ease their pain. The column generated quite a bit of interest and had caught the eye of the resident BBC correspondent at the time who, much to my surprise, came in to the office to interview me on the experiences of Dear Sharon.

The Leader was also fortunate to have respected sports journalist T. M. K. Samat join its ranks. He revealed later in an article that it had been his friendship with me—and my servings of rice and curry to him as he suffered severe homesickness in Hong Kong where we had worked on a newspaper together—that had influenced his decision to join the *Leader* when he returned home and was considering several newspaper offers. He also wrote, ". . . After all, if she believed Lasantha met her requirements for a husband, then, he must have some outstanding qualities, as man and editor."

The mischievous facet of Lasantha's personality would show up in the pages of the newspaper from time to time. Once, he heard that a five-star hotel in Colombo was hosting a Ladies Only night complete with a male floor show. Two of the *Leader*'s young female reporters were assigned to cover it. It didn't stop there. Lasantha asked Mirak Rahim, one of the young, gawky, bespectacled male reporters, to accompany the girls; 'How is that possible? the perplexed reporter queried. "Only girls are allowed in."

"Well, you have to go dressed as a girl," Lasantha told him with a broad grin and a mighty chuckle. After some persuasion young Mirak agreed and the plot was hatched.

On the day of the Ladies Night, three female reporters, all done up prettily in powder, lipstick, mascara and rouge, sallied forth to the venue. Mirak, togged up in glamorous female attire and high-heels, stood out like an awkward stork amongst pigeons but by striking effeminate poses and contriving feminine gait, he still managed to fool everyone. At one point though, the trio thought the cover was blown when they heard a girl in the audience sitting behind them whisper to her friend, "I think there's a man in here." His disguise however remained intact and the cherry on the cake was when, after everything was over and the three reporters waved goodbye to the hosts, one male organiser called out, "I never knew the *Leader* had such pretty girls!"

How Lasantha and the rest of us laughed when we heard of their escapades! Mirak went on to write a piece on a male perspective of a ladies night titled 'I was the only man in the audience.'

There was another time when Colombo was under high security what with suicide attacks by LTTE cadres who had infiltrated the city taking place on a regular basis. Although security checkpoints were dotted all over the city and one had to go through body searches and security checks before entering any government building, it was brought up at an Editorial meeting that loopholes still existed and if someone really wanted to smuggle in an explosive device, it was possible.

Lasantha decided to test the veracity of this assumption. Two reporters, Asgar Hussein and Ruwanthi Ariyaratne, were assigned to visit several key government establishments including Police Headquarters, Bank of Ceylon Head Office and the Supreme Court Complex. In their bags, the reporters carried lunch boxes into which were crammed batteries, wires and other sundry bits of scrap they imagined would generally be used in the construction of an explosive device. The reporters and their 'lethal' cargo breezed through security and gained access to the interior of the buildings without a hitch. The security personnel manning the buildings who checked their personal items merely asked what the boxes contained and when told it was their lunch, merrily waved them through.

At Police Headquarters, even though the metal detectors beeped while searches were being conducted, the mere explanation that all they had in their boxes was lunch, satisfied the security personnel who allowed them to enter the premises. Once inside, the reporters, pretending to be ordinary citizens interested in making representations on the proposed Marine Drive project, even met a Deputy Inspector General.

The other establishments the reporters 'infiltrated' without a hitch were a crowded cinema, the Zoological gardens, a busy shopping mall, a bank, the Colombo Museum and a five-star hotel.

The following Sunday, July 23, 1995, the *Leader* carried the story about the lax security as a lead story on Page One titled 'Colombo sitting on a time bomb,' and as a more detailed investigation complete with pictures on pages 20 and 21, resulting in a lot of red—and angry—faces at the establishments concerned.

Many of Lasantha's enduring friendships were established during those early days at the *Leader*. Once in his Suranimala column Lasantha referred to a young politician from the DUNF which was not taken too kindly. At a function not long after, the man buttonholed Lasantha.

"Give us a chance Lasantha, we young people are trying to come up to do something for the country," he told Lasantha and explained his vision for Sri Lanka.

Lasantha and Ravi Karunanayake became firm friends thereafter.

It was a similar experience with another businessman and emerging politician who featured in one of Lasantha's investigations. The gentleman was annoyed but he came to the *Leader* office one day and gave Lasantha his version of the story. Lasantha was taken with his direct approach. They discussed politics, men and matters and kept in touch thereafter. Soon, the man's entire family became friends of ours; Lasantha especially treated their house as a second home spending a great deal of time with them, discussing politics and current affairs and enjoying their company in general.

Lasantha and he didn't always agree on issues and would have raving arguments but their affection for each other never diminished. M. J. M Muzzamil is today the Mayor of Colombo.

Not every subject of his articles and investigations was that fortunate.

There was one particular gentleman, a Kumaratunga loyalist, who Lasantha exposed in his newspaper as having altered his birth date three times in order to continue in his government appointments. Lasantha was not aware that the man was distantly related to him and after the first article appeared, the mother of the gentleman in question telephoned Lasantha's father Harris and asked that he prevail upon Lasantha to stop writing any more articles about her son. Lasantha was not happy about pressure being applied by persons claiming family ties. Insisting that even if a relative in public office committed an offence he would expose it, he continued with his 'thrice-born' exposures which resulted in the individual having to resign as Chairman Lake House, Secretary Media Ministry and Director AirLanka.

* * *

In the office, the young reporters and sub-editors adored Lasantha. They had great admiration for his work ethic and integrity, but on a personal note, they thought he was a hoot. Lasantha was an irrepressible joker and prankster and would tease and embarrass the young ones or pull their legs by disguising his voice with prank calls. His ear-splitting two-finger whistle which indicated he wanted an office-helper pronto would see poor Sandanam, engrossed in making tea for the staff, almost drop the cups and saucers in his haste to run to his beloved Lasantha *Mahaththya*.

One of those early reporters wrote in a tribute to him, "The first time I had to conduct an interview for a story was at the house of a leading businessman. It was shortly after Lasantha had been attacked for the first time and my mother worried terribly, warning me not to go alone, to make sure everyone knew where I was etc. all of which I naively conveyed to Lasantha.

"After the article was published, I received a call from, (or so I thought) the same gentleman inviting me to dinner and insisting I call him by his first name. My suspicions that it was in fact Lasantha on the other end of the telephone were confirmed when Lasantha walked jauntily out of his office, pleased as punch, with his hands in his pockets, whistling, unable to resist the urge to see for himself what the reaction to one of his never-ending list of practical jokes had been.

"It was not the first and certainly not the last time he was able to successfully impersonate people on the telephone and he played a variety of tricks on even the more experienced journalists keeping the office in fits of laughter."

The girls would tease Lasantha and me, especially when we arrived almost every morning dressed in the same colour. This was never intentional but when the girls teased us, Lasantha would tell them, "Raine watches while I dress and then goes and picks the same colour!"

As Rajni Senewiratne recounted in her tribute article after Lasantha's death, "The memories I have of the two of them who turned the office in to a second home for all of us who worked there, are irreplaceable and unforgettable. Especially those mornings when they would walk in together, their big welcoming grins becoming wider as they were hailed with shouts of laughter because they would inevitably be wearing colour co-ordinated clothes.

"The little bunch of us who worked with them would often tease them saying that we had never seen a happier couple, two people more in love, in their 'old married state,' the little jokes and teasing jibes they shared when passing each other in the office giving us even more ammunition."

There was one time when Lasantha had flowers delivered to me at the office three days in a row. The young ones teased me unmercifully and I extracted a promise from him that he would put a stop to the unending bouquets. He promised he would, and when we got home after work that evening, there it was—yet another beautiful flower arrangement with a maudlin message attached—this time delivered to the house!

After so many years together, Lasantha would still try his prank calls on me as well. Of course I saw through each of them. He was a barrel of laughs and never let an opportunity to tease, pass. At family gatherings, he was the life of the party; my mother, sisters and their spouses—especially my youngest sister Melody's husband—were all at the receiving end of his mischievous antics as were his parents, siblings and their spouses.

Lasantha was funny and entertaining but he also had a heart that melted easily. Disadvantaged children, poverty and difficulties faced by people always moved him and he perfectly understood, and egged me on, when I would hand out assistance to those that needed it. Our friends and colleagues thought I was the one who was always taken in by a hard-luck story but what they didn't know was that Lasantha was hardly any better.

Once we were returning home from Ratmalana with another couple when our car was struck by a vehicle, damaging our car in the process. Luckily no one was hurt and Lasantha got off to talk to the driver of the other vehicle.

When he came back to the car, everyone bombarded him with questions. "What's happening? Do we go to the police? Is he paying for the damage?"

"Those people are from out-station," Lasantha told us. "They had come down to attend a wedding; the driver just got his license."

Then drawing me aside, he said, "I feel so sorry for the fellow, he's terribly shaken up. These are poor people from far off."

He went on to say that he had given the man some money.

This was clearly the other driver's fault and here Lasantha was doling out money to him because he felt sorry for him! However, I wasn't one bit surprised. That was Lasantha.

There were so many occasions when I was in some slaughterhouse or the other feeding cattle who were to be killed, wishing I had enough money to save at least a couple of them. After emptying my purse and counting out my money I would call Lasantha and begin my spiel, "Lasantha, there's this mother and baby . . ." I'm sure every single time he knew what was coming even before I ended the sentence. "Hmm, ok, how much?" he would ask. No begging, no cajoling.

Another time, a salesman came into the office selling packs of educational books; he was a young man with a visible infirmity. His sales talk was so good he made parents believe that if they purchased that series of general knowledge books, their children would turn out to be geniuses. He was quoting an astronomical price which we could not afford. Lasantha came into my room while the salesman was carrying on and after listening for a little while, indicated he would purchase the books and pulled his purse out. After the salesman left Lasantha told me, "I felt sorry for him, that young chap was trying his best to earn a living despite his limitations."

We took the books home and handed them to the children hopefully, but unfortunately no one turned in to an instant genius!

[1] Virtues of the Buddha
[2] The accelerated Mahaweli River diversion scheme

Harris and Chandra's wedding, 1945

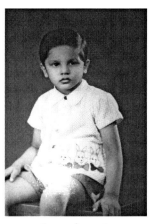

Lasantha at 3

Deputy Mayor Harris Wickrematunge greets Mayor Vincent Perera

Lasantha at 7

Lasantha (at far right) with mother Chandra and brother Anil outside their London flat

Lasantha at 20

Raine and Lasantha at the SUN/WEEKEND

Courting days, Raine and Lasantha

Lasantha and Raine an year before marriage

Wedding of Raine and Lasantha

Lasantha on the campaign trail with Mrs. Sirima Bandaranaike, 1988

Lasantha's election material, 1989

Lasantha campaigning during the run-up to the 1989 parliamentary elections together with another candidate

Lasantha on the political stage

Lasantha and Raine with their first-born Avinash

Lasantha with daughter Ahimsa

Lasantha with youngest child Aadesh

Lasantha and Raine on holiday with Raine's mother and sisters

Lasantha and Raine with their three children

Lasantha and Ranil Wickremesinghe when relations were soured

Lasantha with Ranil Wickremesinghe, Ravi Karunanayake and brother Lal Wickrematunge

Lasantha receiving the first ever Transparency International Award

Lasantha and Raine with their mothers, Chandra (L) and Rani (R)

Lasantha and Raine on holiday in the Gold Coast with their children in 2008

A billboard advertising Lasantha's TV breakfast show

Damaged vehicle, result of 1998 attack on Wickrematunge home

Leader press after arson attack

Lasantha at the Leader X'mas party

Lasantha celebrating his 40th birthday at the Leader office with Raine and the rest of the staff

May 2000: Leader and Peramuna staff receiving news of the ban on Leader Publications

Lasantha interviewing former President and former arch-enemy Chandrika Kumaratunga

Candlelight vigil in Lasantha's memory

The 8-metre monument to Lasantha by Viennese artiste Peter Sandbichler on the Museum Quartier forecourt

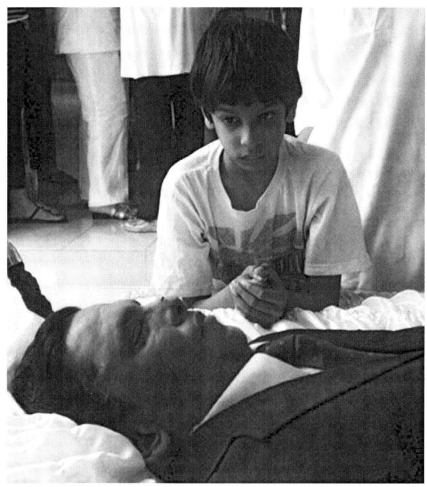

Youngest son Aadesh gazes at his father's body. Picture by Amantha Perera

CHAPTER SIX
Unleashing of the Goons

> *"I detest what you write, but I would give my life to make it possible for you to continue to write"*—Voltaire, French writer and philosopher in a 1770 letter.

THE general elections of August 1994 had propelled into power the People's Alliance headed by the relatively untested Chandrika Kumaratunga. She was sworn in as Prime Minister on Friday, August 19, 1994.

On Wednesday, November 9 the same year, the people once again went to the polls, this time electing Chandrika Kumaratunga as the fourth President of Sri Lanka.

The new President took oaths on Saturday, November 12. That same night she threw a huge unofficial celebration at Temple Trees for about 250 guests that included PA Members of Parliament, Western Provincial Councillors, friends, relatives and party loyalists. Although this event, with no liquor served, ended around 8.30 pm after the President had retired upstairs, more celebrations began soon after most of the guests had left.

This second bash included the President's closest friends, a few relatives and some of her trusted political associates such as S. B. Dissanayake, Mangala Samaraweera and her uncle, Deputy Defence Minister Anuruddha Ratwatte.

An all-night curfew had been declared nationwide beginning from 6 pm and while the rest of Colombo retired to bed early that night, Temple Trees pulsated with heady revelry as the new President and all her trusty lieutenants partied in to the wee hours.

This was *The Sunday Leader* newspaper's fifth month in circulation. We were still inching our way forward in the English newspaper market, trying to find our niche while still battling a host of problems in the Editorial and Production departments. But if the newspaper was relatively unknown yet, that was about to change.

On Sunday, November 20, in his Suranimala column, under the headline 'Dancing at Temple Trees with Countrywide Curfew,' Lasantha wrote a hearty and very detailed account of the celebrations, painting a word picture of a joyous night of merry-making where jubilant guests and their presidential hostess danced to the music of local band Go Public.

Suranimala provided the guests list, wrote how members of the band were transported to the venue during the curfew, the music that was played, what gastronomical delights the menu dished out and even described the moves and gyrations of the revellers on the dance floor. Special mention was made of Anuruddha Ratwatte who it was said waved his walking stick as he strutted in merry abandon.

Word got around on Sunday morning that this new English language newspaper, *The Sunday Leader*, had published juicy details of a presidential bash. After 17 years of rule by one single political party—the UNP—the country had recently elected a brand new lot, most of them fresh faces, and the people were terribly inquisitive to know more about this new mob.

With news of the article spreading, everyone wanted to get their hands on a copy of the *Leader*. That Sunday's edition sold like icy poles on a sweltering day. The newspaper was being handed around in corporate offices where staff took a break from work to pore over the article and have a good chuckle. Lasantha's personal phone rang off the hook. I received a call from a long-lost school friend. I hadn't even realised she knew we were involved in publishing the *Leader*. She giggled and marvelled at the writer's obvious skill in getting all those minute details. "We are having a ball with your paper in office today," (incidentally, a government establishment), she giggled.

With that article, *The Sunday Leader* 'arrived' in Colombo and other main cities. Many loyal readers were born that day. Many enemies were also made during this time, notably, the President and many of those in her merry bandwagon.

The readers too reacted with differing viewpoints. Some were aghast that the nation's highest had indulged in such idle frivolity while a curfew was in force and the people were confined to their homes; others, like the Principal of an international school, were more forgiving. "Good on him!" she wrote of the stick-waving Ratwatte in a letter to the editor.

With the publication of this story, Lasantha's critics jumped at the chance to brand the *Leader* a gossip paper. But the very fact that he could capitalise on the hilarity of a 'gossip story' just as much as he could, in a flash, understand the political implications of another, formed Lasantha's genius. The mischievous facet of his personality was amply represented in his newspaper, as were his politically dynamite stories that bore the hallmark of the highest journalistic standards.

* * *

In the run-up to the general election, Chandrika Kumaratunga had made several promises to the nation about ending censorship and restoring press freedom. In fact, the PA election manifesto stated that the freedom of the individual could not be safeguarded 'without a viable system of checks and balances acting as a restraint on governmental power' and that these checks and balances could be applied with any degree of effectiveness only if there was healthy and vigorous expression of public opinion.

It said, "The PA therefore attaches the greatest importance to strengthening the media and providing a framework within which the media can function independently and without inhibition."

Before long it became painfully obvious that these were hollow words indeed.

From the very inception, the Kumaratunga administration came under the *Leader* microscope. In the very early days, some felt, rightly or wrongly, that, having formed a government as they did after 17 years in opposition, the SLFP and its alliance partners that formed the People's Alliance headed by Chandrika Kumaratunga were entitled to a grace period to prove themselves. Lasantha was stubborn by nature and was not amenable to taking too much, if any, counsel from others. He continued to, week after week, write his exposes´ and investigations on questionable deals, government excesses and presidential gaffes. In his defence, it seemed as if the new government was more than happy to provide him with reams of material to work on.

With time, it was obvious that all these exposures were having a significant impact on the readers. Instead of the bucketloads of government propaganda they had been fed for years in the 'kept' press, or the independent media's half-hearted ear-tweaking, the *Leader* presented them with bold, novel, fare. The people were learning of matters which if not for Lasantha Wickrematunge and *The Sunday Leader*, would have remained as skeletons firmly locked up in the state cupboard. Lasantha's authoritative journalism wasn't the kind that simply ruffled feathers; it ignited public debate. It was his exposes on the government that prodded a lethargic opposition to sit up, take note and move into action.

Lasantha's list of contacts had grown by the day; more and more people with stories to tell, whistleblowers, even complete strangers, emboldened by the Editor's uncompromising stance and proven integrity approached him with information. And Lasantha himself had a nose so sharp it could smell a story a mile away. This coupled with his brilliant and incisive political and legal grasp meant that whether someone came into the office with fat files filled with incriminating documents or gave him just a little verbal tip, if there was a good story there, Lasantha saw it. And he would follow it up like a bulldog after a juicy bone.

Stories would pop up anytime, anyplace. His phone would ring non-stop. In those early days, he didn't have a sophisticated little mobile that fit in to his palm where a conversation could be recorded at the touch of a button. Instead, he had one of those massive cellular monstrosities, and if it rang while he was at the wheel, and the person on the other end was someone calling to give him a potential lead, he would gesture to me wildly to take down notes. I would scramble for a pen and a piece of paper in my handbag and hastily take down whatever Lasantha repeated. Later on I got smart and always kept a pen and writing pad handy in the car specifically for those calls.

In the early years, countless institutions and individuals came under the intense scrutiny of *The Sunday Leader*. Power and Energy Minister and Deputy Defence Minister Anuruddha Ratwatte and several other key ministers and top officials—some of them the President's blue-eyed boys—were subjects of the newspaper's many probes and investigations as were institutions such as the Defence Ministry, Navy, the national carrier AirLanka, the Securities Exchange Commission, the Southern Development Authority and many others. The newspaper carried stunning exposures on dubious tender awards made outside of tender procedure or without cabinet approval, arms procurements steeped in controversy and illegal favours granted to friends and family of those in high places.

In late 1994, *The Sunday Leader* ran several hard-hitting exposures by Suranimala on the controversial purchase of Airbus aircraft for AirLanka. One in particular exposed how the PA government which had made allegations of corruption against the former regime in its Airbus purchase deal, had, just two weeks after assuming office, gone ahead with the same transaction. The article carried in-depth information on the tenders, contracts signed, the re-negotiations, the purchases and the excessive prices paid, all steeped in controversy.

Again, one full-page exposure on the questionable procurement procedure adopted by the Sri Lanka Navy in relation to the purchase of inshore patrol craft running into millions with preference given to one particular bidder also created ripples in the defence establishment.

In December 1994, under the headline 'Russian helicopters and Air Force blunders,' Suranimala also uncovered the story of how the purchase of three Mi-7 helicopters by the Sri Lankan Air Force raised questions about the suitability of these helicopters and the manner in which the deal was finalised.

Lasantha also wrote a series of articles on the Hilton Hotel settlement detailing the sordid backroom manoeuvres and the fact that the agreements signed by the treasury secretary on behalf of the government committed the government to a number of obligations of an unacceptable nature. One article in the series in particular titled 'Shame, shame, Professor Peiris' called for the Justice Minister to resign with honour.

* * *

Lasantha first began receiving threats around one year into publication. First there were ominous telephone calls, some threatening him with dire consequences if he didn't stop writing. Then there were the letters. The first was a note addressed to Lasantha, asking him to stop writing or face the inevitable. Bing! It went in to the dustbin. In those early days, even the lawyer in him didn't see the necessity of filing away these as evidence if ever the need arose.

Characteristically, he laughed each one off. He would come out of his room, walk to the news desk area and announce jokingly, "Chandi Girl (President Kumaratunga) has sent me another love letter," and the entire staff would fall about laughing. He would then go on to describe the sinister warning.

The usual pattern in the office at that time, a year into publication, was that on Mondays and Tuesdays I edited copy for the *Now!* Magazine followed by the TV guide. I would sit with Computer Operator Surejini, directing her on the lay-out of the pages, giving headlines, editing and proofreading. Most days Lasantha and I would leave the office together at the end of the day but sometimes, if I hadn't completed my work I would ask him to go on without me and take an office vehicle later.

It was on one such Monday—February 6, 1995 to be precise—that I was working at the computer with Surejini when Lasantha poked his head in at the door telling me it was time to go home. I started saying I would follow a little later in an office vehicle when something in my head urged me to go with him. I'm not certain whether this was a result of the unease I had been experiencing for a while following a series of hard-hitting exposures involving Minister Anuruddha Ratwatte that the newspaper had run. A sense of impending danger had been buzzing like a bee in my head for a while and I did not want Lasantha to be on his own if anything sinister were to happen.

I told Surejini we would complete the pages the following morning and off I went. We got in to the red Toyota Sprinter we were using at the time and set off home with Lasantha at the wheel. The time was around 5.30 in the evening. We didn't have any inkling that we were being followed or of what lay in wait for us.

On the final leg of the journey, the first dark shadows were falling as we turned down the side lane that led to our house. A few yards away, a white hi-ace van stood stationary, blocking our path. A man emerged from under the vehicle and our first assumption was that the van had stalled, perhaps due to some engine trouble. The man, tall and lanky, then began walking towards our vehicle and when he stood by the driver's side door, once again we both assumed he wanted some assistance with his vehicle.

Just as Lasantha began opening his door, for the first time, I got a proper look at the man's face. I froze. His eyes were red and wild and there was an ominous look about him. Before I could ask Lasantha to shut the door, the man growled *'behepan do!'* (get out) and yanked him out of the car with such great force that it sent him sprawling on to the dirt road. The man then proceeded to deliver him several vicious kicks.

As I watched in total horror, three other men, handkerchiefs tied round their faces with only their eyes visible, emerged from the vehicle in front of us like eerie ghosts. I was still inside our car, petrified, when the three men sprinted towards us and joining the first goon, began beating down viciously on Lasantha with long, murderous poles. I began to scream and moving onto the driver's seat, jumped out of the vehicle into the thick of the assault.

Everything seemed to be happening in slow motion. I just stood there helpless; screaming, shouting for help, watching my husband being pummeled by four thugs. One of the men began beating his weapon down on Lasantha's head while he lay sprawled on the ground shouting. My protective instincts suddenly kicked in, drowning all fear. I jumped on Lasantha and lay over him shielding his body with mine. I instinctively laced my fingers over his head to cushion any blows to the head.

In a second I felt one crushing blow to my back as one of the men attempted to get me off Lasantha's back. The burning pain searing through my body as that monstrous pole with nails embedded in it crashed down on me was unbearable. I saw every star in the universe but at that moment, I know not from where, a wave of courage whooshed through my veins and I gained the strength to face the attacker, and the pain. I resolved to myself, "Even if I receive 100 of these blows, I will not move from here." And I prayed.

Suddenly, with just that one blow to me, the men backed off. Two of them then smashed the windscreen of the car with their poles; another picked up Lasantha's wallet that was lying on the ground; and they all dashed towards the van and took off.

For a few seconds he and I just lay there in terrible shock. Behind us, we heard the agitated voices of people who had heard the commotion and were emerging from their homes. Lasantha stood up unsteadily; he was bruised and bleeding. I had cuts on my hands and there was severe pain in my back where I had received a blow. We stumbled in to the vehicle and as Lasantha turned the ignition on, part of the windscreen collapsed on us in a hundred tiny pieces of glass.

Slowly and painfully we inched along towards the front gate of our home. We didn't want to go inside lest the children saw us in that state. Instead, we parked the car outside our gate and hobbled up to a neighbour's home. Luckily he was outside, preparing to get into his car. Shocked at what he saw and heard, he abandoned his intended journey and rushed us off to the Mirihana police station instead. While on our way, Lasantha called his brother Lal and a few other people and informed them of what had taken place.

At the Mirihana Police Station, Officer in Charge (OIC) Thilak Perera and three other police officers who listened to our complaint drove us back to the scene of the crime to get a clearer picture of what had occurred. Once there, they ascertained that this area did not come under their jurisdiction but that of the Kirulapone Police. OIC Perera then accompanied us to the Kirulapone Police Station where statements were duly recorded.

By this time news of the assault had spread and friends, media persons and colleagues were arriving at the police station. Mahajana Eksath Peramuna (MEP) Leader Dinesh Gunawardena and UNP MP Jayawickrema Perera were the first to arrive. While we were still at the station, Media Minister Dharmasiri Senanayake and Opposition Leader Ranil Wickremesinghe telephoned the OIC of the Kirulapone Police to convey their concern and get more detailed information on the attack.

While his statement was being recorded Lasantha was asked whether he suspected anyone of being responsible for the attack. Lasantha then told the officer that a few days previously, the President's Media Advisor, during a telephone conversation with a *Leader* reporter, had threatened to kill the Editor if anything negative about him was published in the newspaper.

While Lasantha's statement was being recorded, I accompanied officers from the station once again to the scene of the crime, explaining exactly what had transpired there.

From the police station, around 9.00 pm, Lasantha and I were whisked off to the Accident Ward of the Colombo General Hospital where we were met by several MPs including Rajitha Senaratne, Pradeep Hapangama and a wheelchair-bound Anura Bandaranaike. Also present were Kumar and Yogi Ponnambalam, *Ravaya* Editor Victor Ivan and several other friends and *Leader* colleagues. Here, Lasantha and I had our wounds and bruises attended to; I was discharged while Lasantha was warded overnight.

Around 2.00 o'clock that night, Lasantha woke up to a gentle tapping on his shoulder and opened his eyes to the smiling face of Muslim Congress Leader M. H. M. Ashraff looking down at him. Apologising for waking him up at that hour Ashraff went on to express his shock. "We believe in the freedom of the press and it is not confined to mere words," he said.

The assault incident created ripples in the media and was seen as a direct 'hit' at the very heart of free media by goons hired by politically motivated persons. Both a national and international outcry ensued and statements condemning the attack were released by ministers, leaders of opposition political parties, civic groups and representatives of media organisations. Due to the wide TV, radio and newspaper coverage the incident received, those who hadn't until then heard of this trail-blazing Editor and his ground-breaking newspaper became acquainted with *The Sunday Leader*.

This physical attack did not intimidate Lasantha in the least. One day in hospital, and the next he was back at work, writing away, describing the attack in detail in his Suranimala column. In fact, his sense of humour hadn't dampened in the least either. As Sulochana Pieris, a young reporter at the time, was to reminisce in a tribute article published after his death: "I still remember the first time Lasantha was assaulted in 1995 whilst driving home with Raine after work. The next day when all of us visited him in hospital, we were greeted with the same gleaming smile we had come to associate him with. One of us asked how he was feeling and personifying his jovial and high spirited nature, out came the sing-song answer, (referring to the temperature in the room), "Feeling Hot, Hot, Hot" taken from the lyrics of a song which was popular at the time."

* * *

When the PA government notched one year in office, the President commemorated the occasion with a long and winding television address to the nation. To the shocked dismay of many including me, and the amusement of Lasantha, the President dedicated much of her speech to a personal tirade against the Editor of *The Sunday Leader*. I watched the speech with Lasantha at home after which the telephone began ringing non-stop as friends, Lasantha's political and legal contacts and media colleagues, in a show of solidarity, called to discuss the verbal attack with Lasantha.

In her address the President went on to call him many colourful and derogatory names, among them one which stuck—*'mada panuwa'* (worm). She described with derision how years ago, that reporter boy would come and hang around her husband Vijaya, in search of a story.

Anyone else would have, in true wormy style, squirmed with embarrassment at the presidential barrage. Not Lasantha; he had thus far managed to see the funnier side of tough situations. He began referring to himself as 'The Worm' and continued to write with renewed gusto.

More than half the political news stories that were published in the *Leader* came from the Editor. On Friday evenings, he would come in to the sub's room where I would be working on the computer doing Page One and rattle off news stories. Most days he would deliver, off the cuff, the next day's lead story which I typeset at a furious pace.

For as long as he was Editor of *The Sunday Leader*, he wrote news stories, penned his weekly political column and dug his teeth into meaty exposures. In addition, he assigned to other reporters, stories that would rock the foundations of the state machinery, the armed forces and even the judiciary. Those trained by him became clever investigative writers and award-winning journalists themselves.

Lasantha was also the main contributor to the Nutshell column on Page One which comprised several interesting anecdotes from the political arena written in humorous style. President Kumaratunga (referred to as Satellite) featured heavily in the column with many stories about her habitual lateness captured in rib-tickling fashion. In the early years, the President's Social Secretary Padma Maharajah and her sari shop *Vati* were famously lampooned in the Nutshells and word was that the good lady, referred to as Paddy in the column, couldn't wait to get her hands on the Editor's neck!

Others who found themselves 'in a Nutshell' more often than not were Board of Investment (BOI) Chief Thilan Wijesinghe (referred to as the Boi), Mangala Samaraweera (Mangy), Anuruddha Ratwatte (Hot Garden), Army Commander Rohan Daluwatte (Bud Garden), Sanath Gunathilaka (Sonna Boy), Anura Bandaranaike (A-Bee or Crown Prince), Lakshman Kadirgamar (the one to whom nothing is foreign), President's Secretary Balapatabendi (Cheap Belt Wearer) and S. B. Dissanayake (Sporty or Ass-Bee). Cabinet was the cupboard and ministers were referred to as ministering angels.

Following is a typical Nutshell column that appeared in the newspaper.

THE WORM

> *SO A-BEE finally lost his cool, and admitted as much. And what a demented fiasco it turned out to be! And before he made a spectacle of himself, the man was at dinner at friend Ara Soysa's house and was told to mind his tongue lest he open another can of worms (Satellite, please note), but the man insisted he wanted to go ahead and now the joke in the you en pee parliamentary circles is whether they should get ready to re-write the Bard . . . . hell hath no fury like a man scorned . . . .*
>
> *As for us folks, we'll leave that one for The Biography of a Worm!*

A HOUSE, SHE ORDERED

> *AND as for the pruning of the cupboard, echoes of disgust are continuing to reverberate with many of the ministering angels whining away in righteous indignation. And it was Soo-meda, the one who*

looked over women's affairs, that complained to Satellite at the pee a group, that she was in hiding from the electors for the shame of it all. She couldn't stay at home nor at that of her siblings, she noted. Satellite was touched. And promptly ordered that a house be given her.

Chew on that one Wimal, Chew, Chew!

PATIENCE, PATIENCE

AND chew it was on patties and rolls at the presidential abode for red comrade WW and his gang on Sunday night as they waited and waited for Satellite to show up so they may discuss matters commission. But the once young and restless revolutionary types seem to have developed a new patience for Satellite's idiosyncrasies after the accord and was quite pleased to say it was quite ok when the lady breezed in two hours late and flashed her walawwa smile.

BLACK TACTICS

BUT one man who has broken the shackles and is breathing the air of emancipation from the feudal clutches is none other than Ass Bee. Try as they might to woo him back the man has said no is no. But now the latest tactic being used is mail that is black in relation to a house down Hung-oo-runket way. But Ass could only laugh. Go to hell, was his response.

COMING SOON

AND now with the no-confidence in the offing, Satellite is thinking of avoiding a pow wow in the house despite the marriage with the reds. And last week, Bala, the cheap belt wearer, was at Five Villages after the family commemoration and told the hosts to get ready for an election.

Now that's food for thought for the reds, what?

KEEPING COOL

WITH power cuts and mozzies being the order of the day, at least some people are still enjoying Satellite's benevolence. Having held hands for Sri Lanka First, dear old girl Paddy who was appointed director, Hill-ton by Satellite once, told the management, she wanted a room to keep her cool.

And so they obliged. And we are told the other directors are not pleased. In fact, they are rather hot under the collar. And not due to the heat either.

* * *

President Chandrika Kumaratunga and her close coterie of ministers, now into the second year of governance, were livid. To them, Lasantha Wickrematunge and *The Sunday Leader* had become the administration's enemy numero uno.

The President would seize every opportunity, in private and in public, to launch scathing attacks on the errant *'mada paththarakaaraya.'* (muck-raking, rag-sheet journalist). Once, at a cabinet meeting, she referred to what Suranimala had commented on her dress sense and the expenses the national purse must incur on the presidential wardrobe.

"Maybe he is jealous because his wife doesn't have such beautiful saris," she reportedly told her gathering. This was relayed to Lasantha by a 'mole' and he reproduced it in his next week's column. As expected, many were the comments I received, one from Ranil Wickremesinghe, who at a reception at his house that week, came up to me beaming and inquired amidst cackling laughter why the President was so obsessed with my wardrobe.

With most of his stories, Lasantha sought to give the subject of the investigation a chance to give his/her side of the story as well. And that was so when he was preparing to publish a story about the President's educational qualifications acquired in Sorbornne University, Paris. Lasantha had information that these details were not entirely correct. He wrote to Kumaratunga informing her that he was hoping to run a story on her academic qualifications and requested to see copies of degree certificates. In a couple of days the Editor received a reply from the President's secretary. The short and crisp reply informed him in one biting sentence that the President only entertained correspondence from human beings and not from worms!

Of course this massive presidential aberration only provided more grist to Lasantha's journalistic mill and in the following Sunday's edition he gleefully published this bit of correspondence together with his story on the Sorbonne qualifications.

Sometime later, the President's media advisor, film star Sanath Gunathilaka ventured out to offer the *Leader* an olive branch. He approached Lasantha's brother Lal and a meeting was organised at Lal's home. After exchanging pleasantries, Gunathilaka told Lasantha and Lal, the government was willing to help the *Leader* with state advertising if it refrained from publishing adverse stories about the President and himself.

"You can write about anybody else but leave the President and me out of it," he said. Lasantha however was not willing to play ball just because the advertising carrot had been dangled. He told Sanath he would refrain from getting personal but that decision, he said, was not based on advertising. It was up to the government whether advertising was given to the *Leader* or not, he said.

Lasantha continued to write his expose's, many of them embarrassing to the incumbent government. We were certain by now that our telephones were tapped; there was a continuous, almost imperceptible beep on the phone which we were informed by those familiar with telephone surveillance was an indicator our phone was tapped. Our six-year-old daughter Ahimsa found all this very intriguing and while we were at work, she would pick up the receiver and conduct long chats with "Chandrika" who she believed was listening on the other end. One day she 'bartered' with the President. "If you give my school a holiday tomorrow I will ask my father not to write about you."

At school the children were accustomed to comments, especially from their teachers, about their father and his work. Most of them were fans but one teacher in particular was a huge supporter of Chandrika Kumaratunga and didn't take kindly to the exposures the *Leader* was splashing week after week. One day Ahimsa bounced into the classroom to find the teacher seated at her desk poring over the previous day's *Leader*. Seeing Ahimsa she complained, "*Ahhh, hondata deela neda?*" (He has given it, hasn't he?) Not understanding much of what was going on, little Ahimsa smiled sheepishly and took her seat.

Even though Lasantha had this extremely adversarial relationship with Chandrika and her government, he would tell me that some day when Chandrika was out of office, she and he would most probably be good friends.

"I have absolutely no anger or hatred towards Chandrika," he would say. "I'm just doing my job. When this is over we will be yarn-swapping buddies."

In the 90s, a favourite dining place of ours was Canton Seafood Restaurant owned by firebrand UNP MP Sarath Kongahage and his wife Shanthini. The restaurant was patronised by politicians, journalists and other friends of the Kongahages and hence, it was a place where we had hours of fun and merriment. Because of Kongahage's scathing attacks on the government—on the floor of parliament in particular—the restaurant was regarded by the powers-that-be, as a hub where anti-government plots were hatched.

On the morning of Sunday February 16, 1997, we received news that Canton had come under a heavy automatic weapon attack. Lasantha and I rushed to the restaurant where we were met by the shaken couple. The entire restaurant was in a shambles. The raid had taken place a little past midnight on Saturday; a group of men brandishing weapons had burst into the restaurant and opened fire, much to the horror of the last few diners. Sarath Kongahage himself had escaped through a window.

The event was just another reminder that anyone with a dissenting viewpoint was unsafe.

That same year saw a journalist face criminal defamation charges when on July 1, Editor of *The Sunday Times*, Sinha Ratnatunga was sentenced to 18 months in prison for defaming President Chandrika Kumaratunga in a February 1995 gossip column snippet. The sentence was suspended for seven years. Ratnatunga was indicted on two counts of the penal code and press council law which was widely criticised as being an archaic piece of legislation being used to muzzle the press.

That year, Leader Publications moved to new premises in the Collettes Building on D. S. Senanayake Mawatha, Borella.

* * *

It wouldn't be wrong to say that Lasantha's television career was born of a dinner party conversation.

A few months before Lasantha was asked by Teleshan Network's (TNL) News Director to act as mediator on one of the station's political programs, Lasantha and I met with an astrologer. The woman scanned his natal chart, raised her eyebrows and then looked questioningly at Lasantha.

"Soon," she said, "some new avenue of work will begin which will take your name to the four corners of this country."

At the time, we thought nothing about this strange prophesy.

During this time, we had become close friends with Ishini Wickremesinghe and her husband Asitha Perera. Ishini's father Shan, brother of Ranil Wickremesinghe, owned TNL, one of Sri Lanka's private-owned television stations where Ishini functioned as News Director.

Almost every weekend, Lasantha and I would join Ishini, Asitha, Member of Parliament Ravi Karunanayake and his wife Mela to dinner at some restaurant or the other. It was at one of these convivial gatherings of happy chatter and good cheer that Ishini first broached the subject of Lasantha's suitability to host a political program on TNL.

Ishini explained they needed someone with a good political grasp to host *Cross Talks* which had earlier been conducted by *Island* Editor Gamini Weerakoon. After further discussion, Lasantha agreed to come on board and thus began the television chapter in Lasantha's life. Even then we never realised this was going to be the start of a successful run on television for Lasantha that would make his an instantly recognisable face wherever he went.

From the very outset Lasantha did some memorable interviews and hosted many riveting political debates. One of the most talked-of early interviews was the one he conducted with Olympian Golden Girl Susanthika Jayasinghe on TNL's new Sinhala current affairs program *Janahanda* regarding her controversial allegations of sexual harassment against a senior Cabinet Minister.

The interview with Susanthika was relayed live on TNL and I watched the program together with several of our friends at the Canton Seafood Restaurant. We were amazed at how skillfully he conducted the interview and how exceptionally gutty he was in his assertions and the questions he posed. I remember many of those present were very amused at his reference to Susanthika as "*Thamaa*" as if he were addressing a witness in courts. It was a brilliant interview and throughout, he asked his probing questions in such a manner that it prevented Susanthika from making any libelous statements.

Susanthika and Lasantha became good friends thereafter and she would come home from time to time in search of 'Lasantha Aiya' to get advice from him on various issues.

At the time, TNL were putting together plans and ideas for the parody *Always Breakdown* which lampooned all the prominent politicians of the day, portrayed by giant look-alike muppets. Lasantha contributed some of his own ideas to Ishini and the production team on this project just as he provided a great deal of leads to the TNL news crew. When Ishini was arrested by the CID on December 31, 1995 over a news item that was aired, Lasantha was thoroughly disturbed and accompanied her to the notorious Fourth Floor in his capacity as a lawyer.

Just like in his newspaper columns, under the glare of the television cameras too, Lasantha was forthright and totally fearless in expressing his views and revealing stories that embarrassed and angered politicians. Soon he had a devoted audience of men, women and even children, who waited eagerly for his program each week and sat mesmerised for hours on end. The womenfolk were not just enamoured by his eloquence, they admired his mannerisms, his humour and his bright, 'kapati-collar' shirts!

The political debates where Lasantha acted as mediator or was a participant himself, almost always became shouting matches between the panel members and continued into the wee hours. Many nights, especially those when he had castigated a very powerful personality or two on national TV, I would call him up to ensure he was safe. A few times I met him outside the television station, fearful of letting him travel on his own. Most nights, I sat up in fear waiting for him to come home safe.

Lasantha was aware how popular his programs had become and strove to give his audiences what they wanted; sometimes going to mischievous lengths. This was a time when his newspaper was engaged in weekly battles with President Chandrika Kumaratunga, her ministers and her media advisor Sanath Gunathilaka. One of the biggest stories Lasantha uncovered in his newspaper columns at the time was the infamous 'Channel 9 affaire'. This story revolved round a taped conversation he had in his possession wherein the media advisor is heard discussing with a businessman, the setting up of a proposed television station, Channel 9, and makes reference to a 'cut.' Lasantha of course ran with this story both in his newspaper and on television. He published the entire transcript of the conversation in the newspaper and aired it on television.

During the height of the Channel 9 controversy, there were moves to organise a television debate with some of those featured in the Channel 9 drama and a few members of the media participating as panel members. Lasantha, as the man who broke the Channel 9 story and continued to highlight all developments with regards to it, was also invited to participate. After some haggling over which station should host the debate, it was finally decided that one of the State-run stations would do the honours. Lasantha insisted the main players of the Channel 9 drama should be present at the debate.

The debate was aired live and at the beginning, the moderator introduced the panel members and gave viewers a brief background of the story. Lasantha however was unhappy that the participants he had wanted, those implicated in the Channel 9 affaire, were not present. He was itching to voice his displeasure about this glaring 'no-show' and with some difficulty managed to get the moderator to allow him a few minutes to be heard. He then aired his opinion about the unsatisfactory composition of the panel and declaring that he didn't want to be part of such a lop-sided debate, stood up to leave in a huff, throwing his clip-on mike on the table for added effect.

The panelists representing the government began shouting insults after him. "Mada panuwa!" one of them yelled but Lasantha, ignoring these, continued to storm out of the studio. A little while later some of the other panel members too walked out and only the government representatives were left to conduct the debate! It was an unforgettable moment for thousands of viewers who watched the whole drama unfold right before their eyes.

On one occasion, Lasantha was interviewing Muslim Congress Leader M. H. M. Ashraff when the topic moved on to Sanath Gunathilaka and the Channel 9 story. In the process of the interview, Lasantha pulled out a photograph from his pocket and showed it to Ashraff whose eyes widened in surprise. Lasantha chuckled and put the picture away. For weeks afterward, television audiences were clamouring to find out what the picture was all about but of course only a few had the 'pleasure' of seeing that picture which spoke a thousand words!

Several years in to his political programs with TNL, Lasantha was asked by another television station, MTV (owned by the Maharajah Group) to host a breakfast show with a political flavour. Lasantha and MTV boss Raja Mahendran were friends but it was after he began the breakfast show that the two became as close as brothers. Their friendship lasted to his dying day.

Very early in to broadcast, *The Breakfast Show* became a hugely sought-after program. Lasantha's face appeared on public billboards, sitting inside an eggcup with the words, 'Have Lasantha For Breakfast.'

Lasantha's face was now recognisable everywhere. Everyone knew his name. Everywhere, people came up to him to say how much they enjoyed his programs. On one such day we recalled those words uttered by an astrologer a while back. They had indeed come true.

* * *

On Lasantha's 40th birthday, April 5, 1998, we at the *Leader* decorated the office with balloons and streamers. My sister Dream had baked and iced a very clever birthday cake depicting the cover page of *The Sunday Leader* complete with pictures and edible masthead, headlines and text. Everyone had a delicious piece of the *Leader* after Lasantha cut it to a loud chorus of "Happy Birthday."

Two Saturdays later, Lasantha and I along with several of our friends were invited to spend a day of fun and leisure at the home of our friend Gamini Gunaratne in his ancestral home in Dompe. The property includes sprawling gardens where visitors play cricket and take a dip in the cool waters of a small cemented pool before enjoying a sumptuous lunch of typical Sri Lankan village fare. That day, the lunch included a delicious dish of 'kos' or jak fruit which everyone tucked into heartily.

The next day, our youngest child, a son, was born and the joke was that the 'kos' I had tucked into with relish the previous day had advanced my labour, for the baby had not been due for another two weeks.

We named the baby Aadesh Saurav Rahul and he became his father's greatest joy. Under the glass on Lasantha's desk at work, he had several pictures of the two older children and after Aadesh came along, many more were added. Every day after work Lasantha stopped by at a shop on the way home to buy the little fellow a toy and always entered the house shouting "Malli Boy!!!" at the top of his lungs. In office, he regaled the staff with stories of the little chap's every milestone.

Lasantha loved nothing more than spending time with his family; his children were the most important thing in his life. Most evenings at home after work, all three children would be in bed with us, the two older ones prancing about, each one trying to be heard over the other, while baby Aadesh watched all these rambunctious goings-on in wide-eyed fascination. Some evenings we would all huddle in bed watching videos of *Fox and the Hound*, *Lion King* or some other children's animation that Lasantha had brought back from his overseas travels; other times we would all drive off to Pizza Hut or some restaurant, stopping on the way at the video parlour, Lasantha and I picking up whodunit dramas and the children scouting about for cartoons.

Lasantha was always busy, forever on the go, but Sunday was designated as Family Day when we would spend the entire day together as a family. He hated anyone being away from home; the children would sometimes ask to spend the night at a cousin's but their father wouldn't hear of it. When I went overseas for a week's seminar, Lasantha told me it had been the longest week of his life.

Fun and merriment notwithstanding, it was around this time that we realised that government sleuths, goons or both, were on our trail. Driver Lalith reported the presence of suspicious characters hovering in the vicinity of our home. On our way to work we would see strange men standing idly, most often near the Borella cemetery end of our Collettes Building office. Lasantha became quite clever at spotting them and would, in his highly extroverted and unrestrained style, give them a hearty wave as we passed by.

But events proved these were no laughing matters.

On June 17, 1998, less than two months after Aadesh was born, Lasantha, our two older children and I went out to dinner at a restaurant with friends. After our return, the children went off to sleep while Lasantha and I happily settled down to watch a movie in our bedroom where in a corner, the baby slept peacefully in his cot.

Immersed in the intrigue of Harrison Ford's *'Clear and Present Danger,'* we were quite unaware of the very clear danger that was at that moment, very much present right outside our own home.

Suddenly, we were jolted by the sound of a volley of shots; it sounded like very loud firecrackers and I turned to Lasantha and asked, "How come someone is lighting crackers at this time of the night?"

"It can't be crackers," Lasantha replied.

A few seconds later Menika came huffing and puffing up the stairs and burst into our room; "Mahaththaya, mahaththaya, someone shot in to the house!" she cried with absolute terror written on her face.

Lasantha and I rushed downstairs and into the driver's room in the front of the house. Several bullets were embedded into the wall and driver Lalith explained how one had missed his head by a whisker. Window panes in his room were shattered and glass shards lay everywhere.

In the garden, our red Pajero parked in the porch had also received the impact of several bullets with the glass at the rear shattered and the bullets tearing through the back seats. If we had delayed our return home from dinner by 15 minutes, there was every chance we would have been hit by those bullets and been killed. The weapons had been fired through a gap in the front gate of our home.

We immediately informed the Mirihana police and several constables arrived shortly thereafter. Friends too began pouring in. Mangala Samaraweera, the media minister who the *Leader* had always been very critical of, called and asked details of the attack and conveyed his concern. A little while later a minor circus act prevailed when, then UNP MP Mervyn Silva appeared in the house brandishing a pistol and shouting insults at the invisible attackers. This was his way of conveying his concern.

Some 40 empty T-56 bullet cartridges were collected from outside the house proving the intensity of this armed assault.

Although the police promised an investigation would be launched, nothing came of it. We were however provided with police protection in the form of two constables providing guard all-night in the outside verandah area. This continued for a couple of months.

After this attack, Lasantha was included in Amnesty International's endangered list.

An article by Kshama Ranasinghe in *ASIAWEEK* on the attack on our home titled 'Campaigning Editor' quoted Lasantha: "I consider these incidents an occupational hazard. They only strengthen my resolve to continue with my work."

The article went on to say, "In six years of bribery, only once has the political establishment blushed enough to take action. That was in 1996, when Wickrematunge revealed that a senior bureaucrat who was holding the posts of secretary in a ministry, chairman of a publishing house and director of the national airline had altered his date of birth."

The same year as that attack on us, in August 1998 to be precise, another instance of state-sponsored harassment of *The Sunday Leader* occurred. The newspaper had carried a story on July 26 reproducing a letter written to Speaker of Parliament K.B. Ratnayake by two members of the Bribery Commission urging that he remove two ministers from a Parliamentary Select Committee that was probing their own conduct.

Refusing to step down from the committee, the ministers instead engaged in a campaign to remove the two members of the Bribery Commission.

On August 14, 1998, CID officers arrived at the Leader Publications office demanding a statement from the Editor and insisting he divulge the source who leaked the letter about the ministers to the newspaper. Lasantha did not comply with a statement nor did he reveal his source. Thankfully, nothing transpired from that.

The same year as the second attack on us, on February 12, 1998, Iqbal Athas, defense columnist for *The Sunday Times* and his family had been attacked when five armed men forcibly entered their home and threatened him, his wife Anoma, and their young daughter, at gunpoint. According to neighbours, the intruders were backed by some 25 armed men who waited outside the house. The intruders eventually left without inflicting serious injuries.

The attacks on the media continued into the following year.

On July 14, 1999, at least 12 journalists covering a massive demonstration organised by the UNP were manhandled and their cameras smashed. Most of them needed to be treated for injuries sustained at the hands of goons believed to be affiliated to the PA government.

In September that year, Rohana Kumara, Editor of the anti-government Sinhala language tabloid *Satana*, was shot dead inside the trishaw he was travelling in at point-blank range by unidentified assailants.

* * *

Several years after the attacks on us, in April 2002 when the UNP was in office, Interior Minister John Amaratunga directed the CID to carry out investigations in to both, the 1995 assault incident and the 1998 attack on our home. In relation to the assault, the CID team took into custody four persons who had been close confidantes of the former Presidential Security

Chief. It was also revealed that notorious and dreaded underworld killer Baddegana Sanjeewa had been part of the gang that assaulted us in 1995.

Lasantha was willing to forgive and forget. He called me in Australia where I was living by then and told me of the arrests. "I told my lawyer that we don't want to punish these guys," he said. Later however he told me his lawyer hadn't been happy about it as it would have created an unhealthy precedent.

The four assailants were found guilty of simple assault and evaded a jail term much to Lasantha's relief. However among those arrested was a Police Constable (PC) who was previously attached to the head of state's security division and he was due to face an internal police inquiry. If found guilty, he would lose his job. The PC one day arrived at the Leader office to meet Lasantha. After asking for his forgiveness, he told Lasantha he had young children and if he, the sole breadwinner, lost his job, they would be destitute. The mention of children tugged at Lasantha's heartstrings. He took the man to meet Lal and explained the situation. "Damn sin," Lasantha told Lal, "he has kids to feed and educate. I want to write a letter to the IGP stating that I don't consider this man to be responsible for the attack on me and Raine. Instead, it is those who contracted him to carry out the assault that are guilty."

Lal being somewhat of a tougher breed than his younger brother told Lasantha there would be others who had suffered the same fate and that this wasn't a wise course of action to follow. Lasantha however was adamant and the matter ended with Lasantha writing to the IGP in the man's favour.

In a separate incident, underworld figure Mahinda Godage alias Bada Mahinda who was in remand custody for an unrelated offence made a written confession to the Gangodawila Magistrate about his involvement in the gun attack on our home and attempts on Lasantha's life. He was hoping that through his evidence he could be named a crown witness and gain immunity from being prosecuted for his current offence. He revealed to police, details of how he was contracted by a powerful businessman/government official to murder the Editor-in-Chief of *The Sunday Leader,* Lasantha Wickrematunge. The official was someone who Lasantha had done several exposures on from time to time.

According to Mahinda's statement to the police, shortly before the gun attack on our residence, another underworld figure, one Dhammika Perera contacted him asking that he meet with him. When he did, another man known as 'Jackpot Chaminda' was present. At the meeting, Dhammika Perera informed him that a job needed to be carried out at the house of a certain newspaperman.

Mahinda went on to say, the three of them travelled to the Wickrematunge residence in Nugegoda whereupon Jackpot Chaminda alighted from the vehicle and aiming a T56 weapon through the gap in the front gate of the residence, emptied several rounds of ammunition.

According to Mahinda's statement, Dhammika Perera telephoned the official who had given him the order to carry out the attack and told him, "Sir, *vadey hari.*" (The deed has been done.)

Mahinda also said that the same mastermind had ordered him to assassinate Lasantha and following the order, he had carried out two assassination attempts on Lasantha. Both times he had, together with Dhammika Perera, lain in wait for Lasantha as he drove to work in his red Pajero from his Nugegoda residence. According to Mahinda, on both occasions their murderous plan had to be aborted as 'Wickrematunge was accompanied by his wife Raine.' Mahinda said he asked Dhammika not to open fire as 'she too would have run the risk of being murdered.'

I was stunned when I heard this. At functions I had met the 'official' whom Bada Mahinda had implicated in his confession and I remembered having told Lasantha that at one of these events, this official could not look me in the eye and at that time I felt he was responsible for one of the attacks on us.

I was amazed also that Lasantha's life had been saved due to me being present with him in the vehicle. What further surprised me was the information that a vicious underworld hitman had a conscience which prevented him from hitting his target for fear of hurting his wife.

Lasantha' father who had read the entire account of Bada Mahinda's confession in *The Sunday Leader* called me in Australia and expressed his gratitude.

"You not only saved his life in '95. If you had not been in the vehicle with him on those other occasions, my boy would now be dead," he said with great emotion.

* * *

No amount of threats, intimidation or attacks had put a dent in Lasantha's work. He continued with his writing unfazed. By now he had a stunning list of contacts; stunning not merely because of the sheer volume but its mind-boggling diversity. And so the stories and tips poured in. He followed up, investigated and wrote some of them himself, either as Suranimala or under other pseudonyms. Some he passed on to the other journalists at the *Leader*.

Following are the headlines of some of the bigger stories that appeared in the *Leader* in the first few years of circulation. Most of them were in-depth investigations running into full or double-page spreads.

Sad saga of developing the south
Galle Port commission scandal
Another bad 'Show' by the CID
Who's the man behind the smoking gun?
Operation Scapegoat
Ghosts of the past haunt PSD (Presidential Security Division)
"Fiat' Accompli
'Kommis Kakka' in defence contract
Bankrupting the state banks
Uncovering the LTTE safe havens in Nelson Mandela country
CBK accuses SC judge of taking bribe
Defence Ministry Guilty
What hit list?

Chandrika's role in Channel 9 proved
Confessions of a PSD hit man
CID to quiz CBK on 007 handbag
Air Chief nose-dives as Operation Cover-Up backfires
It is highway robbery
Unmasking Mr. Speaker
Dr. JJ's crying shame
A palace for the manor born
Mr. Speaker disrobed
The 'safe house' controversy
Mahinda's fishy businesss
Govt. bungles gas privatisation deal
Case against AirLanka deal proved
Top gangster reveals links with PA
The great AirLanka sell-out
The stink over AirLanka and Sanath's heartache
National security bogey exploded
Alsthom offer on loco deal violates tender conditions
President wanted wheat imports suspended
Anatomy of a tender—How the President forced a show of hand
Galle Port debacle—how the people were taken for a ride
A deal gone sour and being economical with the truth
Another Cricket Googlie
Hilton: the shocking finale

Ghost company and PA-style investment
PSD: the terror machine
Net closes in on the General
Where did the third C130 go?
Ad contracts, lies and videotapes
Bullets are not meant for journalists
Cricket's day of shame
Govt. pays Evans Rs. 250,000,000
UNP's electoral shame
CBK's luxury cars deal exposed
Taking SriLankan to the cleaners
Murder of PSD's Al Capone
Multi-million dollar locomotive deal that derailed train service
Thilanga on the backfoot
Holes and moles in the golf course deal
Case against the High Priest of Justice
Dogs of war make millions risking national security.

* * *

There is an interesting post-script to the story about the February 1995 assault on us.

In February 2012, some 17 years after the assault, I was on a short visit to Sri Lanka where I met one Samarasinha who was a spiritual advisor of sorts. I had gone to meet him with my daughter.

After the consultation was over, I was preparing to leave when he mentioned something about the media. I then told him Ahimsa was the daughter of the slain journalist Lasantha Wickrematunge. Samarasinha stared at me incredulously and asked, "So, you were Lasantha's wife?" When I answered in the affirmative, he motioned us to sit down again. "I have an interesting story to tell you," he said.

He then told me the following.

One evening, around three years previously, a drunk and dishevelled man had walked into his consulting room. The man had told Samarasinha he wished to unburden a huge guilt he had been carrying for years. He had then seen a parcel sitting on Samarasinha's table with my name on it. This parcel contained a monk's robe and an umbrella which I had given my mother in January 2009 before leaving for Australia following Lasantha's funeral, asking that she offer it to a monk. My mother had met Samarasinha by chance at the local temple and even though she did not know him, asked him whether he knew of any monk from a rural area who might make use of the items. Samarasinha had then told my mother he was leaving for Anuradhapura in a few days and that he would take it with him and give it to a monk there. My mother had written my name on the parcel.

This was the parcel the drunk and dishevelled man had seen sitting on Samarasinha's table. He had read my name written on it and asked Samarasinha what the parcel contained to which he had replied it was sent by one Raine Wickrematunge to be given to a monk. The man had then said, "That's who I came here to talk about."

The man then told Samarasinha that he had been one of the gang that had assaulted 'Lasantha and Raine' in 1995. He was suffering from immense guilt because as he put it, he had later learnt that these were good, decent people and he was deeply ashamed at being part of the assault. He had asked Samarasinha whether he could ask for my forgiveness. "She was a brave woman; she jumped on her husband's back and protected him even while we beat her," he had said with great shame. "Please arrange for me to ask her for her forgiveness," he had said.

Samarasinha had then told him he didn't know where I was and that I may be overseas and he should just pray for forgiveness standing by the Buddha image in that room, which the man had then done.

I was amazed to hear this tale and the co-incidental manner in which I had come to hear of it. I told Samarasinha I had forgiven our attackers a long time ago; in fact I told him I had never harboured any anger towards them and that Lasantha himself had not wanted to continue with the prosecution when the men had been finally arrested.

I left Samarasinha's house that day amazed at what I had just heard.

CHAPTER SEVEN
Lasantha Outfoxes the Censor: 'Palaly *not* under attack'

> *"Censorship is to art as lynching is to justice."*
> —Henry Louis Gates, American scholar.

IN Sri Lanka, the euphoria that accompanied the dawn of the new millennium was as short-lived as the celebratory fireworks that lighted up the night sky. In effect, Sri Lanka was ushering in a year which would prove to be one of war, violence and despair. The media was not poised for an auspicious beginning to the year either.

While ferocious battles were being fought in the north and east of the country, the number of LTTE suicide attacks in the city had escalated and bombs were exploding with terrifying regularity. People were fearful of travelling on buses or being caught up in crowded places. Most of them didn't have much of a choice.

The run-up to the new millennium itself had seen a great deal of fresh violence. On December 18, 1999, one event in particular sent major shockwaves throughout the country. A female suicide bomber sought to assassinate President Chandrika Kumaratunga at an election meeting at the Town Hall in Colombo and 26 people including Colombo's Deputy Inspector-General T. N. De Silva were killed. Among the more than 100 injured were three senior ministers and a television crew from Japan. The President herself received major shrapnel injuries resulting in the surgical removal of one eye.

It was a Saturday and the final edition had been put to bed. Lasantha and I were enjoying ourselves at the wedding of *Sunday Leader* columnist Kristen Chen when we heard the news of the attack and rushed to the office to recast Page One with the latest news. A few other journalists arrived at the office and began calling up their police and political contacts for more information. A photographer and two reporters went to the hospital where the President had been rushed for immediate treatment. They were met by her furious Media Advisor Sanath Gunathilaka who berated them and asked them to leave.

On the same day as the attack on the head of the nation, LTTE suicide bomber Skandaraja Ashoka detonated a bomb strapped to his body killing retired Major General Lakshman (Lucky) Algama and 11 persons at a UNP election rally in Ja-ela.

During the war years, Sri Lanka in general and Colombo in particular presented something of a paradox. In the far-flung villages where most of the young canon-fodder soldiers hailed from, all year long, a never-ending trail of bodies made the dismal journey back from the battlefields to the humble homes for their last rites. Grief-stricken mothers lamented by the coffins of their slain sons and heart-broken new widows hugged their young children and wailed. When a high-ranking officer was killed, the streets were adorned with white tissue paper streamers and on occasion, shops closed for the day as a mark of respect for the fallen.

On the other hand, in the capital Colombo, extreme displays of wealth and gaiety that sometimes bordered on the vulgar were commonplace. City nightclubs operated to full capacity as the jet-set tripped the light fantastic while the super-rich, some of them fattened on ill-gotten gains, squandered hundreds of thousands of rupees in casinos and clubs and threw lavish five-star hotel bashes for their children. Each time a bomb went off or there was significant loss of life on the warfront, these same people were momentarily aghast. Sipping imported liqueurs, they intellectualised and analysed the war from the safety of their plush living rooms.

Those caught in-between this vast social inequity went about their lives, earning a hard living, wondering if, when they left for work each day and sent their children off to school, any of them would come back home alive. Such was the frequency with which those monstrous bombs were exploding in the city and suburbs.

The tourism industry, battered and bruised by years of warfare, shuddered and shivered and made desperate attempts to crawl back up after each suicide bomb attack. A handful of politicians were vociferous in their call to put the country on a war-footing. Industrial Development Minister C.V. Gooneratne paid with his life for that strident call. On Wednesday June 7, 2000, the Minister, his wife Shyama and 21 others died in a bomb attack as they participated in a War Heroes Day march in Katubedda, Moratuwa.

Despite *The Sunday Leader* having become one of the government's harshest critics and its biggest thorn in the flesh, several cabinet ministers maintained cordial relations with us. C. V. Gooneratne who I had lunch with occasionally in the Member's Visitors Cafeteria in parliament when I was lobby correspondent, was one of them.

Once, I happened to see Gooneratne and a throng of his supporters on Galle Road as they walked in to shops and business establishments collecting funds to beef up the war kitty. At that moment I realised how vulnerable the

Minister was to an LTTE attack and I made a mental note to convey my fears to him. Within the next two weeks, Gooneratne was killed.

Getting back to the dawn of the new millennium, just five days in to the year 2000, a suicide bomber detonated explosives outside Prime Minister Sirima Bandaranaike's Flower Road office killing 13 and injuring 27 people.

On the same day as this attack, Kumar Ponnambalam, lawyer, leader of the All Ceylon Tamil Congress and vociferous critic of the government was shot dead by unknown persons in Colombo. For all his indignant, highly-charged vituperative—most of it in newspaper articles and letters to the editor in English language newspapers—Kumar was a good-natured soul. What many didn't know was that he who was a strident voice for Tamil rights and was labelled a '*kotiya*' or Tiger, also listened to the classic Sinhala tunes of Amaradeva and C. T. Fernando on his car stereo and was a huge fan of the Sri Lanka cricket team. If the Tigers were the 'boys' to him, the ones that wielded the willow were 'our boys.' Kumar and his wife Dr. Yogi were personal friends of Lasantha and me.

Kumar's killing wasn't the only jolt for us that January. Celebrating her victory in the December 1999 Presidential election, President Chandrika Kumaratunga gave a three-hour marathon interview on state television in early January which was in essence, a focused attack on the private media.

The President accused several media institutions and journalists—notably, Victor Ivan, Editor of the Sinhala-language paper *Ravaya*, and Lasantha Wickrematunge—of attempting to undermine her December 1999 re-election.

Answering questions put to her, the President shocked viewers with her long-winded replies, at times becoming intensely personal in her scathing attacks. Lasantha received the worst of her diatribe.

A few days later news items in the government media alleged that certain businessmen were conspiring with the LTTE to assassinate the President. In response to these, Lasantha and Victor Ivan charged that the reports pointed fingers in their direction. They also said it was suspicious that these news items appeared just days after their castigation by the President on state television.

"The government wants to stifle all dissent," Lasantha stated at a news conference. "This attempt to link us with the LTTE is a direct threat to our lives."

In April that year, Batticalo-based journalist Nellai Nadesan narrowly escaped death when a bomb exploded in his home situated between two checkpoints manned by two militant groups. Earlier, Nadesan who wrote for the Tamil newspaper *Virakesari,* had been threatened with death by an anonymous caller following an article highlighting the atrocities committed by a member of the People's Liberation Organisation of Tamil Eelam (PLOTE).

By May that year, we at the *Leader* were also hit by a bolt; this time one that literally stopped us in our tracks.

Before going in to that story however, I should give readers a brief history of the oppressive media climate that prevailed in Sri Lanka at the time and the events that led to the *Leader* being hit by this veritable thunderbolt.

During the mid 90s, an intermittent media censorship had been in force in Sri Lanka. When in June 1998 a military censor, General Jaliya Nammuni, was appointed, it was perceived as an about-turn by the Kumaratunga administration which had earlier indicated it was considering new constitutional guarantees for free expression. All defence-related reports, photographs and videotapes had to be passed through the military censor.

Despite protests from the local media and concern by international media observers including the New York-based Committee to Protect Journalists, (CPJ), on May 3, 2000, the government further intensified its media blackout. Following a series of debacles in its war against the LTTE, in particular the falling of the northern army base of Elephant Pass to the LTTE, President Kumaratunga, acting under Section 5 of the Public Security Ordinance, promulgated Emergency Regulation 14 which imposed a number of restrictions on publishing and broadcasting. These new laws not only curbed press freedom but in addition banned all protests and industrial action and conferred upon the authorities sweeping powers to block any opposition to the government.

Regulation 14 also armed the authorities with power to ban publications that breached the regulation and to place a sealing order on their premises. Subsequent to the promulgation, the affable and thus far 'media friendly' Ariya Rubasinghe, Director of Information in the Government Information Department, was appointed Competent Authority.

Hardly a week into the appointment of the Competent Authority, the Editor of *The Sunday Leader* was given a rap on the knuckles. On May 9, 2000, the Competent Authority issued a warning to Editor Wickrematunge on the basis that a photograph of an opposition rally and "other news items" published in the May 7, 2000 edition contravened Regulation 14. Lasantha immediately shot off a letter to the Competent Authority asking for clarification regarding the scope of Regulation 14. He queried with dripping sarcasm whether articles highlighting corruption and mismanagement would also be covered under the regulation. A miffed Competent Authority did not respond.

All media institutions and personnel, mindful of reprisals they may have to face if they flouted this new regulation, duly complied. Several newspapers however declared their displeasure of the ban by carrying blank pages. Others left several white spaces in the articles with the word 'censored' printed across.

The Sunday Leader too published highly censored versions of their articles but Lasantha, now in his sixth year as Editor, believed this ban on reporting was counter-productive. Wild rumour and crazy speculation about the war situation became the sworn truth to a people kept in the dark and fed only the highly manipulated official line. The only certainty was that there was heavy fighting going on in the war areas.

Sri Lanka had seen, several years earlier, in 1983 to be precise, how dangerous unchecked rumour could be. Black Friday stood as a stark reminder of this, a day when a bunch of incensed people acting on a rumour that "Tigers had come to the city" went on a murderous rampage.

Lasantha was vocal in his view about the wisdom, or the lack of it, of the ban. He was staunch in the belief that the censorship was not only unconstitutional in that it violated the Article 14 guarantee of freedom of expression but it had been imposed, not to safeguard the war effort but to protect and prop up an unpopular government. He also saw political manipulations in the censor's so-called duties. Determined to expose these facts in his newspaper—the censor's warning he had just received having only added to his resolve—he formulated a brilliant plan.

First, he sat at his office desk and penned two fictitious articles. One blamed the war situation in the country on policies followed by the former UNP government; the other story detailed how the UNP was divided on the manner in which the war should be prosecuted.

He then commissioned cartoonist S. C. Opatha to replicate a cartoon which had appeared in the government-controlled *Daily News* a few days earlier. It showed a scene from a 'UNP Hotel' where Opposition Leader Ranil Wickremesinghe, portrayed as a waiter, is shown waiting on LTTE leader Velupillai Prabhakaran who is preparing to carve Sri Lanka which has been handed to him on a platter.

That same day, May 9, Lasantha despatched to the Censor the cartoon depicting Ranil Wickremesinghe and the articles relating to the UNP.

That evening the *Leader* office received the articles and the cartoons, duly checked. The stories about the UNP had been given the greenlight with just one insignificant deletion. The cartoon too had been passed with a delighted tick of approval.

The next day, May 10, Lasantha duplicated the articles he had sent to the censor with a few changes. In the copies, he substituted 'UNP' and 'Ranil Wickremesinghe' with 'PA' and 'Chandrika Kumaratunga' and replaced the names of UNP Members of Parliament with those of PA Ministers. The cartoon too was changed in that the figure of Ranil Wickremesinghe was replaced by a caricature of President Kumaratunga.

The articles and the cartoon were despatched to the Censor, who, buried under reams of articles sent for his approval—or disapproval—had no idea of the trap that had been neatly laid out by a mischievous Editor. The articles and cartoon duly landed on Chief Censor Ariya Rubasinghe's desk while Lasantha waited in happy anticipation at the *Leader* office, wondering if, and hoping that, his plan had worked.

He need not have worried. The same day the two articles and the cartoon were returned to the Leader offices with a howl of disapproval in the form of pen marks run right across the text on all pages. The cartoon had suffered the same fate.

The Censor or those working for him, were unaware of their colossal blunder. They also had no idea of what awaited them in the form of a full-page article in the following Sunday's edition of *The Sunday Leader*.

On May 14, 2000, Lasantha gleefully splashed the Censor's massive *faux pas* on Page 8 of his newspaper. In a full page story titled, "Censor exposed" by Ariya Borusinghe[1] he explained the Censor's duplicitous actions. He wrote, "Given the Supreme Court judgments that no power can be exercised by any authority arbitrarily, *The Sunday Leader* last week, in the public interest, moved to test the credibility and the manner in which the Competent Authority Rubasinghe exercised his powers in terms of the newly gazetted regulations.

"The Sunday Leader submitted to Competent Authority Ariya Rubasinghe two stories critical of the UNP which he unhesitatingly approved. The following day, the same two stories were forwarded again but by interpolating PA and Chandrika Kumaratunga for UNP and Ranil Wickremesinghe. Guess what Rubasinghe did?"

The page carried the four articles that had been submitted to the censor, side by side. Published on the same page were images of the actual articles and cartoons, very clear for all to see with their 'cut' marks on the ones critical of the PA. The Censor had 'censored' everything critical of the PA but had approved the identical articles and cartoon critical of the UNP.

Lasantha's expose´ of this duplicity was a monumental slap on the face of the Censor. It was an embarrassing gaffe and the Competent Authority's political game-playing lay exposed for all to see. They were understandably livid but there was little they could do about it than silently fume.

The following week, city walls were plastered with posters that read: "*Deshadrohi puwathpath helaa dakimu.*" (Denounce treacherous newspapers).

* * *

By mid-May, the Palaly army camp was overrun by the LTTE but since the censorship prevented people from learning of the real situation, wild speculation and rumour raged. Later, news began to spread about a large-scale LTTE attack on the Palaly army base and the nation was engulfed in a sense of foreboding and fear. Still the country was kept in the dark. There was talk that a very large number of soldiers had perished in the attack.

Lasantha, having amassed all the details of the attack including the number of casualties from his contacts, was bursting to give his readers the real story. The ban on reporting war-related news however stood in his way. If he sent the story to the Censor, there was no doubt in the world of it being axed outright. He needed to come up with an ingenious plan.

As with other news establishments, it was a practice at the *Leader* Editorial to work on Page One of the first edition on Friday evening after most of the other pages had been put to bed. Every Friday evening, I would sit at the computer where Page One had been laid out, giving headlines, editing, cutting and chopping. Lasantha would come in from time to time and instruct the computer operator and me to effect certain changes. He would also rattle off stories which I typeset directly onto the page. And it was in a similar scenario that on Friday, May 19, he came in to the room looking rather pleased with himself as I worked on the May 21 issue.

Waving a few handwritten pages, he asked us to typeset its contents and place the story across on the top of the page below the masthead.

The story went on to describe in detail the overrunning of the camp, how it transpired, how many military casualties it had claimed and all other pertinent details relating to the debacle. But every statement in the article was preceded, by the word *not*. The headline of the story, as directed by Lasantha, was 'War in fantasy land—Palaly *not* under attack.'

I was aghast but had to admit it was a clever ploy. However, I was worried about what the repercussion of this act of defiance would be on the newspaper.

The article of course was not despatched to the Censor for his approval because in theory, it did *not* report news from the warfront. In fact, it specifically said there had *not* been an attack on the camp and so many soldiers had *not* been killed.

This is an excerpt of that article:

> "Heavy fighting was not raging in northern Jaffna peninsula and Tigers were not pounding Palaly with heavy artillery and mortars for the fourth consecutive day. In the so-called attacks, no soldiers were killed nor wounded and several buildings within the base had not suffered minor damages.
>
> "Tigers were not using Kaithady, an area located northeast of Navatkuli as the artillery launching pad to pound the Palaly air base where thousands of soldiers were not under siege by LTTE cadres. In the so-called attacks, the communication tower was not partially disabled, crippling military communications between Colombo and Jaffna for a few hours on Thursday.
>
> "With heavy shelling not being directed at Palaly and areas around the base, the three service commanders did not fly to Vavuniya to co-ordinate counter-offensive measures with their field-commanders.
>
> "Tigers did not enter Kaithady on Wednesday night after 12-hours of so-called fierce hand-to-hand fighting in which more than 40 soldiers were not killed and scores not wounded. The attackers did not breach the forward defence lines of the government forces and did not damage any armoured vehicles nor destroy several gun positions of the army.
>
> "Military officials in Colombo did not say that the situation was very critical and they did not say the stand-off weapons which were ferried to the troops last week were of no use since the morale of the soldiers was very low.
>
> "Jaffna Security Forces Commander Major General Sarath Fonseka did not have to in a last-ditch attempt stall the advance of Tiger rebels order his men to dig bunker lines and mine the areas to prevent Tigers reaching the outskirts of Palaly air base . . . ."

To anyone reading the article, it was obvious what the writer of the news story was trying to convey. The paper duly went in to print and by Sunday morning, readers of *The Sunday Leader* had a full and detailed account of the deadly events in Palaly.

Every Sunday morning Lasantha's mobile and our home phone would ring continuously with friends, family and media colleagues calling to comment on stories that had been published on that particular Sunday. That day people called from all over to congratulate him and marvel at his ingenuity and sheer brass. Lasantha's loud laughter reverberated throughout the house much of that morning as he chatted on the telephone.

But if the Editor thought he had got away with it, he was soon to learn otherwise. The bolt that stopped us in our tracks was about to hit. The very next day, May 22, 2000, the Competent Authority wrote to Leader Publications stating that the May 21, 2000 article was published in breach of Regulation 14 (2) (b) (i) because it dealt with the operations of the security forces but had not been submitted for prior approval. Furthermore, it said, the article was "prejudicial to the interest of national security and the preservation of public order." A printing/publishing/distributing suspension of six-months from the date of the order was issued on Leader Publications and the printing facility.

The same day police officers stormed the Leader Publications press in Ratmalana and surrounded it, shutting it down.

The events of that day are branded in my mind forever. It was a Monday, a relatively quiet day in a newspaper office that publishes two Sunday papers. If no major news story has broken, those busy in the office on a Monday are usually the reporters and sub-editors working on the entertainment tabloid.

All 16 pages of the *Now!* Magazine were required each week to go to production by Tuesday evening so as to free the press for the features section, main section and any advertising supplements coming later in the week.

That Monday, I sat at the computer in our office in Borella, editing a copy that had just come in. Suddenly Lasantha burst in to my room; one look at his face and I knew something disastrous had just occurred. "They have sealed the press," he said breathlessly. We both rushed in to the news room. Everyone—desk heads, reporters, sub-editors, photographers, typesetters and layout artists from both the *Leader* and *Irida Peramuna*—stared dumbfounded as Lasantha explained that a little while earlier police had sealed the Leader printing facility in Ratmalana.

Ten minutes later Lasantha's brother Lal who was now Chairman of Leader Publications, came in and addressed the staff. The Sinhala paper had not flouted any censorship regulations but with the suspension imposed on Leader Publications, they had become victims of collateral damage.

Lal provided the staff with more details of the closure and the events that had led to it and asked everyone to report to work every day if they so wished. "We will continue to pay your salaries," he promised.

Lasantha informed the staff that Leader Publications would fight the ban in courts.

For the next few weeks everyone faithfully turned up to work each day. There were no stories to write and no newspaper to print but everyone reported to work anyway. There was doom and gloom written on faces; the staff—many of them with dependent families—wondered in despair whether the two papers would ever be in circulation again.

Lasantha and the management were not going to sit around licking their wounds. Their lawyers immediately filed a fundamental rights application in the Supreme Court stating that their client's right to equality under Article12(1), 14(1)(a) and 14(1)(g) of the Constitution had been infringed by the shut-down of the paper. The respondent was 'Ariya Rubasinghe, Director of Information and the Competent Authority, et al.'

On June 2, the Supreme Court agreed to hear the petition and during the preliminary hearings the presiding judge questioned the legality of the government's emergency censorship regime. With this slap in the face, President Kumaratunga ordered the ban be reduced by several months and on June 26, the government announced that the Leader Group could resume publishing their newspapers on July 31.

Before that could happen however, on Friday, June 30, the three judge bench of the Supreme Court who had heard the case, in a unanimous decision ruled that because the appointment of the competent authority charged with enforcing emergency censorship regulations had not been submitted to parliament for review within seven days as required by law, the respondent had no power or authority to act under Regulation 14 and hence "the document dated 22 May 2000 addressed to the petitioner was a nullity and was of no force or avail in law."

In addition, the state was ordered to pay Leader Publications, who had won the day on a legal technicality, 100,000 rupees in court costs. Jubilant *Leader* and *Peramuna* staff left the courthouse and rushed off to the Leader Publications office to start work on the following week's editions.

With the 'nullity' of the Competent Authority thus being judicially declared, the ban on another newspaper, the Jaffna-based Tamil daily *Uthayan* too was automatically dissolved.

On May 19, the government had banned *Uthayan* stating the paper had violated censorship. It later charged in a press release that "this newspaper has been maliciously and detrimentally publishing information that is biased to the LTTE and which is geared to disenchantment among the members of the armed forces and the general public of Jaffna."

The Supreme Court's ruling had implications on all of the Censor's actions; therefore, new regulations backdated to July 1, the day after the verdict on *The Sunday Leader* case, were forthwith issued and Ariya Rubasinghe re-appointed as the government Censor.

On July 4, in an interview with The Associated Press, Rubasinghe said the government had re-imposed some of the earlier restrictions on the media as some checks on news reporting were necessary. Rubasinghe also met with editors and senior journalists to explain the provisions of the revised regulations.

The revised decree proscribed "any matter which pertains to any operations carried out or proposed to be carried out by the Armed Forces or the Police Force, any statement pertaining to the official conduct or the performance of the Head or any member of any of the Armed Forces or the Police Force, which affect the morale of the members of such forces, and any material which would or might in the opinion of the Competent Authority be prejudicial to the interests of national security or the preservation of public order."

Two days later, in a letter to President Kumaratunga, the Committee to Protect Journalists (CPJ) pointed out that the Supreme Court ruling on the *Leader* case was an opportunity for the government to end censorship and that the government's failure to do so 'belied earlier commitments to relax the repressive media policy.'

In an order dated September 5, 2000, the government temporarily suspended Regulation 14.

During the time of the *Leader* closure, media-government relations had been further strained. In June, a news report was published and broadcast by state-run media outlets accusing four journalists of having links with the LTTE. The journalists named were Dharmaratnam Sivaram who wrote a blunt and upfront column under the pseudonym Taraki, BBC Tamil Service reporter and head of the Tamil Media Alliance P. Seevagan, *The Sunday Leader* defence columnist Roy Denish and *Irida Peramuna* (*Leader*'s sister paper) Editor Saman Wagaarachchi.

In a joint statement issued on June 6, the four journalists expressed the view that the news reports had been "very clearly designed and deliberately calculated to instigate extremist elements and contract killers against us and our families."

Meanwhile, on the same day that the government temporarily suspended Regulation 14, a judge from Colombo's High Court, armed with the country's archaic criminal defamation laws, sentenced Lasantha to two years in jail on charges of criminally defaming President Chandrika Kumaratunga in relation to an article published in *The Sunday Leader* in 1995. The defamation charge had been filed in response to an article titled '*A Promising Government*' that Lasantha had published in *The Sunday Leader* of September 3, 1995. The article was a scathing attack on the President accusing her of not fulfilling her election promises which prosecutors said implied President Kumaratunga was corrupt.

The sentence was suspended for five years.

Condemning the sentence, CPJ Executive Director Ann Cooper said at the time, "No journalist should ever face the threat of jail for something he or she writes. With a potential jail term hanging over his head for the next five years, Mr. Wickrematunge is bound to think twice before writing anything critical of the government. The press should be given the widest possible latitude to criticize public officials . . . . If criminal defamation laws can be used by a President to silence journalists, the media will not be able to play its watchdog role."

Both Editor Lasantha and his brother, Publisher Lal were indicted under Section 480 of the Penal Code. However, Colombo High Court Judge, Andrew Somawansa, while finding the Editor guilty of the offence, acquitted the Publisher.

If the CPJ had feared that, "Mr. Wickrematunge is bound to think twice before writing anything critical of the government," Lasantha was going to put all those fears to rest. He dug his nose deeper into dodgy affairs of governance and came up with bigger and even more embarrassing stories each week.

Earlier, in June that year, a CPJ delegation had met with Foreign Minister Lakshman Kadirgamar and Media Minister Mangala Samaraweera who had expressed some interest in facilitating media access to conflict areas.

But on September 8, Rubasinghe announced that reporting on the military remained subject to censorship under regulations issued in June 1998 and November 1999.

Just a month later, another journalist was to pay the supreme price for carrying out his noble craft. On October 19, Jaffna-based journalist Mylvaganam Nimalarajan who had been filing reports to various news organisations about the vote rigging and violent tactics in the parliamentary elections was shot by an unknown gunman while he sat at his desk at home engaged in writing yet another article. A hand grenade was also hurled into the house. Nimalarajan's parents and young nephew were also injured in the attack. Nimalarajan died of his injuries in hospital.

During the five weeks of *The Sunday Leader* ban, the annual awards ceremony organised by the Editors Guild of Sri Lanka recognising journalistic excellence took place. At a ceremony in Mt. Lavinia Hotel on Sunday June 4, 2000 represented by journalists from the country's Sinhala, Tamil and English press, the Guild presented awards to those who had excelled in their craft the previous year. *The Sunday Leader* won seven awards including Journalist of the Year, Young Reporter of the Year and the award for human interest reporting. Honourable mention under the Scoop of the Year category went to "the story titled 'Government pays Evans Rs.

250 million' about a story of a deal gone sour, a payment of 250 million rupees from the state to an aggrieved foreign company by Suranimala of *The Sunday Leader*." Chief Sub-Editor Romesh Abeywickrema accepted the award on 'Suranimala's' behalf.

Not only had the efforts of the *Leader* in consistently publishing and breaking major stories been recognised by our peers, but so had the manner in which we presented them. My July 18, 1999 lay-out on a double-spread exposure titled 'Channel 9: the drama spills over to cabinet' won the main award for design and lay-out. Under the category Best Designed Page of a Newspaper (colour) *The Sunday Leader* was recognised for 'displaying a complicated and controversial story with the use of colour pictures and typographical techniques in a manner that was easy on the eye and easy to read.'

This award was a feather in our cap because The *Sunday Leader* lagged behind those with more sophisticated and advanced printing facilities and hence the finished product was not up to mark. Despite this, our design and lay-out had won the day and we were proud of that recognition.

Among those invited by the Guild to present awards was the ever-smiling Ariya Rubasinghe.

That same year, Lasantha's pioneering investigative journalism was recognised internationally when he won the first ever Integrity Award from Transparency International, the global coalition leading the battle against worldwide corruption.

Transparency International said, "Lasantha Wickrematunge has earned a reputation for courageous investigative journalism. He has been dedicated to exposing corruption in all branches of the Sri Lankan government and his exposes´ have dealt with issues ranging from petty to grand corruption in areas such as privatisation and arms deals. When government authorities shut down his newspaper in May, he fought back and succeeded in having the presses re-opened. Lasantha Wickrematunge has earned great respect abroad for his contribution to the anti-corruption movement. International recognition may counterpoise the ill-treatment he has experienced at home in Sri Lanka, a country which he is trying to serve through his determined investigation of the truth."

In August that year the government had announced that parliamentary elections would be held on October 24. In a violent election, the PA returned to power but lost its majority. Just over a year later, as a result of the instability in its governing alliance, elections were called again and following another blood-soaked campaign trail, on December 6, 2001, the PA lost its hold on governance. The United National Front (UNF)—an alliance of five parties—formed a government with Ranil Wickremesinghe at the helm as Prime Minister. It was an uneasy governance with the President and the Prime Minister representing two opposing political parties.

With the greens in power, rumour and speculation was rife that Lasantha would accept an offer of some plum position from the new government. Before the election there had been a great deal of talk that he would enter parliament on the National List and that he was eyeing the post of Justice Minister. Some whispered he wanted to be Sri Lanka's next High Commissioner in Australia. There was no truth in any of this although a few offers had been made to him by the UNP leadership who often sought his advice and admired his strategising and analytical genius. Lal meanwhile was aware that if Lasantha accepted an offer, *The Sunday Leader* would suffer. It was the general perception by this time that Lasantha Wickrematunge carried *The Sunday Leader* on his shoulders and that the paper would never be the same without him or in the worst-case scenario, collapse, without the clout of his journalistic brilliance and dynamism.

Lasantha's very close friend Gamini Athukorale who was the Transport, Highways and Civil Aviation Minister in the new government was very keen that Lasantha take on the post of Chairman, SriLankan Airlines. Lasantha was not ready to accept such an appointment because, not only did he understand this would not be a good reflection on him as a journalist but also because journalism was his first love and he was not about to renounce it just yet.

One night we were at dinner at Professor G. L. Pieris' residence and Gamini who was also a guest that night, continued to coax Lasantha to consider the offer. I remember asking Gamini jokingly why he was trying to make controversial appointments to which he replied there would be no controversy if the right man was appointed for the right job.

There were those who encouraged Lasantha to accept the offer and others who were vehemently opposed to it. I for one was not one bit happy about him accepting a political appointment and losing his integrity as a journalist. Lasantha shared this belief and informed his friend that his conscience would not permit him to accept the post.

Lasantha and Gamini remained extremely close friends until the latter's untimely and sudden death from a heart attack on January 1, 2002. The good-natured and politically savvy Gamini's death was felt deeply by both the United National Party, his family, friends and constituents.

If the UNF government was under any illusions that Lasantha's close ties with the party meant they would be safe from the harsh glare of the *Leader* spotlight, they were to learn otherwise. After *The Sunday Leader's* intense scrutiny of PA governance and its leader in particular, Lasantha had been branded as a UNP journalist. But now it was the UNP's turn to face the music and miscreants found themselves splashed across the *Leader* pages come Sunday. So much so that one Deputy Minister who the *Leader* exposed in an investigative piece as having intimidated and haggled foreign investors and insisted on an illegal payback in the form of a 20% share from a US$ 2.5 million investment, ranted that he would like nothing more than to kill the Editor himself.

* * *

About three years prior to all this drama, in 1997, a major change had occurred in Lasantha's life. He had converted to Born Again Christianity. Lasantha's three sisters in Canada were all Born Again Christians whose well-meaning mission in life was to convert the rest of the family, and on their trips to Sri Lanka they would spend a great deal of time preaching the gospel to us. My faith in Buddhist wisdom however was unshakeable. In keeping with my concept of universal spirituality I respected Christianity just as I did all great religions of the world but I found the extreme views and basic intolerance propounded by certain groups offensive.

During one of Lasantha's trips to Canada, the conversion plan for 'Malli' was put into action. Someone purportedly became possessed by the 'devil' and began screaming abuse and chasing Lasantha around the house. In the melee, another person snatched his protective talisman which a Buddhist monk had given him, and this bit of 'evil witchcraft' was duly hurled in to the bin.

This disquieting experience convinced Lasantha he should embrace Born Again Christianity; he returned to Sri Lanka with a copy of the Holy Bible in his hand and a grin on his face. Inside the Bible, one Pastor Angelo had written: "Lasantha, this day is the first day of your life. Welcome in Jesus' name. God has placed you in a position of greatness. He will use you everything." (sic)

Lasantha began reading the Bible in earnest and engaged in prayer each day. Psalm 91 became his daily spiritual guide giving him peace and calm in a roller-coaster life.

Lasantha had, ever since his TV debut in 1995, and his reputation as a brave and crusading Editor, won thousands of followers, among who were hundreds of ardent female fans. After his conversion, many were those who rushed to him with Bibles, advice, and even invitations to accompany them to various churches. One went as far as to tell him, "Lasantha, you are not married in the eyes of the Lord. I have been sent by God to be by your side."

Only a few months earlier he had given me a birthday card in which he ended a long and sentimental message with the words, "The happiness you have given me in our 15 years together is enough to carry me to my next birth."

With his conversion, he no longer believed in any 'next births' or involved himself in Buddhist practices in our home. Our family was split on matters spiritual.

* * *

It was during the time when the UNF government was settling in to governance that the children and I went to live in Melbourne.

The decision to move had first been made in early 2000. Lasantha and I could no longer ignore the fact that the safety of our family was being hugely compromised; we took stock of the situation—it wasn't just he and I who were in harm's way. We had three children who were at risk also. I was in constant worry about our daughter walking with Menika to her Montessori each morning imagining all manner of terrifying scenarios. After all, veiled threats had been made against us, his family, as well.

My sister in Australia meanwhile was coaxing me to explore the possibility of moving to Australia. Lasantha and I sat down one day and did all the necessary paperwork to apply for migration. A few months later, after having attended an interview at the Australian High Commission in Colombo, we were issued with residency visas. Although we as his family wanted him to be safe, Lasantha was adamant that he wanted to stay on and continue with his work. His idea at the time was that the kids and I should live in Melbourne and return when things were more settled.

It was not easy making the decision to move. I was leaving behind family, friends and of course *The Sunday Leader*. Here, Lasantha and I had started off from a little Editorial of five or six people and ended up with a large and beautiful *Leader* family; we had experienced the highs and lows, we had paid with our blood and sweat for the success of the paper; we had seen our presses shut down and savoured victory in court, we had been beaten black and blue and shot at, vilified in public; won awards and accolades and the admiration of the people; there were a million memories that made up the *Leader* story, and I was leaving it all behind.

That February we had a rollicking farewell luncheon party at our home in Nugegoda for the staff of *The Sunday Leader*. Everyone had a good time singing, dancing and merrymaking. Lasantha, carrying three-year old Aadesh, performed his clowning gyrations on the dance floor accompanied by a very animated Leader Publications security guard and a bunch of inebriated office-helpers. Despite all the merrymaking and laughter, there was the underlying sadness that I would not be a part of that good old *Leader* family again.

Going in to the *Leader* office to say my final goodbyes on that last day, there were tearful pleas from many of the young ones that I return soon. I was greatly touched to see that they had brought me thoughtful and beautiful farewell gifts, some which they had made themselves. Fernando, Gayal, Sanjeewa, Mangala and the others in typesetting, the pagemakers, photographers, peons and drivers, were all near to tears as they made me promise I would not stay away too long. Simeon, our factory coordinator began bawling. It was not easy leaving all those wonderful people. I realised then, how much I loved them, one and all.

On February 22, 2002, we departed Colombo, spent two days with my sister Desiree and her family in Malaysia and arrived in Melbourne on February 25. My sister in Melbourne had already prepared a shortlist of houses we could rent. We chose one located close to schools, shopping and transport; Lasantha signed the rental agreement and the very next day we moved into our new home. The arrangement was that Lasantha would return to Sri Lanka to continue as Editor and visit us from time to time.

---

[1] A play on the surname Rubasinghe, Boru = deception

CHAPTER EIGHT
A President's Fury

> *"There can be no higher law in journalism than to tell the truth and to shame the devil."*—Walter Lippmann, writer, reporter, and political commentator.

MAHINDA Rajapakse and Lasantha Wickrematunge first hobnobbed in the late 80s. Mahinda was then a young and active SLFP Member of Parliament and Lasantha, a lawyer, newspaper columnist and Private Secretary to the Leader of the Opposition.

Mahinda had served in Mrs. Sirima Bandaranaike's government from 1970 to 1977 as the SLFP member for Beliatte. In the 1977 general election when the UNP rode to power in a landslide victory, Mahinda found himself in the political wilderness having lost his seat to the UNP's affable gentleman politician Ranjit Atapattu. Fortunately for Mahinda, just months after the electoral loss, he passed out as an attorney-at-law and was able to build a practice in Tangalla in the Hambantota district in southern coastal Sri Lanka.

The 1989 general election is significant in the story of Mahinda and Lasantha in that both were fielded as candidates by the SLFP and ran for election, Mahinda contesting from the Hambantota district and Lasantha, the Colombo district. With that election, Mahinda was back in the parliamentary saddle, this time as an opposition MP. Had Lasantha been elected to parliament like Mahinda that year, their story would have been very different to what is being written today.

Soon after the SLFP election defeat the Leader of the Opposition Sirima Bandaranaike invited Lasantha to be her private secretary, an offer he accepted without reservation. With this new position, Lasantha was required to spend a considerable amount of time in the opposition leader's chambers in parliament and consequently, his ties with Mahinda and other SLFP members of parliament were consolidated. A few years later however, choosing media as his primary calling, Lasantha resigned from the post.

Mahinda, a scion of an old political family from Medamulana, Weeraketiya in the deep south was a grassroots man with an acute understanding of the pulse of the people. He was back in parliament at a time when the UNP government was engaged in a massive anti-JVP onslaught and it fell upon some of the younger SLFP MPs such as Mahinda to rally popular support to oppose government excesses and spearhead the agitation over human rights abuses. Aligning himself with both human rights issues and labour rights, he together with Mangala Samaraweera and a few other party loyalists, took leadership in challenging autocratic policies with people-power movements such as the Pada Yathra (foot pilgrimage) and Jana Gosha (noise protest). Mahinda was also instrumental in taking details of the country's deplorable human rights violations all the way to the UN. In September 1990, on his way to Geneva to attend the 31st session of the working group on Enforced or Involuntary Disappearances, Rajapakse's bags were searched and 533 documents and 19 pictures seized. Rajapakse later filed a fundamental rights application in court.

Even during the SLFP's lowest ebb in the early 90s when opportunistic politics and crossing the floor was the rave, Mahinda never once flagged in his loyalty to the party. His steadfast devotion catapulted him to a position of potential prime minster in the latter part of the Chandrika Kumaratunga administration. Dynastic politics, internal bickering and backroom politicking however ensured the journey to the top was fraught with obstacles. When Mahinda Rajapakse finally clawed his way to the Prime Ministerial office on April 6, 2004, Lasantha, counting ten years to the day as Editor-in-Chief of *The Sunday Leader*, welcomed the man warmly in his editorial the following Sunday.

"We at *The Sunday Leader* cannot hide our pleasure at welcoming Mahinda as the country's next Prime Minister," it said. The editorial went as far as to refer to the new Prime Minister by his first name.

Indeed, Rajapakse and the Editor had always been on first-name basis. Infact, they had been on even more casual 'machang' terms. The close ties formed in the 80s had solidified during the tenure of President Chandrika Kumaratunga under whom Rajapakse served as a senior minister.

The friendship had been a thorn in President Chandrika's flesh and she more than once referred to Rajapakse as 'the reporter' suspecting he was the 'leak' in the ranks supplying all the inside details of Cabinet and other closed-door meetings to Lasantha.

Whoever Lasantha's sources were, like all good journalists he did his utmost to protect them. In the privacy of their homes, Lasantha and some of his political contacts were yarn-swapping buddies—but when they met at public gatherings, they studiously ignored each other.

But there was one very public occasion when there was no way Lasantha could ignore his friend. It was June 21, 1998 and Lasantha was on his way to Ratnapura to attend the funeral of the father of UNP Member of Parliament Gamini Athukorale. Lasantha was travelling with Ravi Kumararatne, CEO of tea firm Asia Siyaka. In the hamlet of Lellapitiya along the Ratnapura-Embilipitiya road, the duo were forced to slow down as a result of a traffic jam caused by a road accident. Upon alighting from their vehicle, Lasantha and Ravi came upon a visibly upset Mahinda Rajapakse sitting by the roadside with his face in his hands. One of his back-up vehicles had been in a smash-up with a bus and his favourite personal security officer was dead; his mangled body still stuck in the windscreen of the vehicle. Rajapakse had been returning to Colombo having attended the funeral house to offer his condolences to the Athukorale family.

Lasantha walked up to Mahinda and spoke with him, noting how devastated he seemed by the horrific crash and the death of his security personnel. After spending some time talking to Mahinda, Lasantha and Ravi then resumed their journey to the Athukorale funeral house.

There was one time, in the mid-90s, when Lasantha suspected he was being followed by sleuths assigned to dig out his contacts. The powers that be were mostly interested in finding out whether, as suspected, Minister Mahinda Rajapakse was plying Lasantha with cabinet secrets and other matters of a sensitive nature.

Lasantha came up with a simple plan to outsmart the surreptitious trail and from then on, every Thursday—the day after the weekly Cabinet meeting and the day he wrote his Suranimala column—he would wake up at 5.30 in the morning and drive to the 'mole's' home to gather the 'meat' for his column. Every Thursday I woke up with him and prepared him a cup of tea while he had a hurried shower before setting off.

A few months into Mahinda's ascension to the Prime Ministerial seat, cracks began to appear in his relationship with Lasantha. The friendship could not withstand Lasantha's editorial outspokenness and his exposures of certain transgressions in the Rajapakse ranks.

In fact one big story in *The Sunday Leader* on July 3, 2005 titled, 'The disappearing tsunami millions from the PM's fund,' immediately put the two former allies on a collision course. The story was political dynamite and gave extensive details of how tsunami funds that had poured in to Sri Lanka from foreign donors had allegedly been channelled into an account of which the signatories were four persons connected to Prime Minister Mahinda Rajapakse.

The story detailed how officials had allegedly re-directed tsunami funds running into millions into the private account 'Helping Hambantota' in direct violation of a Presidential directive that no accounts should be opened for any tsunami monies.

Hambantota was the Prime Minister's electorate and The *Sunday Leader* observed that 'setting up this account would give Mahinda a free hand to use the monies which were meant for the rehabilitation of Tsunami victims from all over Sri Lanka, to nurse his own southern electorate.'

The follow-up stories on Helping Hambantota grew in intensity each week in *The Sunday Leader* under the headlines 'For PM, Charity Begins at Home,' 'PM Looks for Mole,' 'Cabinet Note and Documents that Damn PM's Defence' and *'Cabinet Fixes PM on Tsunami Scam.'*

In its story "PM looks For Mole' the *Leader* reported what had transpired at Temple Trees, the Prime Minister's official residence on the morning of Sunday July 3. Apparently, pandemonium reigned. Completely thrown off—balance by the revelations in the *Leader* that morning, Mahinda had, the article said, summoned his official staff and demanded to know how confidential financial documents and copies of cheques had ended up in the media. Accusing everyone there of working for the opposition UNP, Rajapakse ranted that all suspicious officers would be transferred.

Ironic, one might say. Perhaps at that moment, Rajapakse had a déjà vu moment thinking back to the times when he had been in that unenviable position being accused of leaking information to the press.

"Rajapakse was also keen to find out how the information had reached the press and he assigned some of his most loyal officers to find out how the information had been leaked so expertly," the article continued.

"He soon came to the conclusion that it was none other than the accountant of the Prime Minister's Office who had informed the media of these details. All of the Premier's advisors were of the opinion that Rajapakse issue a clarification immediately to avoid the issue getting out of hand . . . . But the UNP had different plans. The main opposition decided to request a debate in parliament regarding the matter after calling for explanation."

The opposition UNP also lodged a complaint with the CID about the private account and the Prime Minister's alleged hand in it. The heat was turning on the Prime Minister, and the CID, having sought permission from court to investigate the allegations, moved in to conduct their inquiries into the account.

Prime Minister Rajapakse meanwhile lodged a Fundamental Rights Petition in the Supreme Court following which a Supreme Court bench headed by Chief Justice Sarath Silva ordered the CID to call a halt to the investigation temporarily. Rajapakse's lawyers informed court that the CID began investigations based merely on reports in *The Sunday Leader* and its Sinhala edition *Irudina*. They further said that Cabinet had been kept informed of the 'Helping Hambantota' account.

The Sunday Leader reported that President Chandrika Kumaratunga had ordered that the funds deposited in the controversial 'Helping Hambantota' account be transferred to the National Fund for Disaster Relief account at the Central Bank.

Mahinda Rajapakse was furious with Lasantha. It didn't help that *The Sunday Leader* continued with exposures on the Prime Minister. One story in particular on August 14, 2005, under the headline 'Mahinda's Highway Robbery' provided details of how Rajapakse had allegedly converted a rural road rehabilitation plan into a political program by using funds received from the Japan Bank for International Cooperation to garner political mileage for himself.

Despite these and the whole sorry saga of the Tsunami funds scandal, President Kumaratunga, whose second term in office was ending that December, named Mahinda Rajapakse as the Presidential candidate for the forthcoming election.

Lasantha and Mahinda were now enemies but they were to run into each other at a function hosted by a legal luminary. The hall was filled with politicians, diplomats, judges, lawyers and members of the business community and the media. The former friends ignored each other all evening but at one point Lasantha was in conversation with a senior lawyer when, seeing Mahinda standing nearby, the gentleman drew the prime minister into the circle and smiling widely said, "I believe you two know each other," and advised that they should let bygones be bygones. Lasantha and Mahinda laughed politely, made some small talk and the circle then broke up.

It was during the run-up to the Presidential election that Mahinda made overtures to Lasantha inquiring whether he would consider handling his Presidential campaign together with his brother Basil Rajapakse. The shrewd tactician in Rajapakse perceived the wisdom of having Lasantha in his camp. He had seen the pressure *The Sunday Leader* exerted not only on Chandrika Kumaratunga and her government but on himself as Prime Minister and did not want a repetition of that while he was at the helm.

Lasantha did not take up the offer. Rajapakse was to later deny he made such an offer.

Before that election, two attacks on the media occurred. The first was the shocking abduction and murder of popular journalist Dharmaratnam Sivaram, also known as Taraki after the pseudonym he used in a newspaper column.

Sivaram was abducted on April 28, 2005 by four men in Bambalapitiya who bundled him into a SUV even as his friend watched in horror. His body was discovered the following day. The brutal murder created a huge outcry both nationally and internationally.

On October 2005, the *Leader* was to suffer the dire consequences of some aggrieved party's ire. An armed gang broke into the Leader Publications press in Ratmalana and set bundles of newspapers on fire. The gang also assaulted the publication's manager and demanded that printing of the newspaper be stopped.

In the Presidential election held on November 17 that year, Mahinda Rajapakse defeated the UNP candidate Ranil Wickremesinghe and on November 19, 2005, was sworn in as Sri Lanka's fifth President. In his address to the nation as the newly elected head of state, Rajapakse promised to build a new Sri Lanka as a new leader with a new policy.

"I won't be the owner or the ruler of the country, but its protector," he promised.

In its editorial that week *The Sunday Leader* congratulated Rajapakse on his victory. "Last Thursday's election will go down in history not just as the most 'peaceful' but also the most skewed in Sri Lanka's history," it said. "Victory must surely taste bitter-sweet in Mahinda Rajapakse's mouth as the weight of the responsibility that has been thrust upon him begins to tell. But a victory it nevertheless was, and we join the country in congratulating him."

". . . . For its part, the UNP must give effect to the pledge it made to seek a national government if it won. It has a duty to support Rajapakse sincerely in the peace process and the process of constitutional reform while at the same time providing him with the sternest opposition should he go astray."

Just eight weeks later, the country was to learn the extent of a head of state going 'astray.'

On the morning of Wednesday, January 11, 2006, at 11.13 to be exact, Lasantha's mobile phone rang. The caller informed Lasantha that the President wished to speak with him and when eventually Rajapakse came on the line bristling with untamed fury, he barked in Sinhala, "*Thamuse monawada Shirani gena liyala thiyenne*? (What have you written about Shiranthi?)

Genuinely unaware of anything about the first lady having been published, Lasantha inquired from the President what exactly had been written and whether he had himself read it.

The President was apparently acting on a 'tip-off' received from an Indian diplomat that a story involving a trip he had made to a hallowed Hindu temple in India with his wife, was published in *The Sunday Leader's* Wednesday edition, *The Morning Leader*.

The temple in question, in Kerala, India, expressly forbids non-Hindus from stepping inside its premises. The fact that President Rajapakse's wife Shiranthi, despite being a Catholic entered the holy precinct, had created quite the brouhaha among the Hindu fraternity. The President being a Buddhist had no entry prohibitions as Buddhism was considered a philosophy and not a religion.

Borrowing extensively from the lexicon of Sinhala filth and making several references to the Editor's mother, the President then ranted, "*Umba mata gehuwa, den magey genitath gahanawada?* (You hit it me, now you are hitting my woman as well?")

Not mincing his own words Lasantha queried as to what the article in question had stated to which Rajapakse screamed further abuse and threatened him, "*Mama umbava vinasa karala thamai ivara venne!* (I will stop only when I have destroyed you!)

Lasantha informed the President that he didn't usually get intimidated by threats to which the President screamed, "Pariah! . . . You are not scared! . . . . I will show you what it is to be scared . . . . I treated you well all this while. You don't know who Mahinda Rajapakse is!!! You watch what I will do to you . . . . You hit me even during the election. Pariah . . . you are hitting even now . . . I will destroy you!"

The line went dead thereafter.

Lasantha immediately despatched two letters, one to the Inspector General of Police and the other to the President himself.

> "My dear President," he wrote, "I was shocked and surprised by the tone and content of your telephone call to me at 11:13 this morning. I cannot imagine that the occupant of the highest office in our land could utter such foul, lewd and disgusting words: indeed the language of the gutter. It is unbecoming and disgraceful of you to have uttered threats against me, and I want to repeat the assertion made by me during your hysterical ranting that I will not be bowed by them. You, more than any other politician, have paid lip service to human rights and the building of a decent society in Sri Lanka. It is all the more shocking then, that you should conduct yourself in such a low manner.
>
> Given the office you hold, I have no doubt it is well within your power to do me harm, whether or not through the abuse of the state machinery that lies at your disposal. I have therefore no choice but to give your threats the widest possible publicity in the hope that this will persuade you to desist from the course of action you are clearly contemplating, to eliminate me or do me harm.
>
> No doubt you will deny the content of the conversation that took place this morning as you would a request made to me prior to the Presidential election inviting me to run your election campaign

with your brother, Basil Rajapakse which I politely declined. You have no choice but to deny the threat made, given the lip service your public persona pays to the upholding of decent values.

You know better than anyone that *The Sunday Leader* was infinitely more critical of your predecessor, Chandrika Kumaratunga, than it has been of you. Yet, she never stooped to the level you have, even though she was reported to have given ear to a plot to "kill an Editor or two."

Leader of the Opposition, Ranil Wickremesinghe informed me that you had spoken with him at around 1 p.m. on the same subject which was within a matter of two hours of threatening me, and asked him to request me to desist from publishing in future any story you consider provocative. You have specifically mentioned the publication of a story relating to your wife, Shiranthi. I have no idea what story you are referring to: you failed to tell me, and you evidently failed also to tell him. Yet, I wish to remind you that should you have anything to convey to me, your purposes would be best served by informing me directly rather than threatening me in vile language.

Given our long acquaintance, you should know better than anyone that I am not one to be swayed by third parties. I take this opportunity to also remind you in that context your request to me as Prime Minister to refrain from publishing details of the 'Helping Hambantota' account in July 2005 and my refusal to oblige you. Indeed, when there is news that it is in the national interest to publish, be assured that nothing will prevent *The Sunday Leader* from publishing it.

I urge you even now to respect the great office to which you have been elected, and to conduct yourself with the dignity and decorum the people and Sri Lanka have a right to expect of you. It does not become the presidency that you should threaten journalists or indeed, plot violence against them.

With best wishes for the new year,

Yours sincerely,
Lasantha Wickrematunge
Attorney-at-Law,
Editor, The Sunday Leader

In his letter to the Inspector General of Police, Chandra Fernando, Lasantha detailed the telephone call from the President and said he considered it a grave threat to his life in the light of the number of journalists murdered in recent years.

> "At 11:13 a.m. today I received a call on my mobile phone from telephone number 2392047. Speaking in Sinhala, the operator told me that she had a call for me from His Excellency, the President. The number is registered on my mobile phone, a certified copy of which can be furnished if necessary. A man then spoke to me in English, and asked me to hold the line as His Excellency the President wished to speak to me.
>
> Shortly thereafter, President Mahinda Rajapakse came on the line. I recognised his voice because he has on several occasions spoken with me by telephone, including after his election as President. I have known President Rajapakse and associated with him for more than 20 years prior to that and am well acquainted with his voice.
>
> I made a contemporaneous note of the conversation, in Sinhala, which I attach hereto, together with a translation in English.
>
> As you will see from this note, President Rajapakse used foul, abusive and threatening language unbecoming of the high office he holds. He told me repeatedly, "What have you written about Shiranthi in the *Leader*?" However, when I asked him, "What is it you are referring to? Have you read whatever it is you are referring to?" he replied with the words, "I know what to do to you." He continued to mouth vile and defamatory references to my mother and threatened to destroy me, "wait and see what I am going to do to you." As the President continued, apparently in a state of hysteria, I told him not to threaten me and that I will not give into such threats. I have no choice but to interpret the President's words, however, as a threat to my life.
>
> Further, one of the most prominent businessmen in our country (I shall disclose the name to you if it is necessary to aid your inquiries) recently informed me that the President had told him that he intends to "destroy" me. He interpreted this as a threat to my life. So seriously did he take the threat that he spoke also to my brother, Lal Wickrematunge and another mutual friend, and requested them to convey this message to me and urge me to take care.

I am therefore bringing this matter to your urgent attention and requesting you to take immediate steps to ensure my security given the serious nature of the threats made by the President of the country who is also the Commander-in-Chief of the security forces and Defence Minister. I also request you to investigate this matter fully and I am willing to furnish you with such information as may be necessary to facilitate such an inquiry.

I wish to remind you that I consider this a grave threat to my life especially given that several journalists have been assassinated in recent years, including Mr. Rohana Kumara, Mr. Mariyadasan Nimalaranjan and Mr. Dharmaratnam Sivaram. In some of these cases, the murders were preceded by threats made by leading politicians. The threat made against me by President Rajapakse was, however, more serious and immediate than any of those directed at the above late journalists. You will also undoubtedly be aware that there have been two previous attempts on my life, one involving firearms: and in the latter case, despite complaints to the police, no action has been taken.

In the run-up to the Presidential election of November 17, 2005, *The Sunday Leader* press at Ratmalana was torched. Shortly after his election, the President was also reported as having told Mr. S. B. Dissanayake that he will use the judiciary to jail some journalists. I have grave apprehensions, therefore, that President Rajapakse will use the machinery of the state to harass and intimidate me, and possibly even take my life.

The President had also within two hours of the threatening call to me spoken with the Hon. Leader of the Opposition, Mr. Ranil Wickremesinghe and requested him to speak with me as well and urge me to refrain from writing articles he considers provocative claiming his (the President's) patience was running thin. Mr. Wickremesinghe communicated to me the President's message. The telephone conversation initiated by the President to the Leader of the Opposition subsequent to the threat issued to me is further proof that the President did speak with me in the morning.

I would be grateful if you would kindly arrange therefore, without delay, to provide me with adequate security against this threat.

In the hope that it will result in additional pressure on President Rajapakse to desist from the criminal course of action he appears to be contemplating, I am copying this letter to the heads of foreign missions in Colombo, the Leader of the Opposition and the Presidents of the Free Media Movement, Transparency International and Bar Association of Sri Lanka.

Yours faithfully,
Lasantha Wickrematunge,
Attorney-at-Law,
Editor, The Sunday Leader

Soon after his angry outburst it must have become painfully obvious to the President that *The Morning Leader* that day did not in fact carry any story about a Presidential visit to a temple in India.

That Sunday, January 15, 2006, the *Leader* ran an article detailing the President's telephone call together with an English translation of the Sinhala words uttered in anger by the President. This article ignited the interest of the Indian media with headlines screaming 'Has Sri Lankan First Lady broken Guruvayur tradition?' (*Indian Express*), 'Sri Lankan First Lady breaks Guruvayur tradition' (*newindpress.com*) and 'Temple in upheaval over Sri Lankan First Lady's faith.' (*Rediff.com*).

The website *Rediff.com* quoted Guruvayur temple's Chief Priest, Chennas Raman Namboodiripad as saying, "If she is a Christian, she committed a grave religious mistake by entering our temple and praying here . . . . If the Sri Lankan President's wife is a Christian, the temple is duty-bound to perform (re-perform) all the *poojas* from December 30 (the day of the visit) to the present date."

"We will also have to undertake cleansing because if non-Hindus enter the temple, we cleanse the holy precincts with a set of purifying religious rituals."

The article in Rediff.com quoting Temple Administrator K. Anil Kumar said the Sri Lankan President and his wife were allowed to worship at the temple after the temple authorities confirmed with the state government that the couple was of the Buddhist faith.

The President had, by making the call based on hearsay to Lasantha Wickrematunge, given rise to a hornet's nest and also given the Editor an invaluable lead that all was not well with the President's visit to the Guruvayur temple, a lead which he followed up with great delight. And in its issue on January 22, 2006, *The Sunday Leader* carried a full-page article about the temple fiasco. It included a picture of a grinning President seated cross-legged and offering *thulabharam*[1] with the help of temple *poosaris*[2].

The article read, "This newspaper never intended to publish the details of President Rajapakse and his wife Shiranthi's disastrous visit to the famous and sacred Guruvayur Temple in Kerala at the tail-end of their failed visit to India earlier this month. In passing we had mentioned President Rajapakse had gone there for a special *pooja* for which he had to shed his *saluwa*[3] and don a *vetti*[4]. However we refrained from giving any further details. Today we are compelled to do so to point to the motive for his fit of rage."

The article admonished that the President and his advisors didn't seem to believe in doing their homework before visiting a hallowed temple in Kerala—"a place so sacred only Hindus are allowed in and that too with nothing but a *vetti* to cover themselves. Steeped in history and spiritual legend, the Krishna temple is the fourth biggest temple in India in terms of the number of devotees per day. The temple dedicated to Lord Krishna, popularly known as Guruvayurappan, is famous all over India as a pilgrim centre."

"President Rajapakse who had made a large number of vows was also eager to engage in one of the *poojas*. For this, barebodied and sans *saluwa*, he donned a *vetti* and proceeded forth. Well and good. But who should accompany him but his charming wife Shiranthi, who being a Christian and Catholic was not allowed anywhere near the sacred temple in terms of the hallowed traditions of the temple."

"But at the time of the *pooja* no one in the temple was any the wiser and the *pooja* was conducted and temple activities went on apace. However word gets around and Keralites in general, the Indian media and more importantly the temple administration were buzzing with the news that a Catholic had stepped onto sacred soil. The temple administration was to immediately write to the Indian High Commission in Colombo and ask for clarification and confirmation as to whether the Sri Lankan First Lady was indeed a Catholic.

"President Rajapakse got wind of this letter from the Indian High Commission and panicked. The President was told by High Commissioner Rao, (Nirupama Rao) that the story about Shiranthi visiting the temple was all over and if reported in Sri Lanka and got back to India would cause "a lot of problems."

"According to what Rajapakse was to later tell confidantes, Rao had also said the only paper that might carry the story is the *Leader*."

"If Rajapakse had only done his homework. If only the very efficient Sri Lankan Foreign Ministry had given him a do's and don'ts list. In fact they could have got such a list off any old website or tourist brochure.

"But President Rajapakse need not have gone far to learn the spiritual etiquette. All he had to do was call Indian High Commissioner Nirupama Rao, a Keralite herself, and ask her advice. She would have certainly known the spiritual sensitivities surrounding Guruvayur. But he chose not to do that."

Concluding, the article said, "However, it is obvious that the President is a man who given enough rope will hang himself. If the highest in the land is now to act on the basis of mindless gossip and Chinese whispers, what is to become of this nation? Surely, the Commander in Chief may order a war without verification on a baseless rumour of an incident in the north? He is also a man capable of issuing threats to the media while talking about democracy and human rights. He has proved himself a man who will sooner make this country a banana republic than a democratic one."

The President was to later admit he did indeed talk to the Editor but insisted he had not used foul language nor issued any threats.

Three weeks later in early February, 2006, Lasantha, on his way to attend the Geneva peace talks between the government and the LTTE, was harassed by immigration officials at the Bandaranaike International Airport.

At the Immigration counter Lasantha was told a computer alert had been received from the National Intelligence Bureau, (NIB) and a long-winded line of questioning ensued. An infuriated Lasantha whipped out his mobile phone and called Raja Mahendran, head of Capital Maharaja Organisation which owns MTV and Sirasa Radio. Within minutes Lasantha was broadcasting his plight on Sirasa Radio. Airport authorities then received a hasty message asking that he be let through, a mere five minutes before his flight was to leave.

It was later revealed that the NIB had issued orders to prevent "one Wickrematunge" from leaving the country.

The February 5 editorial in *The Sunday Leader* addressed the Editor's experience at the airport and the issue of media harassment in general.

It said,

> "Last week, in travelling overseas through Bandaranaike International Airport, your good Editor was detained for half an hour, on the basis there was a computer alert from the National Intelligence Bureau, as explained by the immigration officer. Returning to the country, the same treatment was meted out. This time, when asked what the problem was, the Editor was told, "It is taking time for the NIB clearance to come."
>
> "Ironically, just days earlier, Anton Balasingham, the chief negotiator of the LTTE that murdered President Premadasa, Indian Prime Minister Rajiv Gandhi, Presidential candidate Gamini Dissanayake and given the very allegations of this government, late Foreign Minister Lakshman Kadirgamar, had been whisked through

the VIP lounge at the BIA by the very same NIB and flown to a secret destination in the Wanni courtesy the Sri Lanka Air Force (SLAF). And even as their spectacular intelligence failures have led to the unnecessary deaths of countless soldiers and civilians, the NIB was focusing its undivided attention on what? Harassing a passing newspaper Editor!

"Well, President Mahinda Rajapakse, if you think we're going to stop in our tracks because you choose to abuse the power vested in you in this way, you had better think again. The state can harass, the state can kill, but cry freedom we will.

"And not to be outdone, into this fray stepped Wimal Weerawansa, taking time off from applying gel to his hair and whispering into his ill-gotten cellular phone. His grouse was that foreign investors were fleeing the country in the wake of our article that Colombo was imminently threatened by an LTTE attack. It seemed that foreign investors are given (and quite right they are, too) to taking us more seriously than they do the government, which has strengthened security in Colombo for a four-year high, with checkpoints and pickets everywhere.

"Too busy chatting up the Indian High Commissioner, Weerawansa has had no time to check with the US Embassy that it had indeed told US companies to locate themselves outside of the Fort area, which is considered to be at high risk. Worst of all, he has evidently not read the NIB reports that have clearly informed the government that there is an imminent threat to Colombo from the LTTE. We have not published these up to now, but even if only to inform Weerawansa, we do at least one of them now on the opposite page. More will be on offer in the coming weeks if Weerawansa so wants.

"In any event, it is both ironic and touching that Weerawansa should choose to allege that *The Sunday Leader* is hand in glove with the LTTE. We have never espoused the creation of Eelam, something that Weerawansa's erstwhile leader, Rohana Wijeweera, touted very hard indeed during his Presidential campaign of 1982. We have never bombed parliament or shed blood in the sacred precincts of the Dalada Maligawa as Weerawansa's JVP has.

"Was it not the JVP who set fire to and destroyed public property, beheaded innocent civilians, butchered Buddhist monks, murdered policemen and soldiers, attacked the Katunayake airport, enforced curfews under threat of murder and brought industry to its knees driving away foreign investors and drove away the Indian

Peace Keeping Force (IPKF) to ease the pressure on the LTTE? And the cardboard Sando he is, Weerawansa has the gall to accuse us of helping terrorists and driving away investors when he and his party epitomises terrorism. And given the low value the JVP places on human life, the party obviously does not want the media to keep the people informed of possible threats to their lives.

"The fact of the matter is that Weerawansa is simply trying to cover up his own nakedness by attacking us . . . .

". . . . Desperate in the straits in which it finds itself, the government of Mahinda Rajapakse has chosen to kill the messenger. Be our guests, gentlemen, be our guests. Journalists have died before us, and more will surely die before the evil preached by the Weerawansas of our time are done."

The harassment of the *Leader* and its Editor did not stop with that incident.

---

[1] A ritual where people make a vow to God offering one's weight in such things as coconut, coconut water, butter, sugar, fruits, silver, gold or any other material.
[2] An officiating priest in a Hindu temple
[3] Shawl
[4] An ankle-length cloth tucked around the waist

CHAPTER NINE
A Move to Arrest the Editor

> *"To the press alone, chequered as it is with abuses, the world is indebted for all the triumphs which have been gained by reason and humanity over error and oppression."*—James Madison, 4th US President.

ON April 25, 2006 a violent event occurred that rocked the defence establishment and sent major shockwaves throughout the country. A suicide bomber targeted the Army Commander, General Sarath Fonseka as he was leaving army headquarters in Justice Akbar Mawatha in Colombo. General Fonseka who was seriously wounded underwent several major operations and was put on a ventilator before making a slow and painful recovery. Most of the 11 people who died in the attack were his bodyguards and young soldiers.

The attack came at a time when Norway was in the midst of brokering peace negotiations between the Sri Lankan government and the LTTE but with the attack on the army commander and retaliatory action by the government forces, there were fears in some circles that the country would once again be pushed in to the dark abyss of open warfare.

In December the same year, Defence Secretary Gotabaya Rajapakse narrowly escaped death when a three-wheeler carrying explosives attempted to ram into his convoy on Dharmapala Mawatha in Colombo. The assassination attempt failed although two commandos who prevented the vehicle from reaching its target were killed instantly in the massive explosion.

The government had its hands full dealing with a deadly terror machine but it always had that bit of extra time to deal with 'errant' journalists. A few weeks after the assassination attempt on Gotabaya Rajapakse, the government made a move to arrest the Editor of *The Sunday Leader* for 'endangering national security' by publishing in a lead story in its Christmas eve issue, details of a luxury bunker to be built in Colombo's high security zone.

In its story *The Sunday Leader* reported that a 400-million-dollar luxury bunker with modern living quarters was being built for the protection of President Mahinda Rajapakse and his family at a huge cost to taxpayers. Due to security considerations, the story refrained from divulging the location or the names of the companies involved in the construction work. The plans for the bunker were publicly available.

Four days after the story was published, the Criminal Investigation Department (CID) was instructed by the Defence Ministry to arrest the Editor of *The Sunday Leader*. The arrest would be justified, or so they believed, by the new emergency regulations which had widened the scope of existing regulations and rendered applicable the Prevention of Terrorism Law which overruled the normal law that safeguards basic rights such as the freedom of speech.

Earlier, the government had gone to great lengths to inform the media that the newly promulgated emergency regulations would not be used to stifle the media.

Several weeks before the story was published, Lasantha, as Editor, had received a letter under the signature of Defence Secretary Gotabaya Rajapakse outlining procedure to be followed by the media in reporting security-related issues. Rajapakse wrote that any information relating to the security forces should be clarified from the designated authorities, one of who was the Director General, Media Centre for National Security, Lakshman Hulugalle.

Accordingly, prior to publishing the story on the Presidential bunker, Lasantha called Hulugalle and inquired whether the newspaper was flouting the new emergency regulations if it published such a story. Hulugalle said he had not heard of any luxury bunker but confirmed that if the facts were correct, the newspaper could go ahead and publish the story. On December 24, *The Sunday Leader* under the headline 'President to get Rs. 400 million luxury bunker' carried some details of the proposed underground hideout but refrained from divulging information that could be useful to the enemy.

According to the story that appeared in a subsequent edition of *The Sunday Leader* following the whole arrest fiasco, when the Defence Ministry instructed the CID to arrest the editor, they in turn sought the advice of the Attorney General's Department on the matter. Having read the *Leader* article about the presidential bunker, Solicitor General, President's Counsel C. R. De Silva advised the CID there was no legal basis to make an arrest as the regulations did not apply in an instance such as this. The CID officers who were by now coming under increasing pressure caught as they were between the devil and the deep blue sea, prevailed upon the Solicitor General to convey this bit of cautionary advice to the Defence Ministry. De Silva not only complied but reminded those at the ministry that the new regulations had been introduced not to punish the media but to deal with a deadly terror situation.

The Defence Ministry however was not about to give up its call for an arrest. On December 28, the government-controlled *Daily News* published on its front page a snippet titled 'Sleeping with the Enemy' questioning the failure of the Attorney General's Department to take action against the newspaper and its Editor. The Defence Ministry also voiced its displeasure indicating the CID officers could either carry out the directive or look for other work. The CID, in a bid to cover their backs then requested a written directive from the Defence Ministry but the request went unheeded. DIG, CID, Asoka Wijetilleke knew the ramifications of by-passing the AG's Department ruling on the matter and making an illegal arrest. Not wishing to get his junior officers in trouble, he decided he and Director, CID, Sisira Mendis would carry out the order. He also wrote a note which said he was instructed by the Defence Ministry to make the arrest.

Radio stations, in particular Sirasa Radio, who had been informed of the arrest move, began airing this bit of news in their bulletins. With the story thus disseminated, journalists, diplomats, opposition politicians and well-wishers began flocking to *The Sunday Leader* offices. President's Counsel Ranjit Abeysuriya in whose chambers Lasantha had, many years previously been a junior, and Attorneys Nalin Laduwahetty and Ranil Prematilleke were also at the newspaper office. Lasantha's mobile phone and the Leader phone lines went into overdrive with calls coming in without a moment's break.

Despite the very real threat of being arrested within minutes, Lasantha's jovial nature prevailed. "I have never had so much publicity in my life!" he joked. On a serious note he charged that the anti-terrorism laws were not being used to deal with terrorism but rather as a tool to shackle the media. "As far as I know these new laws have never been used to arrest a terrorist," he told those gathered.

Lasantha also told journalists that if arrested he would file a fundamental rights application in the Supreme Court. He would not seek refuge in hospital as was the usual practice when a prominent personality was taken into custody, he said. "Nor will I flee abroad. I will face this crisis and live up to our newspaper's motto "Unbowed and Unafraid."

Lasantha called Lakshman Hulugalle, Director General, Media Centre for National Security who had given Lasantha the greenlight to go ahead and publish the story. Hulugalle said he knew nothing about the arrest move and promised he would look into the matter and get back to Lasantha. He never did.

With the news of the impending arrest gathering momentum in Colombo, UNP General Secretary Tissa Attanayake went on air condemning the move and stated that his party had supported the new emergency regulations on condition they would not be used against the media. Two more leaders, Vasudeva Nanayakkara and Wickramabahu Karunaratne, expressed similar sentiments.

UNP Leader Ranil Wickremesinghe meanwhile was a few hours away from boarding a flight to travel overseas. Having heard of the unsettling developments and wishing to convey his displeasure, Wickemesinghe made a call to President Rajapakse but was told the President was resting. The President's brother and Presidential Advisor Basil Rajapakse however was up and about and taking calls from concerned individuals. Some callers advised that an arrest would be counter-productive. Others felt the government would unnecessarily be making a hero of the Editor by making an arrest.

Subsequently President Rajapakse communicated to the UNP Leader that he had been unaware of the move to arrest Lasantha and that he had directed the order to be withdrawn. Thus, while the CID officers were on their way to make the arrest, orders were received from President's Secretary Lalith Weeratunga that the arrest move be called off.

In Melbourne, I was sitting by the phone nervously, waiting for Lasantha to call with the latest news. When he did, he spoke calmly, explaining that the CID was expected to arrive any minute to arrest him and that the newspaper office was filled with friends, well-wishers, politicians and even diplomats who had heard the news of the imminent arrest and wished to record their solidarity with him.

Lasantha explained to me what needed to be done in the event he was arrested. He said he had already spoken to a friend about arranging for our eldest child Avinash, who was living with Lasantha at the time, to be flown to Melbourne. I was extremely worried about the implications of an arrest if there was one and asked him whether we should fly back to Colombo. Lasantha said he would keep me informed of developments.

Lasantha had always told me that if ever he was arrested and thrown in jail he would make use of that time to write his memoirs. The very idea of a tortured writer locked up in a cell scribbling away by candlelight in the dead of night painted a very romantic picture and we would joke about it, but when the possibility actually presented itself, it was far from appealing; it was disturbing to say the least.

The following Sunday, in its editorial titled 'Curbing Terrorism or Eliminating Democracy?' the newspaper took the government to task on the arrest drama.

> ". . . . When the Rajapakse administration brought in the new emergency regulations that made even the Prevention of Terrorism Law applicable, *The Sunday Leader* in its editorial pointed out to the danger of these regulations being extended to cover the media. The government spokesman made hurried statements that it will not

apply to the media. A few weeks later the ministers and their cohorts are singing a new tune; no one is above these laws.

"What the media is concerned about is they can be taken into custody under the blanket cover of passing information to the LTTE for any report. Even the report of an opening or closure of a road could be construed as passing information to the LTTE and the journalist concerned arrested. Considering the subservience of the police to politicians in power, anything is possible these days . . . ."

* * *

All the threats and harassment suffered throughout 2006 did not have a dampening effect on *The Sunday Leader* or its Editor. The newspaper continued to each week present its avid readers with more ground-breaking stories.

Then an event occurred which made the Wickrematunges realise how far those in power would go, how every conceivable avenue would be explored, to silence the *Leader*. Deputy Minister of Tourism Faizer Mustapha had called up Lal indicating he wanted to come over for a chat with him. When he arrived at the *Leader* offices, Mustapha asked Lal to step in to his vehicle which was being driven by his chauffeur. "We can chat while travelling," he told Lal. To Lal's surprise, the chauffeur drove on to Temple Trees where they were met by the President who proceeded to have a relaxed chat with the duo. The President remarked that Lasantha should have 'joined him' in a political sense and suddenly posed the question as to whether Lal was willing to sell Leader Publications. When Lal in turn asked who was interested in buying the paper, Rajapakse looked at both Faizer and Lal and smiled, "I will put somebody and buy, no?"

Rakapakse asked Lal to keep mum about the meeting but the next day the Sinhala language *Lankadeepa* newspaper carried an account of the meeting. When Lasantha who was overseas returned, he was furious at what had transpired and asked Lal whether he was thinking of selling the newspaper. Lal replied he hadn't even thought about it and the matter ended there.

The year 2007 was to bring more surprises the newspaper's way. Before going in to that however, I should give readers an idea of the stories that were being published in the *Leader* in 2007. Following are some of the headlines;

- **President's square project that came a cropper**
- **Yoshita Sails Away**

The story was about the President's second son, naval cadet Yoshita, who had been the subject of much government media hype since 'the President was sacrificing one of his own sons to the war effort.' The *Leader* exposed details of how Yoshita was shipped off to the UK on a full naval scholarship in Dartmouth, just two weeks after joining as a cadet officer of the Sri Lanka Navy.

- **The politics behind the *Mawbima* arrest and the secret SLFP-LTTE deal**
- **Sri Lanka's thriving abduction industry**
- **Abductions and the white van syndrome that haunt a people**
- **UDA subsidiary a den of corruption**
- **Bribery, corruption, *bheeshanaya* and domestic squabbles come home to roost**
- **Navy in tender bender**
- **Government's rank gamble with the family silver**
- **Rights violations take centre stage**
- **The war against the media**
- **Taking the food out of the Farmer's Mouth**
- **Mihin leases an Airbus at a monthly rental of Rs. 110 million**
- **When Percy and his ministers went to town**
  This was the story of Presidential excess where over 20 million rupees was spent on a junket trip by various officials and their friends to travel to the Caribbean Islands for the Cricket World Cup matches.
- **President's Tiger deal exposed**

This, and a follow-up story had far-reaching consequences. According to these stories, in an interview with the newspaper, the former Airport and Aviation Chief revealed details of a pre-Presidential election deal with the LTTE. In a statement to the Terrorism Investigation Division, he also said he had been requested to establish a link with the LTTE to co-ordinate the Presidential election strategy for the north-east.

- **And the winners are, the Rajapakse Bros**
  This was the story about the formation of a new company to operate a controversial new airport. It revealed that the company would operate along the lines of other controversial private companies paid for by public monies—Mihin Lanka (Pvt) Ltd, and Lanka Logistics and Technologies Ltd.
  The Sunday Leader charged that Mihin Lanka was maintained as President Rajapakse's private airline while Gotabaya Rajapakse was

the foremost subscriber director of Lanka Logistics which controlled all the state military procurements. The chief executive officer of the company was another relative of the Rajapakses.
- **Controversy over US$3 billion offer to govt.**
 Details of the President's decision to consider a dubious proposal for a US$ 3 billion capital infusion to the country by a broker from Australia, which potentially fell into the category of money laundering under the Prevention of Money Laundering Act of 2006.
- **Who Profited From the MiG Deal?**
- **Lid blown on ghost company that did the MiG deal**
- **Swindling the war-battered farmers**
- **Unearthing all the President's men and their mega projects**
- **The mighty rush to milk NLDB**
- **Government hand in abductions racket bared**
- **Gun-toting Malaka (a ministerial son) goes berserk again**
- **How the govt. attempted to fix Malaka's case**
- **How the public paid for Malaka's remand time**
- **New taxes and MR's New York binge**
- **Payment vouchers to Tiger companies for the vote swindle surface**
- **Meet 'First Brother' Basil**
- **Statistics that lie in defence of the realm**
- **Govt. caught out over Prima deal**
- **A President's act of vengeance**
- **A foreign policy nightmare that haunts the President**
- **Trainee foreign pilots fly Mihin**

* * *

By 2007 former adversary Chandrika Kumaratunga and Lasantha were friends. The acrimony was gone; the very public spats buried. Chandrika was no fan of Mahinda Rajapakse and she more than appreciated the exposures Lasantha was splashing in his newspaper on the Rajapakse brothers. Thus, bonded by a common animus, the former enemies developed a friendly and cordial relationship, meeting from time to time and keeping in regular contact with long mobile phone conversations. It was a classic case of politics making strange bedfellows.

In fact Kumaratunga was to once tell Lasantha, "What a pity we spent those years fighting. I shouldn't have listened to the stories people were telling me. You and I could have worked so well together."

In September 2006 *The Sunday Leader* had published an interview with Kumaratunga in which she charged that President Rajapakse was putting her life at risk through 'numerous acts of commission and omission.' To a question posed by Lasantha as to whether she considered aligning with the JVP in 2004 the single biggest mistake in her political career, Chandrika replied, "No. The single biggest mistake I made will reverberate for generations and which is relevant at this very moment, I cannot speak about now. But, yes the alliance with the JVP was also a big mistake."

* * *

In October 2007—in another act of aggression toward *The Sunday Leader*—one of its reporters, 22-year-old Arthur Wamanan and his mother were arrested and incarcerated by the CID based purely on a statement made to the CID by a government Minister. His mother was arrested because Wamanan's mobile phone was registered in her name.

The previous Sunday the *Leader* had published under the headline, 'Minister gets Gem Authority to pay wife's roaming charges,' a story about the Minister's hand in an alleged misappropriation of funds. Following this the Minister claimed that on October 19, 2007, Wamanan had telephoned him and demanded five million rupees in exchange for suppressing the story.

The CID's intention was to hold the young reporter for a fortnight but fortunately, the glare of publicity the story attracted forced them to produce him in court. The magistrate chastised the police officers asking that they refrain from misleading court by making foolish allegations.

That Sunday's editorial in *The Sunday Leader* took the Minister in question to task over his 'amateurish concoction.' The journalist had been thrown behind bars for checking with the Minister and seeking his side of the story, the editorial wrote. "What is more," the editorial said, "the CID's knee-jerk reaction sends a message to journalists throughout Sri Lanka to publish without verification, or to verify at their peril. If that is what the government wants, so be it."

Elsewhere in this same edition, the *Leader,* recounting the arrest and hailing the stand of the magistrates, wrote, "We said it before and we will say it again. If there lies any hope for the people of this country, that hope lies within the judiciary. All a nation on the brink of an abyss of despair needs is a few good men and women. All this country needs to rid itself of this culture of barbarism and impunity is an upright and independent judiciary coupled with public outcry."

The following month, in the early hours of November 21, 2007 to be exact, the Leader Publications printing press in Ratmalana was attacked by around 10 pistol-waving thugs who proceeded to destroy the press having earlier forced the workers to kneel down and hand over their mobile phones. The men then set ablaze the press and some newspapers due for distribution that morning and hurled petrol bombs before fleeing in their four-wheel drive vehicles.

Lasantha was spending time with us in Melbourne when he was informed of the attack which was the second act of vandalism on the press in two years. When interviewed by Sri Lankan media establishments on the phone, Lasantha termed the attack a 'commando style' operation and questioned how such a high-handed act of aggression was possible in such a high security zone. The press is situated in close proximity to the Ratmalana military and domestic airport. That day Lasantha spent much of his time communicating by telephone and e-mail with his staff instructing and assisting them with the stories to be published with regard to the attack and on Sunday, *The Sunday Leader* put out a leaner version of the paper "to highlight the determination and courage of the newspaper's loyal and dedicated staff to bring you this newspaper." Several pages were in black and white due to technical problems that had arisen due to the attack.

The editorial that Sunday read, "The *Leader* does not claim to be an infallible sacred text. It is a newspaper, but unlike many in existence in Sri Lanka, one which strives hard to find facts which affect the lives of the people and the country and is not afraid to publish and comment on them, irrespective of the persons involved. We respect views that we are not in agreement with and go along with the thinking of Voltaire, the French philosopher: I disapprove of what you say, but I will defend to death your right to say it.

"We have not gone after small fry but the big whales, the highest and the biggest. We have named them and exposed them the political rogues in saintly clothes with trays of flowers in hand and ill-gotten gains in their bank accounts, the death merchants who preach patriotism, spend state funds for dud armaments and collect millions of dollars abroad, unqualified profligate wastrels who reach high office by licking sandals and being toadies to the powers that be and spend thousands of dollars for luxury suites in star class hotels while the poor at home don't have money to buy bread, brazen thugs who disgrace the nation by picking up fights in night clubs and encouraging their progeny to do so, pious hypocrites who are supposed to have given up all worldly pleasures and dupe gullible women of their sainthood while being unable to move without their tax free luxury limousines, and state officials who have diddled billions of rupees of state funds have been some of our subjects. Only such nefarious characters and their like would like to see *The Leader* stop publication."

The Sunday Leader also published in the same edition a "Rajapakse Media Scorecard' courtesy of the Movement Against Media Suppression, which was a damning indictment on the President's record on the media.

Journalists killed	13
Abductions	03
Imprisonments	05
Banned Channels	05
Blocked websites	01
Newspapers closed	03
Suppressive laws	03
Threats/harassments	Countless

That year (2007) Sri Lanka was named by media watch-dog the Press Emblem Campaign (PEC) as the third most dangerous place for journalists after Iraq and Afghanistan. Giving more justification to this deplorable ranking, many more assaults on the media took place come 2008.

In March 2008, Gotabaya Rajapakse who had been furious with *The Sunday Leader* in general and Lasantha in particular since 2007 when the *Leader* carried a series of expose's on arms deals, sent a letter of demand to the Editor of *The Sunday Leader* stating that his reputation and goodwill had been damaged due to two articles published in *The Sunday Leader* and claimed Rs 1000 million in damages.

The articles in question were 'MIG deal crash lands' published in *The Sunday Leader* of July 15, 2007 and the story titled 'Lid blown on ghost company that did the MIG deal' published in *The Sunday Leader* of July 29, 2007.

Legal proceedings were duly instituted[1].

The Mount Lavinia District Court issued an interim order restraining *The Sunday Leader* from publishing any news item concerning the Defence Secretary.

Also in March 2008, journalist J. S. Tissainayagam was taken into custody by the Terrorism Investigation Division of the Sri Lanka Police. He was held in custody without charge for six months. In August he was charged with inciting communal disharmony for an article written and published three years earlier in the *North Eastern Monthly*. In September, he was sentenced to 20 years in prison.

In May the same year (2008), Keith Noyahr, Associate Editor of *The Nation* newspaper (published by the Rivira Media Group) who wrote the

'Defence Matters' column was abducted as he returned home from work. He was subject to hours of merciless and intense beatings and torture before being released. The last column he wrote before his abduction was titled 'An army is not its commander's private fiefdom.'

In June the same year Sri Lanka Press Institute journalist Namal Perera narrowly escaped being abducted but suffered knife wounds and a severe beating when he was set upon by a gang of unidentified men in Kirulapone, Colombo. His friend Mahendra Ratnaweera who was with him at the time also suffered injuries.

Despite the harassment he and the Leader Group had endured and the attacks fellow journalists in other media organisations had suffered, *The Sunday Leader* under Lasantha's stewardship continued to highlight cases of governmental corruption, transgression and misdemeanor, inviting more state displeasure with each passing week. Among the stories the *Leader* exposed in 2008 were the oil hedging scam which would potentially cost the country 400 million dollars and the Central Bank's part in it, the SAARC summit blunders and the huge Rs. 2,800 million cost to the taxpayer, the diplomatic nightmare in Washington after a relative of the President was appointed as Head of Mission, the woes of SriLankan Airlines and the Defence Ministry's move to set up a private security firm with shares held by the Defence Secretary, Treasury Secretary, Defence Ministry lawyer and four Additional Secretaries of the Defence Ministry.

In its issue of February 24, 2008 the newspaper published a story under the headline 'The Rajapakse 'connection' and a multi-million dollar deal.' It said, "Damning documents and details have emerged to prove that the government has yet again moved to place the interests of President Mahinda Rajapakse's family before the state and the public, in a well thought out move to persuade state telecom operator SLT to shell out millions of rupees to yet another family company.

"The shocking details will show that the family company was set up for the specific purpose of securing a multi-million dollar deal with SLT while withholding vital approvals from SLT to force it to go into business with the Rajapakse family business." The story continued into a full-page exposure.

In its issue of March 2, 2008, under the headline 'Milking the country dry *Chinthana* style,' Lasantha wrote, "The government, in the latest of the *Chinthana* tender benders is moving to accept a Rs. 3 billion offer from an Australian company to import 15,000 cattle heads and upgrade the farming infrastructure of the National Livestock Development Board (NLDB) despite the Board itself advising to the contrary." Again, the story ran into a full page.

Several exposures on Mihin Air were also published in 2008. A story titled 'BoC dumps a billion rupees on ailing Mihin' on May 4, 2008 said, "Astounding evidence has surfaced, implicating several high ranking officials at the Bank of Ceylon (BoC) in what can only be described as a scam to keep the desperately bankruptcy-bordering Mihin Lanka afloat.

"Documents in the possession of *The Sunday Leader* prove not only that the bank kept doling out money by the hundreds of millions to what is effectively an asset-less shell company, but also that moves were made at the highest level by the bank to wipe out over Rs. 117 million in interest owed by Mihin to BoC on over Rs.1 billion of high interest overdrafts.

"Several sets of internal minutes and memoranda prove beyond doubt that bank officials knew that they were acting in bad faith, to say the least, in dumping their depositors' money into a dead loss enterprise."

Another expose' on May 11, 2008 titled 'Mihin, BoC directors face court action' said, "Following *The Sunday Leader*'s exclusive expose last week of the Bank of Ceylon's virtual dumping of one billion rupees of public depositors' funds into the defunct Mihin Lanka, several public advocacy groups have begun to prepare to take legal action against the directors of both Mihin and the Bank of Ceylon (BoC), who are personally liable for their actions under the Companies Act Number 7 of 2007."

On June 29, 2008 in an article titled 'Mihin pondering the 'new deal,' the newspaper said, "*The Sunday Leader* has learnt that a scandalous agreement was signed last week at the Aviation Ministry premises in the presence of Aviation Minister Chamal Rajapakse, to look at the prospect of selling off Mihin Lanka's landing rights to a Malaysian company, Mindflow Technologies . . . ."

The newspaper continued with its investigations into Mihin Lanka.

Several stories on questionable tender awards were also published in 2008. On July 6, 2008 a story titled 'Tender Bender in Railway' explained how two Railways authorities had been exposed in an ill-begotten attempt to manipulate a tender for new railway locomotives that ran into tens of millions of dollars. 'The Security Threat over NIC Tender Bender' published on November 9 exposed the controversy surrounding the tender for a new national identity card costing billions in taxpayer money while putting the security of the country at risk.

Throughout 2008 Lasantha highlighted 'white van' abductions, human rights violations and exposed duplicity in the war effort targeting in particular those at the helm. He accused the army commander of playing a numbers game and of being economical with the truth when it came to war casualty figures. On September 21, *The Sunday Leader* carried a full-page article titled 'A General on the Loose' wherein he proved the vast disparity in official figures announced from time to time. Other headlines screamed 'Playing Russian Roulette with the Soldiers,' 'Lies, Damn Lies and Statistics' and 'Govt's War of Attrition.'

In the article titled 'A General on the Loose,' the writer accused the General of politicising the war for the benefit of the party and the President. The article then quoted General Fonseka from an interview he had given state-run *Sunday Observer* in the run-up to the North Central and Sabaragamuwa Provincial Council elections: "The military is no doubt entitled to get political mileage especially after capturing areas like Vidattalthivu and Mannar. Most probably we will capture many more places before the elections."

In October that year (2008) a Reporters Sans Frontiers (RSF) initiated World Press Freedom Index Survey of 173 countries placed Sri Lanka at No. 165 and stated, "Asia still has the biggest representation in the 10 countries at the bottom of the ranking. Most of them are dictatorships, but they also for the first time include Sri Lanka (165th), which has an elected government and where the press faces violence that is only too often organised by the state."

Sri Lanka was followed on the list by China, Iran, Cuba, Turkmenistan, North Korea and Eritrea. Ahead of Sri Lanka were countries such as Pakistan, Afghanistan, the Palestinian Territories and Somalia.

That same month the government gazetted new regulations pertaining to private television stations. The regulations posed the very real threat of the stations' licenses being revoked and was seen as an attempt to control the independent electronic media.

Lasantha's very last Suranimala column titled 'Cabinet defies Supreme Court as LTTE spoils Killinochchi party' reported: "That the government is totally dependent on the war for political survival there is no gainsaying and the senior-most minister in the administration D.M. Jayaratne no less admitted in an interview with this newspaper the previous week, the war is being marketed for political gain . . ."

Elsewhere in the column Lasantha wrote of what transpired at an emergency cabinet meeting. The President, he wrote, spoke of a package of tax benefits and relief he had put together and wanted Cabinet approval so that the benefits could be passed on to the people. The President then told the gathering that all he had said would probably appear in the next edition of *The Sunday Leader.*

The article continued, "No sooner the President made that comment, Minister Fowzie interjected; "Even your kitchen cabinet meeting was reported in detail (in *The Sunday Leader*) the previous week."

"Taken aback the President countered stating he does not have a kitchen cabinet and went on to make a long statement, the content of which only went to prove, he had in fact met separately with a select few the previous week to discuss the Supreme Court order as exclusively reported in this column . . . ."

The Suranimala column had given readers exclusive reports of internal matters of state and provided fly-on-the-wall style details of high-level closed door meetings and Cabinet confabs for almost 20 years. The column of January 04, 2008 was to be the very last.

That Sunday's investigation story headlines read 'Economic Gloom the Stimulus Package Failed to Brighten' by Risidra Mendis, Nirmala Kannangara, Arthur Wamanan and C.B.M. Joseph, 'Mihin: Chamal's to Fly, Yet ours not to Reason Why' by Sonali Samarasinghe, 'Water Board's Purification of a Dubious Supplier' by Dilrukshi Handunnetti and 'The Presidential Omissions' by the same writer.

That first week of January 2009 Lasantha was his usual adrenaline-driven, ever active self, steering his staff towards producing another brilliant edition of the *Leader*. Some reminisced in hindsight that a dark shadow of worry furrowed his brow yet no one could ever have imagined what lay ahead for their beloved Editor.

---

[1] The case is still continuing in the District Court of Mt. Lavinia with Lal Wickrematunge, Publisher as Respondent.

CHAPTER TEN
The Murder of Truth

> *"Assassination is the extreme form of censorship."*—George Bernard Shaw, Irish playwright.

"WHEN Killinochchi is re-captured is when they will kill me."

In conversation with his brother Lal in late December 2008, Lasantha uttered these chillingly prophetic words. He was not foreseeing the future like some crystal ball gazer. He was simply putting into perspective his logical analysis of the political and military situation vis a vis his own battles with the government.

The Sri Lankan armed forces had for several months been locked in heavy fighting with the LTTE in their final onslaught against the terrorist group. In a country that had endured some quarter century of terror at the hands of the LTTE, the armed forces were finally poised on the edge of victory and the people were jubilant. The soldiers and the military high command waging war against the enemy were venerated as the saviours of the nation. *The Sunday Leader* dared to go against the tide as it were and continued to highlight the massive humanitarian disaster that was unfolding in the conflict zones, the plight of the Tamil civilians caught in the crossfire as well as the abductions and killings taking place in the south. It was an unpopular cause to espouse and Lasantha was labelled a 'terrorist lover,' a traitor, and worse.

Lasantha and I had discussed his anti-war stance many times. While I felt indebted to the armed forces who were sacrificing their lives to rid the country of a ruthless terror machine, Lasantha felt the human price was too heavy to be ignored. There was frustration at what he perceived as the sheer short-sightedness of the people and their rulers. He saw racism entrenching in the media with the vernacular press in particular given to pushing extreme lines.

In an interview he gave a newspaper he had noted that there were "restrictions on the coverage of war, non-disclosure of the battle casualties of late, concealment of human rights violations and a reduction in the reflection of the suffering of the IDPs. (Internally Displaced Persons)"

In the same interview he remarked that "new perceptions are being created that every Tamil is a LTTE sympathiser," that in the prosecution of war "there appears to be rejoicing of aerial bombardment to the extent of overlooking collateral damage to civilians. That's a horrible mindset to reach."

Lasantha also believed there was a social obligation to journalism that could not be ignored but was being overlooked because it was deemed unpopular. "One must state the truth and create spaces for diversity and democracy. That may not be a popular choice but it is a must," he insisted.

On December 21, just 18 days before his murder, Lasantha wrote in his Suranimala column, "Having placed all its eggs in the war basket, the government was totally dependent on success in the military front to survive politically, in the face of a crashing economy due to mismanagement and extravagance, and the stiff resistance faced in the Wanni has now placed the Mahinda Rajapakse administration on a razor's edge."

A few days later, on January 2, 2009, the army's 57th Division led by Major General Jagath Dias and the Task Force 1 of the Sri Lanka Army led by Brigadier Shavendra Silva liberated Killinochchi town in a blaze of glory. The logic behind Lasantha's statement to his brother about being killed "when Killinochchi falls" was that his enemies would find this an opportune moment to strike because the country would be so intoxicated by this massive war victory that his murder would go relatively unnoticed.

The LTTE's administrative capital and Eelam's de facto capital Killinochchi first fell into LTTE control in 1990. Though operations Sathjaya I and II saw the army regain the town in 1996, two years later Killinochchi had once again been recaptured by the LTTE.

By January 2009 Lasantha was certain that an attack on him was imminent. He was living in our Kandewatte Road, Nugegoda residence with our 17-year-old daughter Ahimsa and devoted childhood nanny Menika while the two boys were with me in Australia.

Ahimsa was going through a period of emotional upheaval and acute stress and Lasantha was tackling single-handed the responsibility of taking care of her while also attending to the hundred other pressing matters on a professional front.

Lasantha called me up in Melbourne more often than usual; we would discuss everything from Ahimsa to the situation in Sri Lanka. Each time he called he would make it a point to talk to his sons who he adored. When MTV Channel's main transmitting centre in Depanama, Pannipitiya came under attack in the thick of the night on January 5, Lasantha was greatly distressed. A gang of approximately 20 men armed with T-56 rifles and explosives had destroyed the centre's main control room. The intruders held staff members at gunpoint, opened fire within the building, lobbed hand grenades and damaged property and vehicles. Two synchronized clocks froze at 2:35:31 when a massive explosion believed to have been caused by a claymore mine ripped through the building.

Lasantha was in deep slumber when a call came through informing him of the attack. Hastily throwing on T shirt and pants he rushed to the scene in his slippers. There was devastation written all over his face as he condemned the attack when interviewed by a journalist on camera. Lamenting the obvious non-tolerance of any alternative viewpoints he warned that all media institutions in the country should brace themselves for more attacks. He was not to know that the very next attack was going to be on him just 48 hours later.

Lasantha had for several years hosted a regular breakfast show on MTV and appeared on its political programs. He also had a very close and cordial friendship with Raja (Killi) Mahendran, head of Capital Maharaja Organisation which owns MTV.

The same day as the attack on MTV Lasantha called me in Melbourne to convey the news. He was angry and bitter, yet his spirit was unbroken. I could sense the defiance in him, the same defiance that shone in his eyes the very first time I saw him as he sat in the waiting room of the *SUN* office 27 years previously.

There were ominous shadows cast of what was to come. Lasantha had been receiving death threats, on the phone and in the mail. One of the last he received was a page of *The Sunday Leader*, painted over in red with a warning scrawled across.

That Lasantha himself had a sense of foreboding was somewhat evident in certain things he said and did. Thirteen days before he died, he spoke to me about writing his last will. He followed it up with an e-mail which said, "I have given all the details to the lawyer. I will courier you a copy once it has been finalised."

Unknown to many, he had also started writing an 'editorial from the grave' addressing those he thought would be responsible for his murder. This brilliant, now legendary piece of journalism received worldwide publicity and acclaim after it was first published in *The Sunday Leader* three days after his assassination.

* * *

The last time Lasantha visited us in Melbourne was in September 2008, three months before his murder. After the hugs, kisses, gift-giving and general chatter, he engaged in the 100 kisses ritual with his 'baby,' 10-year-old Aadesh, who he absolutely adored. This game entailed Aadesh and dad frolicking around with dad hugging, tickling and squeezing the little fellow who would be screaming with laughter and begging to be released. Dad would then say he would stop once he got his 100 kisses. This was a customary bit of boisterous fun they consistently engaged in on Lasantha's arrival in Melbourne.

Once, during that final trip, we were standing in line to pay for our purchases at a shop. Lasantha was standing with his arms draped around Aadesh. From time to time he bent forward and planted kisses on Aadesh's cheek. A lady standing behind us in the queue thought it was very sweet.

"It's so nice to see a father who obviously adores his child," she said, "especially these days when you hear so many horror stories about children being abused."

Lasantha glowed while Aadesh glowered. He didn't like all this very public displays of affection!

During the same trip, early one morning Lasantha stirred; I looked over to find his gaze fixed on Aadesh who was sleeping on our bed. Lasantha's eyes glistened with unshed tears. I asked him what he was thinking.

"It breaks my heart to think that if something happened to me I won't see them again, ever," he said wistfully. "The only happiness I now get is spending time with the kids. If I die, you must promise me you will take good care of the children; I know you will be a wonderful mother but if something happens you will have to be both mother and father to the children. I want you to give them everything they have enjoyed so far in life."

"Nothing is going to happen to you Lasantha," I replied and continued as an after-thought, "If something does, I will take good care of them . . . and I will make sure they will never forget you." I then chided him about his lax security. I was happy however that he had traded his evening constitutional on the streets of Nugegoda for a safer option—a treadmill at home; something I had been begging him to do for years.

"That's what I love about Melbourne, it's so peaceful," he said.

Indeed, he loved his walks whenever he was in this Melbourne suburb with its pretty homes, carefully clipped lawns and rainbow coloured flowerbeds, as if the pretty illustrations from childhood storybooks had come alive in all their caricatured charm. Most days he would ask me to accompany him as he set off for a walk—track-pants, peak cap and all—and we would chatter away about all manner of things as we strode the maze of little side-streets.

Despite Lasantha and I having divorced a couple of years previously, we had remained the closest of friends and the bond we shared had only become stronger. In fact he would always tell me that in his prayers each day, he first asked for my happiness. "Every day, you are very first person I pray for," he would tell me. "I pray for you even before I do for the children or my parents."

At the time Lasantha last visited, I was editing the SriLankan SOCIETY Magazine, a glitzy people and events quarterly catering to the Sri Lankan population in Australia. It was Lasantha who first came up with the idea of a magazine and was always at hand like the Rock of Gibraltar if ever I needed support and advice. During his last trip, he arranged for me to have a story about cricket star Lasith Malinga's experience with spiritual healer Eliyantha White which I ran as my cover story in the next issue.

On February 8 that year (2008) Lasantha had written to me about Eliyantha White who he said was the President's friend and physician and that he himself had sought treatment from him for his high-blood pressure. He was also planning on taking Ahimsa to meet him. Lasantha had also sought White's help for some treatment for his brother. At the time, Lasantha's relationship with the President had still been acrimonious but Lasantha told me the President had supposedly directed White to help Lal saying, "*Lasanthage aiya ne,*" ("After all he's Lasantha's brother").

Lasantha wrote in that e-mail: "There is a doctor who is also a faith healer . . . . He is Mahinda's doctor. He is the man whom Mahinda sent to meet me through another friend saying he wants to get friendly etc. He is the one who attends to all his medical needs. He keeps a low profile and not many people know him or about him. He cures cancers etc.

"Anyway I'm taking some treatment from him for my pressure. He said some of my nerves on the right side of the brain were damaged leading to the pressure. The medicine involves applying some oil for three days and some *kasaya* and stuff."

"My friend Pasan whose relation he is, is the person that brought him to me. I of course refused to meet Mahinda because he can always kill me thereafter and say we were once again friends and that I had even met him."

That was in February; in September when he was in Melbourne, he still had not mended fences with the President.

On September 27, Lasantha left for Colombo after his two-week holiday with us. Never in my worst nightmares did I imagine this was going to be the last time I would see him alive. We had had such a wonderful time; taking the kids shopping, dining out, visiting friends, chatting, laughing, talking of events in Sri Lanka and generally having a good time. Lasantha was extremely careful with his diet in Colombo but here in Melbourne he relaxed the rules, loosened his belt a few notches and dug happily into my cooking.

As he left, he hugged us all and cried his eyes out. The boys were embarrassed but suffered silently their father's time-tested idiosyncrasy.

Lasantha promised us he would be back in April in time for Aadesh's birthday.

From the airport he called us again telling us how much he was already missing us. I don't know if Lasantha felt that this trip was going to be his last; but certain things he said and did make me wonder about that, even now.

Three months before Lasantha's trip to Australia, in June 2008, the Defence Ministry had launched a virulent attack on journalists who were printing "crap" stories on the war which were not complimentary to the government.

An article appeared on the Defence Ministry website labelling these writers 'cowboy defence analysts' and 'enemies of the state.' It said that the ministry "does not wish to entertain mere doomsayers who always try to undermine the soldiers' commitment." It further said it would take "all necessary measures to stop this journalistic treachery against the country."

Despite these, Lasantha and the President, through the intervention of Eliyantha White and other mutual acquaintances, buried the hatchet.

* * *

Three months after this final visit to Melbourne, on December 27, he and journalist Sonali Samarasinghe who had just a few days prior, registered their marriage, hosted a function for family and friends. Despite the merriment however, there seemed to be something weighing heavy in his heart.

Every single day he called us in Melbourne and hung on the phone with the boys and me and elaborated both on the phone and in e-mails what I should do in the event of his death. I was disturbed, but since I had received e-mails from him prior to this titled, "What to do in the event of my death" and "What to do in an emergency," I didn't read too much into it.

Once, on the phone with me, he again jumped to the subject of his death.

"I have told Lal that if I die, my body should be kept at a funeral parlour," he said. This was a change of heart because I had had an e-mail from him a few weeks earlier in which he said, "When I die I want my body to be sent to medical college."

This same e-mail was full of sadness, regret and unhappiness about his father's failing health. "What's the use of this life?" he wrote. "Life is not worth living. Thatha is also very weak and they don't know how much longer he can hold out. His system appears to be packing up slowly. What use is this life. He did everything for us and now he is helpless and we can't do anything to save him. He was so active but can't even go to the toilet alone . . . . Just imagine how he must feel. And then when I picture Malli (Aadesh) waving goodbye to me at the airport when he left Sri Lanka I want to tear my heart out. I am ashamed because I too am a weak man much before age has caught up with me. I have ruined my children's lives. This newspaper gave me so much but has taken so much more away from me."

In November 2008, he called me from India.

"I am at the shops," he said, "I want to buy you a sari."

I told him I didn't need too many saris in Melbourne.

"That's alright," he said, "I'm buying you one anyway."

I cautioned him not to spend money on an expensive sari which I might not wear too often.

"Don't worry about that," he replied. "There's a black one that I like, it has a red flower design on it."

I could hear him talking to the shop assistant as he proceeded to purchase it.

The sari arrived in December, through my mother who was visiting Australia. He had also sent me a Phil Collins CD with the song *Against the Odds*. I wore the sari to the '08 New Year's Eve dance, just eight days before he was killed.

After he got back from India he wrote to me about how depressed he had been returning to Sri Lanka from India and that he had wished he didn't have to come back to Sri Lanka. A few days later he told me casually that he had dreamt of my father who passed away in 2001, handing him a white shirt.

From the time I had got to know Lasantha 27 years previously, he had spoken of death as just another experience. Something he had mentioned more than once was the fact that he wanted to be "the first one to die in my family—even before my parents." This was because he felt he would not have the emotional strength to cope with the death of a loved one.

The Wickrematunges had always been an emotional family. Even tough old father Harris was quick with the waterworks when it came to sensitive family matters. In Melbourne Lasantha would watch Aadesh's school plays with tears streaming down his face. Each time he left Melbourne he would bear-hug us all and sob like a child. I remember at least a couple of occasions he cried at funerals, one of them being when his childhood best friend Shivanka's father passed away.

On Thursday January 1, 2009, Lasantha sent me a text message that read, "Happy new year and all the best. I love you guys so much. Will call when I get to office." When he called, he told me he was sending me the supplementary card of his credit card through my sister-in-law who was arriving in Melbourne. The next day he called to find out whether I had received it. He wanted me to, while he was still on the telephone, destroy the old card and sign the new one because as he said, "you are such a harum-scarum!"

As usual I joked that I was going shopping with the platinum card.

"I hope you will," he replied. "At least justifies me sending the card to you." The last was a reference to the fact that I hardly ever used the card in Australia mindful of the vast disparity in the exchange rates. In fact, on December 30, 2008 in an e-mail to me he wrote, "Even though you seldom use it, it is useful to have for an emergency."

When Lasantha called me on January 7, I was almost out of the door and told him I would talk to him the following day and passed the phone to my son. That night he called again and we talked about the situation in Sri Lanka and about Ahimsa. He was also worried about his sons. He began talking about the old days. He sounded wistful. "I wish we could all get in the car and go out to dinner again as a family like the old times," he said.

I never dreamed at that moment this was going to be the last time we would speak to each other again; that in less than 24 hours, he would be dead.

On January 8, I woke up as usual and started pottering around the house. Hearing a loud crash I rushed to the bathroom to see a torrent of water gushing down from the ceiling. I thought it was a disaster. I had no idea of the biggest disaster yet to come.

* * *

In Sri Lanka, Lasantha woke up at 6.00 am to the sound of his phone alarm and prepared for work. After his shower, he ironed a white shirt and black pants, dressed and went downstairs for breakfast. Ahimsa who had been listening to Pink Floyd's *Great Gig in the Sky*—ironically a song about preparation for death—joined him at the table as was her usual habit.

Father and daughter had become extremely close in the last two years and were inseparable. They would sit and chat for hours on end about anything and everything and tease each other unmercifully. He would strut around doing his Arnold Schwarzenegger impression, he would relate to her anecdotes from his early life; father and daughter would sometimes pore over family photo albums and talk of the old times when the kids had been little. Lasantha would sometimes get emotional and his daughter would either tease him or try to comfort him. The standard family joke was that one minute he would be sniffing despondently and the next, the phone would ring and he would in a trice regain his composure and speak animatedly, usually ending the call with, "Ok machang, I'll be there in 20 minutes."

Despite getting married, Lasantha continued to live in our Nugegoda home with our daughter. Father and daughter never seemed to tire of watching *Friends* and Lasantha would joke about a massive crush on actress Jennifer Aniston. They would religiously watch the 2008 US primaries and election trail, cheering madly as Barak Obama notched up each victory.

Lasantha told his daughter he was thinking of doing a TV show on the lines of the David Letterman Show with a studio audience present. He said he wanted it to be a laid-back show with a mix of politics, current affairs and humour.

About two weeks before his death Lasantha told his daughter he felt there was some supernatural entity in the house.

"Shall we get a monk to bless the house?" he asked her. Lasantha had written to me a few days prior asking for the contact numbers of a Buddhist monk closely associated with our family.

When her father left the house each day, Ahimsa worried about his safety and begged him to take care. Lasantha would tell her, "Don't worry, if assassins came to me with guns I wouldn't run away because I know God is protecting me."

This notion that he was constantly protected was firmly implanted in his mind after a pastor in Canada told him that God would protect him throughout his life and there were two angels watching over him at all times.

On the face of it, his implicit faith in divine protection was paradoxical. On the one hand, he felt he could be done-in by his enemies any day. And he was prepared for it. He wrote an editorial predicting it. He had told me and his children that it was better to die once with integrity and honour than to die a thousand deaths as a coward. Yet, he also firmly believed nothing could touch him because divinity's watchful gaze was forever focused on him.

On that final day, Ahimsa, who had had an uneasy night with hardly a wink of sleep, sat with her father at the dining table while he drank his mango juice freshly prepared by Menika. He ate his bread, butter and *seeni sambol* while Menika hovered around preparing his cup of tea.

Lasantha usually had his tea in the hall while chatting to Ahimsa but on that particular day he was in a hurry to leave. It was a Thursday, the day he wrote his Suranimala column, and he had a busy day ahead of him. He also had a meeting scheduled with UNP leader Ranil Wickremesinghe for 11.30 that morning.

As he prepared to leave the house Ahimsa clung on to him asking whether he would be back for lunch. As was the case on most days she cajoled her father to part with some money so she could send the driver out to buy some food. When they reached the door, she kissed him and cautioned him as she always did, asking him to take care.

The last Menika saw of Lasantha alive was as he got into his vehicle with his mobile on his ear.

A few minutes later, Lasantha's driver Dias came calling out to Ahimsa. He explained that he had left his mobile phone in Lasantha's car and needed to retrieve it. He asked Ahimsa to call her father and ask him whether, if he went to the Nugegoda junction, he could collect the phone. Ahimsa then called and spoke to her father and this was arranged.

A few minutes prior to leaving our house, Lasantha had received a call from Sonali asking that he come to her residence in Battaramulla as she needed to get some medication for her maid.

Soon after Lasantha left, a three-wheeler operator who resided close to our home informed driver Dias that he had observed some suspicious looking men following Lasantha's car. Two men on a motorbike, he said, had been hovering outside a small shop in the vicinity of the house, one of them casually puffing on a cigarette. When Lasantha passed by in his car, one of the men had muttered in Sinhala, "He just left." The smoker then butted his cigarette out and they revved up the motorbike engine and took off, following the car.

While in Battaramulla, Lasantha received a call from a worried *Leader* employee who told him Dias had informed them of what the three-wheeler driver had observed. Soon after, a motorbike with two persons on it whizzed past Lasantha's car and disappeared into an empty lot.

After getting some medication from the Pelawatte Pharmacy, Lasantha dropped Sonali off at her home and headed for Ratmalana where the *Leader* offices are located. On the way he called driver Dias and asked him to meet him in Nugegoda where he handed over the driver's phone and some documents in a file.

Wending his way through rush-hour traffic in Ratmalana, Lasantha realised he was being followed, this time by eight men on four motorbikes similar to Bajaj pulsars. (The number of motorbikes and assailants has not been firmly established; varying reports have given the number as four, six and eight assailants).

Lasantha then called up his friend Malik Samarawickrema, one-time Chairman of the UNP, and apprised him of the situation. Samarawickrema advised him to go to some safe place immediately. Lasantha also called Eliyantha White and asked him to inform President Rajapakse of the goons following him. It was later revealed that White did call the President but had been told he was in the shrine room. Lasantha then tried to reach Killi Mahendran; Killi later said his mobile phone rang with the caller identification showing Lasantha's number but the line went dead thereafter.

It is not clear as to what happened next although eye-witnesses recalled that the car had stopped behind a bus that had come to a halt. Lasantha's silver Toyota bearing registration KC 1098 was found adjacent to the boundary wall of Attidiya Model Primary School, near Bakery Junction on Attidiya Road. The car was straddling a street crossing.

What is clear however is that the men smashed open the windscreen and the driver's side window and stabbed him on the right side of his temple before fleeing.

There are conflicting reports about the weapon that was used. Even eyewitnesses who saw the assailants as they fled were unable to identify the weapons they carried as they were wrapped in newspaper.

Early reports were that a gun was used but doubts arose soon after. No spent cartridges were found on the scene nor did forensic investigators find traces of a gun having been fired. Adding to the theory that a gun was not used was the fact that there did not appear to be an exit wound on the skull. At first doctors surmised that the bullet may still be embedded within. However, since there was no tearing of skin on the surface, this was ruled out. The Judicial Medical Officer's report however said that death was due to, "cranio cerebral injuries following discharge of a firearm."

The fact that there were no major external injuries to Lasantha's skull seemed to indicate that some other type of weapon may have been used. Some believed it could have been a sharp instrument such as a prod similar to that used to stun and kill sheep which they said, explained the two tiny scars, about an inch and a half apart, on the exterior of the temple while the skull was crushed from within.

It was also revealed that his heart was not functioning when he was brought in to hospital and could be pumped only after a pacemaker was attached.

One of the people who came to Lasantha's aid soon after he was attacked, 33-year-old mechanic Prasantha Rajapakse, giving evidence in Mt. Lavinia Court on July 2, said from where he was standing, he could see a car at a standstill on the opposite side of the road and he observed someone standing on the right side of the car and another near the left window of the car. He could see the men "doing something" to someone inside the car. Prasantha didn't see a weapon but saw one of the men holding an object covered by newspaper. Curious to see what was going on, Prasantha walked up to the car just as the two men were moving towards a motorbike that had been parked nearby. The men were wearing black jackets and had black helmets on. They then got on the motorcycle and headed towards Ratmalana.

Prasantha told court he peeped into the car and saw a man lying there with his head leaning on the left door. He was bleeding from his right ear and was facing upwards. The driver's side window and the windscreen were smashed.

"I noticed that he was bleeding profusely from the head and he was finding it difficult to breathe. I asked some people standing around to help me carry him to a van that was parked there and asked the driver to take him to hospital," he told reporters soon after the crime was committed. Prasantha himself did not go to hospital but left it to the Good Samaritans in the van to do the needful.

While all this was happening Lasantha was clutching his mobile phone. On the way to the hospital the phone began to ring. The person on the front passenger seat of the van answered the phone and advised the caller that if he was a friend of the owner of the mobile phone he should come to the Kalubowila Hospital.

While being transported to hospital Lasantha moaned in pain and mumbled weakly that his chest was hurting. The young man who sat in the back-seat of the vehicle holding Lasantha continuously rubbed his chest.

It was only when the van reached the hospital and people began milling about shouting excitedly that they realised the man they had brought to hospital was journalist Lasantha Wickrematunge.

"We have always admired him as a fearless man who stood for the rights of the people. We were all sad to find out that it was this man who was shot," one of the men who brought Lasantha to the hospital later told a *Sunday Leader* journalist.

The van that transported Lasantha to hospital was driven by one Nathan from a courier company who had been on his way to Avissawella for a delivery when he was held up in a traffic jam in Attidiya.

"We stopped to look and when we heard there was an injured person, we allowed the people to carry him to our van. Along with two other people and my sales manager, we drove straight to the Kalubowila Hospital," he told journalists from *The Sunday Leader*. Nathan also said he hoped the injured man would pull through because "there was an air of innocence about him."

Lakmal Nanayakkara, a computer operator attached to *Irudina*, the *Leader's* Sinhala edition, was on a bus travelling towards Ratmalana when a major traffic jam on the road near Attidiya Junction brought the bus to a halt. From the bus he watched as a man was carried out of a car and transported into a van. Recognising the car and fearing the injured man was none other than Lasantha, he scrambled off the bus hoping to get into the van. Just as he alighted from the bus however, the van took off.

Journalists from *The Sunday Leader* who rushed to the scene of the crime reported seeing a notepad and file containing documents lying on the front passenger seat of Lasantha's car but sometime later these had mysteriously vanished. When questioned about these, police gave conflicting reports, initially insisting that only a phone headset had been recovered and that they did not know anything about a file and a notepad. Police immediately cordoned off the area.

Lal, who had been informed of the attack by Leader Publications driver Upul, rushed to the scene where he saw Lasantha's damaged car. In a state of shock, he inspected the vehicle. He then rushed to the Kalubowila hospital where hundreds of people had gathered; friends, relatives, *Leader* colleagues and journalists from other media establishments, politicians, police officers and members of the general public were all thronging the hospital. When Lasantha was transferred to the operating theatre, the crowd was so massive that at one point, hospital staff carrying the stretcher were unable to move forward. There were loud orders asking the waves of people to give way and amid the pandemonium of cameras flashing and people yelling, Lasantha was rushed in for emergency surgery. His pulse was a low 43, he had an injury to the right temple, he had suffered a fracture to the base of his skull and he was bleeding from one ear. Tearful and traumatised faces watched in horror as bare-bodied and inert with a bloodied bandage tied around his head, Lasantha was rushed through to the theatre. One man in the crowd began wailing, "Aney Lasantha mahaththaya . . . . aney Lasantha mahaththaya."

The doctors at the hospital and other specialists who were brought in battled for three hours to save his life. *Leader* journalists and friends waited outside the operating theatre, hoping and praying he would pull through.

Meanwhile, in a bizarre twist, the President, who had received a message about the attack, handed a protective talisman to Eliyantha White and asked him to place it near Lasantha's head on the hospital bed. This was duly done. Despite the herculean efforts of nearly 20 doctors working feverishly to save him, around 2.15 pm, Lasantha breathed his last. The surgeons threw down their gloves in despair; one of the doctors then came out, threw his hands in the air and proclaimed, "Lasantha Wickrematunge is no more!"

An anguished roar tore through the waiting crowd. *Leader* journalists sobbed. The media went into overdrive. When the news was relayed on radio and television, the country was plunged into shock. The opposition went ballistic. For a long time nobody could quite believe that Lasantha

Wickrematunge was dead. He had been the go-getter, the livewire, the trail-blazer, the crusading journalist, the trusted face on television, the upholder of free speech and the brilliant political analyst who fearlessly, in his no-holds-barred fashion, strode a path no Sri Lankan journalist before him had. And now, in one fell sweep from a coward's weapon, he had been silenced forever.

Politicians and prominent media persons, thoroughly shaken-up by the events, were interviewed on camera in the hospital premises. Most felt the perpetrators of the crime were close to the powers that be.

SLFP (M) Leader Mangala Samaraweera when interviewed by a television crew said he felt he needed to fall down on his knees and ask for forgiveness from the people of the country for playing a part in installing such a brutal regime.

Executive Director, Centre for Policy Alternatives, Dr. Pakiasothy Saravanamuttu who was also Lasantha's friend and *Sunday Leader* columnist for many years said, "What has happened to Lasantha Wickrematunge today is an absolute atrocity. This is the second attack on media institutions and media personnel who have dared to be independent, who have dared to have dissension. Clearly, it is part of a plan . . . There is no option but every peace loving, democracy caring citizen in this country needs to come out and send a very clear message to those who think they can do these things with impunity and destroy what is precious and valuable in this country. A very clear message has to go out to them that this must stop and that those who perpetrate crimes like this must be brought to justice and will be brought to justice. The culture of impunity is corroding this country and destroying us as a functional democracy."

Media activist Sunanda Deshapriya, speaking to a television news crew said Lasantha was easily one of the most courageous journalists in the country and denounced his murder in the harshest terms. "We have lost Lasantha at a time when we needed him the most," he said.

After the Judicial Medical Officer conducted an autopsy, police filed a "B" report in Court. A "B" report informs Court of the progress of an investigation and what processes have been followed in the investigation.

* * *

At home, Ahimsa still had no clue as to the horrific events unfolding; feeling somewhat restless, she called driver Dias to find out why he had still not returned from Sponge with the short-eats she had asked him to bring.

"Where are you?" she asked when Dias answered his phone.

"I'm in hospital," he replied but said nothing further.

Instantly, fear gripped her heart. By nature she was always fearful of disasters befalling loved ones and she had a dreaded thought that her father could have been in danger of some sort. Overcome by a sense of panic, she hung up the phone.

Menika then turned on the television and just as Ahimsa replaced the receiver, they both heard the TV anchor relaying the news that Lasantha Wickrematunge had been shot and was undergoing surgery in hospital. At that moment something snapped in Ahimsa's mind. Although she collapsed to the floor in shock, she soon took hold of herself, telling herself over and over again that it was a false report and she was overacting as a result of sleep deprivation and stress. A little later, pulling herself together she ran to call her aunt in Canada.

By then the news had broken and the whole family was aware of the events.

"God won't let anything happen to him. You must pray more than ever," her aunt Rukmani said amidst sobs.

Family and friends began arriving at the house and were huddled in conference as to how they were going to break the news to Ahimsa who had by then got into bed and was refusing to come out of the room. Although she had heard the news on the television, she was still in complete denial. In her mind, it was all a mistake and her father was going to return home in his customary manner, they were going to laugh off the reports of the attack and then cosy themselves to watch television together.

Those gathered outside her door decided to let my brother-in-law break the news to her. He opened the door, went up to the bed and told Ahimsa she couldn't stay in the house anymore as it was unsafe. He asked her to get a change of clothes. Reluctantly, Ahimsa complied.

When she returned with some clothes, he asked, "Do you have anything in white?"

"Why?" she asked.

"For the funeral," he replied.

"What funeral?" she screamed.

Her uncle then informed her that it was none other than her father's funeral.

Even as she took her bag of clothes and left the house to be at her aunt's, Ahimsa was in denial. She did not believe a word she had been told. All night she paced the floor like some demented robot. At first dawn, she insisted on being taken back home.

* * *

In Melbourne, I had received a few calls from Sri Lanka informing me that Lasantha had been attacked. I jumped on the phone to call home and a hysterical Menika came on the line. She said she had just heard the news but didn't have any details. I then called Mela Karunanayake, wife of UNP MP Ravi Karunanayake who amidst sobs told me he had been shot but she didn't have any details either. Ravi was in hospital she said, and she would call back as soon as she heard something.

In the meantime I was receiving text messages telling me Lasantha was being operated on and that he was stable. Friends and relatives began arriving at our home and I decided to leave for Colombo immediately with the two boys. Family members rushed about organising our air tickets and travel documents. It was while I was thus preparing to leave that people began calling with news of the worst. I didn't believe it; I was certain this was just the rumour mill at work. "No, it isn't true," I insisted, "He is stable and still being operated on."

The phone rang again and this time it was my brother-in-law Ananga calling from Sri Lanka. I thought it strange that when I answered, instead of speaking to me, he asked to talk to my sister Fern. As I watched the expressions on her face and heard her voice drop to a concerned whisper, the painful, gut-wrenching truth dawned on me. I remember screaming in utter anguish like some demented soul and crying uncontrollably. I still couldn't believe it. The sadness and devastation I felt was indescribable.

Within the hour, Avinash, Aadesh and I were on our way to the airport. All the way to Singapore, I stared out of the window in utter misery. Memories were flooding my mind and I could see Lasantha's smiling face each time I closed my eyes. Avinash sat in stony silence while 10-year-old Aadesh watched cartoons on the small television screen.

At the Singapore Airport where we had several hours of transit time, I sat in the lounge, still benumbed with shock and sadness. Avinash sat alone away from me staring into space while little Aadesh played about. I erroneously assumed that he was aware of the events but that he hadn't quite grasped the finality of death. Being the youngest, Lasantha and I had both petted and pampered Aadesh a great deal and still considered him a baby.

A little later Aadesh came running to where I was sitting. "Now when we go to hospital, Thathi will ask me for 100 kisses, won't he?" he asked, smiling happily. That was when the painful realisation hit me that he wasn't completely aware of what had happened. In fact he seemed very excited about the prospect of seeing his father again. I had been so consumed with my own grief that I had not taken the time to explain the tragic events to him. I had assumed that because of the pandemonium that had reigned in the house, both he and Avinash were aware of the worst.

For a few seconds I struggled to find the words to tell our darling little boy that his wonderful, funny, loving father was not going to be around anymore. I yearned to delay telling him, to give him a few more minutes of pain-free time. But I hugged him close and explained to him as best as I could, that his father was no more. I didn't expect his reaction. He jumped up in shock horror as if stung by a snake. "NO! NO! NO!" he screamed. "It isn't true!" He began to wail and I felt my heart breaking into a million pieces. "No, it can't be!!" he cried in anguish.

"How do you? When did you know? What happened?" he began bombarding me with questions while his little body was wracking with sobs. After a while he sat by me and cried softly as I held him in a tight embrace. On the plane ride to Colombo he stared into space, not saying a word.

Before boarding the plane to Colombo however, there was more drama at the Singapore airport. As we waited to board the plane, staff from SriLankan Airlines sought me out and handed me a telephone. On the other end was my sister calling from Sri Lanka. She was asking me to turn back and return to Melbourne citing some obscure security situation. A close friend got on the phone next; she too tried to dissuade me from coming to Colombo.

"I don't care what happens to me," I told them. "I have to see Lasantha. My children need to see their father. We are not turning back."

"You don't understand, you have to turn back. It's not safe for you to be here," they said.

"Ahimsa needs me," I countered.

"Ahimsa is fine. She is also worried about you . . . it's best you turn back," they insisted.

"I will not deprive my children of their last farewell to their father," I shouted. "I need to see him, my children need to see him and have their closure. We are not turning back!!"

It was several days later that I learnt this had been a sinister, heartless plot by an individual who didn't want us to be in Colombo during the funeral and had conveyed some outlandish story to my friend and sister in a bid to keep me and the children away.

Arriving in Colombo, everything seemed surreal. Driving towards our home, a home that was to me, awash with a million happy memories, I was beginning to feel so overwhelmed with grief that I feared I wouldn't make it to the front door. But for the children's sake, especially for Ahimsa's sake, I had to hang on to every ounce of strength I possessed.

Ahimsa had given everyone strict instructions that the minute I came home, they were to wake her up immediately, whatever the hour. She also told them only her mother and two brothers were to enter the room and that she needed some time alone with us.

When I entered Ahimsa's room, she was still in a deep sleep; I hated to wake her up and throw her back into that painful, dark, abyss, but finally she stirred and opened her eyes. The moment she saw us she hugged me and her brothers and began to weep as if her heart was broken. United in our grief, we sobbed until the shadows outside lengthened and we had no more tears left to cry.

* * *

The next several hours passed by in a haze. People came, people went, the phone never stopped ringing; to me everything seemed unreal. I was not thinking; just responding to people and events while a constant raw knot of grief choked my heart. I looked at my children's faces wondering what anguished feelings would consume them when they saw the body of their father.

Lasntha's three sisters arrived from Toronto and his brother Anil and his wife flew in from Bremen, Germany, all of them grappling with their own grief. Their lovable, funny, kind, generous 'Malli' was dead and it was more than they could handle.

Being back in our family home where the children had grown up was emotionally draining for me and the children because Lasantha had been such a big part of that house and it held close within its walls so many memories for each of us. Now, he was no longer there. Our old family pictures were still hanging all over; in Lasantha's bedroom, our wedding picture sat on his bedside table. A colourful wall plate with a picture of him and me, looking so young and laughing happily—done in Hong Kong all those years back—sat on a bookshelf. The clothes he had worn the previous day hung on a chair in the room with his familiar Bulgari aftershave still lingering.

That night, the three children and I all huddled on Lasantha's bed; it was an uncomfortable, restless sleep and more than once little Aadesh muttered in his sleep or stirred and woke up in the dead of night. In the morning he told me someone had been stroking his head as he slept.

Around 10 am, friends, family and *Leader* staff began flocking to our home; they were all there to accompany the children and me to Sonali's home in Battaramulla where the body lay. Sixteen cars left our home but despite the moral strength offered by all those dear, loving souls, dread was gripping my heart as we neared the funeral house. I wondered whether I'd have the strength to see Lasantha in that state.

I was still in a daze as I watched from the car hundreds of people dressed in white walking along the decorated road, towards the funeral house. I was touched to see that most of these were ordinary people, wizened old ladies, mothers and children carrying umbrellas to shield themselves from the sun, men of all ages, talking to each other, shaking their heads as if in disbelief. Most of these were people who had never known Lasantha personally but had come to love and admire him through his newspaper and television work, and were now trudging the miles to pay their last respects to a hero of their times. At that moment, I felt so much gratitude for all these people; I imagined how moved Lasantha would have been to know that he had inspired so many people from all walks of life.

I remember now, with the same searing pain that I felt then, the moment our children and I saw him lying in that cold, dark coffin. The two boys screamed involuntarily; I think above all it was the shock of seeing their father lying dead like that. As the boys and I sobbed, Ahimsa wailed and fell to the floor. All five of us were reunited, but under what gut-wrenching circumstances!

Someone told me later that in those minutes of utter grief and despair as the children and I huddled together by his body, everyone present in that room had cried with us.

Back home, I realised that for the children it had been a doubly traumatic experience; seeing their father in that state was sad enough; but having to see him lying in what they saw as a strange house, added to their feelings of confusion and despair. I knew then why Lasantha had called me up a few weeks previously and told me he had informed his brother that in the event of his death, he wanted his body to be placed in a funeral parlour. He had been thinking of me and the children.

That night I had a very uneasy sleep. Around 4.30 in the morning, I got out of bed in the dark, huddled on the couch in the bedroom and cried silently as the three children slept a few feet away. At that moment I truly felt Lasantha's spirit by me, trying to comfort me. I kept talking to him telling him how much the children and I loved him. I promised him I would take good care of the kids. I then told him, "Lasantha, the children need to see you at home, please, please come home."

As morning light slowly crept in through the windows, I heard Menika pottering about downstairs. An hour or two later Lasantha's brothers Lal and Anil walked in. As we talked, out of the blue, Lal asked me whether I would like to have the body brought to a funeral parlour for the day. I told him that would be wonderful if it could be arranged. Lal then proceeded to call the parlour, spoke to someone there and put the phone down. "The parlour is busy the entire day," he said gloomily, and my hopes for the children fell.

"Would you like to have the body brought home?" he then asked. My heart leapt. My only thought was of the three children and how, having their father home, would give them a modicum of comfort amid the pain.

Arrangements were then made to bring the body to Kandewatte Road. I silently thanked Lasantha. It was just a few hours before that in the darkest depths of despair I had pleaded with him to "please come home."

Emotionally draining though it was, Ahimsa and the boys gained some solace from the opportunity of seeing their father at home and saying their final farewells to him in private. Ahimsa especially insisted she wanted to spend half an hour with him alone.

And alone she sat there, in the very hall where just a couple of days before, she had sat with him chattering away and giggling at his jokes; this time sobbing uncontrollably as she talked to him and said her goodbyes to the father she loved so much.

* * *

With the mood in the country being what it was and the opposition crying murder from rooftops, it was obvious that the funeral scheduled for Monday, January 12, was going to be nothing short of a political circus.

A mass demonstration had been organised and thousands of people were due to take part in a monumental show of solidarity with the slain Editor. The UNP's Colombo district organisers in particular were planning a massive show of strength which saw procession numbers swelling to several thousand.

At 12.00 noon on Monday, January 12, the cortège left the Battaramulla residence of Sonali Samarasinghe for the Assembly of God, People's Church in Kirimandala Mawatha, Narahenpita where a one hour service was held.

Thereafter, the funeral procession consisting of journalists, politicians, friends, human rights groups and representatives from various organisations, made the long, sombre walk to the General Cemetery, Borella, following the hearse carrying Lasantha's mortal remains.

Among the political leaders who walked in the procession were UNP Leader Ranil Wickremesinghe, SLFP (Mahajana) Wing Leader Mangala Samaraweera, SLMC Leader Rauf Hakeem, Democratic People's Front Leader Mano Ganesan and Left Front Leader Wickremabahu Karunaratne.

With the mood of the people being what it was, the funeral procession soon turned into a protest march as hundreds of incensed, inflamed people shouted anti-government slogans, waved placards, chanted, and burnt an effigy of President Rajapakse. Members of political parties and organisations such as Women United for Democracy and the United Federation of Labour among dozens of other civil groups, in impassioned displays of outrage, called out for an end to tyranny. 'Defend democracy! Stop political violence and killings now!' they chanted as others shouted slogans directly blaming the powers that be for the horrendous crime.

Many wore black armbands; others waved black and white flags; some carried dark-hued balloons. Swollen with mourners and protestors, one section of Baseline road had to be closed down for traffic. Hundreds of people lined the streets watching the procession and paying their respects as the hearse slowly passed by.

Lasantha's loyal lieutenants, the staff of *The Sunday Leader*, walked alongside the vehicle bearing their general's body, grief written all over their faces. Lasantha's body had remained at the *Leader* offices for a little over half an hour the day after his murder and many of his colleagues felt this was inadequate considering that *The Sunday Leader* had been Lasantha's whole life, the great passion he lived and died for.

As they approached the roundabout near the cemetery, staff members of *The Sunday Leader*, *Irudina* and representatives of other media organisations carried the casket on their shoulders, raising their right arms in a determined pledge to continue the work of Lasantha Wickrematunge.

As the procession advanced towards the main entrance of the cemetery, some began dashing coconuts, invoking punishment on those who were responsible for the reprehensible murder.

Among the dozen fiery and impassioned funeral orations delivered was that of Ranil Wickremesinghe who in a hard-hitting speech warned that the death-knell of democracy had rung loud and clear and cautioned the people of similar killings in the future. "Let us forget our differences and make Lasantha's dream of creating a democratic and corruption-free nation a reality," he said.

SLMC leader Rauf Hakeem said Lasantha had used his pen fearlessly to expose corruption and injustice when many others were fleeing. He said this period in Sri Lanka's history would be remembered as one of the darkest times of all.

Lasantha's brother and Chairman of Leader Publications, Lal Wickrematunge called on all journalists to unite in the common goal of fulfilling Lasantha's dream of creating a better nation.

German Ambassador Jurgen Weerth, speaking in his capacity as the Dean of the Diplomatic Corp said, "Today is a day when one remains speechless. Maybe we should have spoken before this. Today it is too late. Today is a day when humanity has lost a major voice of truth. But what remains is his legacy and what he meant to each of us. As Dean of the Diplomatic Corps may I extend our deepest condolences to the family, the staff of *The Sunday Leader* and all here who have had the privilege to call Lasantha a friend as have I."

As the shadows lengthened and darkness began to fall, the mourners lighted candles while the sense of doom and gloom increased with every dark shadow that descended.

* * *

Our three children, Avinash, Ahimsa and Aadesh, felt their father's last days on earth had been swallowed up in a very public frenzy, which, given Lasantha's public standing, was unavoidable. On the day of the funeral, Ahimsa in particular was unhappy when faced with the prospect of being smothered amidst thousands of people and flashing cameras when all she wanted to do was say goodbye to her father in peaceful privacy.

We decided that at the cemetery we would keep away from the last rites and orations and the glare of cameras and say our final goodbyes to Lasantha at the gravesite. It was already dark when the casket was brought and the reality hit us that this was the last time we would ever be in the presence of our beloved's earthly remains. It was a very traumatic, highly emotional experience. Seeing the casket being lowered into the grave was one of the worst experiences in my life. I remember being held by family members and old friends from the SUN. It was fitting that some of the ex-SUN journalists were there, for it was together with them that Lasantha and I had first walked the path of journalism as two young people in the bloom of youth.

Even now I don't let myself think of Lasantha, lying there under the ground. It is too distressing. Lasantha had a phobia of being buried; he wanted to be cremated, he always said. When I brought up the issue with a family member before the funeral, he said since it was a police case, the body could not be cremated. It is something that, to this day, has troubled me greatly.

Seven days after his death, we organised a *dana* (alms giving) at home for monks from the Wijewardenarama temple in Nugegoda; it was attended by friends, relatives and *Leader* staff. Among the monks were some who had participated in an all-night *pirith* ceremony several years prior when we had first moved in to that home in much happier times.

* * *

A few days after the funeral, two of Lasantha's close friends Pasan Madanayake and Gamini Gunaratne came to see me with a message from

Mahinda Rajapakse. The President, they said, wanted to meet me and convey his sympathies; would I go to Temple Trees? At first I refused. When they persisted, I told them if he was keen on meeting me, perhaps he could come to see me at my house. The two then returned with the message that security considerations prevented the President from visiting me.

I mentioned this to a few close confidantes. They had mixed feelings. During this time, I was firmly of the opinion that the President had nothing to do with the murder; those close to him, perhaps, but not the President. After all, I knew Lasantha and he had become friends again and talk was that he had infact been invited by Lasantha for the recent bash. Even in his last editorial, Lasantha predicted the President himself would be anguished by his death.

The events that had occurred at Singapore's Changi airport too were still fresh in my mind. There were those intent on creating mischief, and in the event this line of attack continued, I needed my own line of defence. My children were left with just one parent now; for their sake, I had to protect myself from any vicious attacks stemming from an egocentric mindset.

Lastly, Mahinda was not completely unknown to me. It had not been a personal friendship but I had met him socially, and as a journalist covering parliamentary proceedings I had interviewed him during his Jana Gosha days, when he was a simple, unassuming parliamentarian who thought nothing of meeting a reporter in the casual press room and giving a candid interview. I had the urge to look him in the eye and ask him about the murder and about the murder inquiry.

More than all others, it was this last reason that finally pushed me to agree to meet with the President. On the designated day, Eliyantha White picked me and my youngest child Aadesh and took us to Temple Trees. When I met the President, the first thought that crossed my mind was how different he now looked to that affable, simple man I had known. We sat and talked for a while, about Lasantha and about the murder; he threw up some theories. Finally I asked him about the murder inquiry.

"Of course we will see that the inquiry is thorough and quick," he said, and looking at Aadesh, he continued, "After all, these children need to know what happened to their father."

Soon after I returned to Australia, a picture of the meeting between the President and I was splashed in the state media and I was branded by some as a traitor.

It was a difficult few weeks that followed the publication of the picture. As I worried over the whole fiasco, especially certain reactions, one night I dreamt of Lasantha stroking my head. He simply said, "I'm sorry about what they are doing to you."

The children, mostly Ahimsa, and I continued to have very vivid dreams of Lasantha. Some nights we would feel his presence in the room and on several occasions she thought she saw him in the bedroom.

Some months after his death, Lasantha once again appeared to me in a dream. He seemed worried. "I came to tell you about the accident," he told me, staring directly in to my eyes.

"What accident Lasantha?" I asked.

He simply repeated the same sentence, "I came to tell you about the accident." At that point, I woke up and pondered the implications of the dream; what had he been trying to convey? Then it dawned on me; he was warning me about an accident! I told my family and friends about the dream but thought nothing further of it.

Two weeks later, I was driving home after my volunteer work with a local charity organisation when my car got into a huge smash-up with another car. It was an unnerving experience and both cars were left write-offs but fortunately the other driver and I both escaped without a scratch.

After that incident, I laughingly addressed an invisible Lasantha, and told him firmly, "The next time Lasantha, I need dates!"

* * *

Things were never the same at *The Sunday Leader* after Lasantha's death. The truth of what everyone had always feared, that no one could ever walk in those shoes, became painfully real. Leader investigative journalist of many years Frederica Jansz was appointed Editor of *The Sunday Leader* and the staff rallied round, trying in earnest despite their grief to continue Lasanth's work.

Gaining inspiration from a giant picture of Lasantha smiling down at them, the young journalists plodded on, infusing their work with everything their wonderful boss had ever taught them.

As Chief-Sub Romesh Abeywickrema wrote, "It's close upon 13 years now that I have constantly heard him call out, 'Copies, copies! How's the story? Pages pages!' and as I sit today staring at the door to his empty office, knowing that no more will that cheery baby face be peeking out from it shouting something or the other, no more guidance on how to get about things, no more constant jokes, no more his copyrighted brand of humour, no more the pat on the back when the going gets tough that I slowly realise that life as I know it is never going to be the same again."

Leader journalist for several years Marianne David later remembered, "With Lasantha leading us, we never had to worry; we were never uncertain. We would stand with him, confidently. He inspired loyalty and devotion and we believed in him fervently. He never let us down. Not once. I have often been teased about how much I adore Lasantha. No harm. I always did. And I always will. He taught me so much. And the day that we walked, hand in hand, behind the hearse carrying his lifeless body was a day that I hoped would never dawn.

"But even though Lasantha may have left the land of the living, for those of us who love him, he will always be alive in our hearts, sporting that mischievous, boyish, now heart-rending smile."

CHAPTER ELEVEN
Aftermath

> *"Although we are opposition members we still did not have the courage to take on the government as Lasantha did*—Rauf Hakeem, Leader of the Sri Lanka Muslim Congress.

WHILE the country slowly and painfully came to grips with the murder of Lasantha Wickrematunge, condemnations of the attack began pouring in to media institutions from all quarters. The cold-blooded slaying of a high-profile journalist stunned not just the ordinary citizenry, but local and international media and human rights organisations, political groups, the diplomatic community and the business world.

Outrage and anger over the brutal killing was growing, as was the complete and utter despair over the impunity that prevailed with regard to violence, abductions and murder. The general perception was that forces loyal to the government had carried out the attack on Lasantha by enlisting the services of a goon squad. In fact in parliament, the UNP had questioned whether a separate unit existed within the Army, set up for the express purpose of carrying out offensives on the media.

The President, quick to absolve himself of any blame, went on record saying he had been a very dear friend of Lasantha. His statement condemning the murder was given priority on state television and radio newscasts. The President said he was devastated by the death of his close friend and that he had ordered a thorough inquiry into the murder so as to enable the perpetrators of the crime to be brought to book speedily.

For about two months before his death, Lasantha had been meeting Rajapakse at Temple Trees, generally at night, with a couple of Rajapakse loyalists. Lasantha however did not attend any functions or breakfast meetings the President held for representatives of the media.

When Lasantha's passing occurred, the President was in the midst of a meeting with representatives from associations dealing in coconut, coir and poultry. While in the midst of discussions, an urgent call came through to the President and he was heard asking, *"Oluwatada weduney?"* (Did it hit the head?).

A day after the slaying, the President's speech marking the army's re-capture of Elephant Pass from the LTTE was aired on television. In this address, in stark contrast to the buoyancy he had displayed in his January 2 address announcing the capture of Killinochchi, Rajapakse appeared solemn; he went on to explain that there were elements trying to discredit him and the government in the wake of the wave of military successes. The underlying message was that Lasantha's murder and other recent attacks on the media had been the work of conspirators intent on tarnishing the government's image in the face of its growing popularity following the military victories.

Despite Rajapakse's rush to claim that he and Lasantha had been good friends, on January 14, when the President invited media heads and newspaper publishers for a meeting at Temple Trees, there was no display of any residual affection for the memory of the Editor. On the contrary, Lasantha had been an 'informant' he said, and it was Lasantha who had first told him of Karu Jayasuriya's defection from government ranks back to the UNP. He also went on to present several theories on how and why Lasantha was murdered, hoping once again to deflect any blame.

Later, whispering in another newspaper Editor's ear, he referred to the funeral and commented, "Raine was distraught wasn't she?" The Editor and he then shared a private joke and a visibly jolly Rajapakse moved on to other topics of interest.

The Defence Secretary meanwhile was coming out all guns blazing. When Gotabaya Rajapakse heard the news of Lasantha's murder, Gotabaya was in Jakarta and according to the *Sunday Times* political correspondent, he responded to the news with, "*Den ithin maawa allai.*" (Now they will blame me).

Back in Colombo, he wasted no time in making a grand TV appearance and having congratulated the armed forces on their victories on the warfront, launched a scathing attack on sections of the media who he labelled as traitors. MTV journalist Chevaan Daniel was among those Gotabaya singled out for harsh censure. He then charged that the MTV attack on January 6 was a self-inflicted assault for insurance purposes. No mention was made of Lasantha's murder.

Earlier, in an interview with the British Broadcasting Corporation's Chris Morris, Gotabaya had taken a frivolous attitude to the murder, desperately attempting to paint the Editor as a 'tabloid journalist.'

"Who is Lasantha Wickrematunge?" he ranted. "There are killings all over the world . . . why are you asking only about him? He is someone who was writing to tabloids."

Trying in earnest to contrive a hollow laughter, Rajapakse then said Lasantha had been criticising previous leaders even more virulently than he did the current regime and any one of them could have killed him.

When the interviewer asked him about allegations there were death squads within the Defence Ministry, Rajapakse eyed him like a stunned mullet and muttered, "What about . . . . ? What?"

Regaining his composure, he explained that when Lasantha had criticised him in his newspaper, he did the right thing by taking the matter to court.

Not everyone in the government however was acting like a bull in a china shop. Media Minister Anura Priyadarshana Yapa at a Cabinet press briefing on the day of the murder expressed the government's shock over the assassination and said the President had ordered a full inquiry into the killing. He also said it was the President who had organised the despatch of some of the best doctors from the National Hospital to Kalubowila Hospital when Lasantha was fighting for his life.

Meanwhile, political parties, civil organisations and media groups threw themselves into feverish activity planning massive campaigns and protest rallies to highlight the prevalent culture of media suppression and the need to restore democracy in the land.

UNP parliamentarians and activists were naturally dismayed by the death. Many of them were very closely associated with Lasantha and were fond of him as an individual. They also recognised the political mileage that Lasantha's death presented and the tremendous opportunity that had been thrown open to haul the Rajapakses—under whose watch the murder had occurred—over the coals.

On Friday, January 9, the UNP carried out a protest outside the Fort Railway Station and a protest in parliament with around 20 UNP MPs sitting in the well of the house in front of the Speaker's rostrum. Red and black shawls draped around their necks, they carried placards laying the blame for the murder squarely at the government's feet. Among the MPs was Thalatha Athukorale, sister of Lasantha's close friend Gamini who had died of a heart attack in 2002.

In keeping with the grim mood, UNP Leader and Lasantha's close confidante Ranil Wickremesinghe had a red scarf tied across his mouth symbolising the gagging of the media.

Funeral arrangements were worked out meticulously by friends; some UNPers were in favour of Lasantha's body being taken in procession beginning from Kotahena—the Wickrematunge homeground and political turf—and all through the Colombo North electorate. This plan to extract the maximum political mileage did not eventuate.

On Monday January 12, the day of the funeral, a large group of lawyers representing the Bar Association of Sri Lanka, gathered at the gates of the Superior Courts Complex at Hulftsdorp as a sign of protest against the assassination of their colleague Lasantha. They carried pictures of Lasantha and placards that read, "Protect Democracy," "Who is Next?" "Protect Freedom," "Respect the Rule of Law" and "Hands off Lawyers." The walls nearby were plastered with posters depicting a smiling Lasantha.

A spokesman for the BASL recalled that when Lasantha's house was fired at in 1998, the BASL had passed a resolution condemning the attack. He stressed that this was "not a political demonstration by or against any one particular party, group or individual but a furtherance of the oath and duty to safeguard and protect the rights and liberties of the citizens of the Republic, to express absolute dissent and contempt of society against all moves to suppress, curtail or shut out the basic fundamentals of a democracy such as the freedom and right of a citizen to form, hold and promote his/her own opinion without fear or being discriminated, persecuted or killed for it."

The joint opposition comprising the UNP, SLFP (Mahajana Wing), Sri Lanka Muslim Congress, United Socialists Front, the New Samasamaja Party and the Development People's Front, decided to hold continuous protest campaigns throughout the country highlighting the suppression of the media by the Rajapakse regime. They also organised three major processions in southern Galle, culminating in a massive agitational rally in the Galle town.

The UNP also called for an international investigation into the assassination of Lasantha.

On Thursday, January 15, several civil society organisations held a silent vigil opposite Viharamahadevi Park to protest against the killing of Lasantha. It was a sombre, melancholy occasion as participants lit candles in front of a portrait of the Editor's smiling face which glowed from the reflection of the hundreds of tiny flames.

The JVP, who had earlier condemned the murder, decided to hold countrywide protest campaigns and awareness programs to muster the support of the people against media suppression. They were joined by the Working Journalists Association, Intellectuals for Human Rights, University Teachers for Human Rights and the Patriotic National Front.

The Daily Mirror editorial the day after the murder read, "Lasantha's killing poses a serious threat to society as a whole, and raises a question on how secure it is for any of us anymore. His killing must deserve our condemnation not merely because it denied a journalist his right to an opinion, but more because it denied the people their right to know. These are not the workings of a society even close to democracy leave alone a path to progress.

"It is an undeniable truth that Sri Lanka is one of the most dangerous locations for journalists to operate in. The level of killings, abductions, threats and intimidations to journalists is a sad manifestation of how intolerable we have become, as a society, to opposing views. The long term consequences of such intolerance cannot be condoned by any right thinking people, because therein lies the degradation of society as a whole, and the threat to every citizen.

"No amount of condemnation, official or otherwise, can compensate for the inhumanity that made this killing possible. And it is not only the cruelty of the killing and the inhumanity of the process that led to the death that we must condemn. It is the very elements of a social system that allows for such deaths to take place and also provides refuge to the culprits of such heinous crimes that we must find a means to end."

"If dissent, as they say, is an act of faith in a democracy then it failed both Lasantha the journalist and us as a people, miserably yesterday. The cowardly act lay bare the fragility of the democracy we believed we could find refuge in and the vulnerability of anyone attempting change."

The Nation in its editorial on January 11 said, "Wickrematunge's killing must be condemned in the strongest possible terms. It is a cowardly act committed by persons who feared *The Sunday Leader* Editor's tenacity and determination and his commitment to the causes he espoused.

"We have been assured the killing will be probed. We appeal to all those responsible for the inquiries to act promptly and independently, with fervour rather than fear or favour. To bring the culprits to book and shed light on who is responsible would be the only means of salvaging Sri Lanka's reputation as a law abiding nation—or else, we would descend to the level of a Banana Republic that disposes of dissent with summary executions."

The murder also evoked an international outcry.

Jyoti Thottam writing in *TIME* magazine for which Lasantha was a freelance contributor, said, "His death has galvanised the growing anger among the press and other civil-society groups in Sri Lanka about restrictions on free expression in the country and intimidation of the media. Just two days earlier, the offices of Sri Lanka's largest private broadcasting company were attacked in the middle of the night."

US Congressman and co-founder of the Congressional Caucus for Freedom of the Press, Adam Schiff, paid tribute to Lasantha on the Floor of the United States House of Representatives by reading excerpts of his last editorial.

"I rise today to honour, Lasantha Wickrematunge, a brave journalist who was gunned down while driving to work in the Sri Lankan capital of Colombo. Threats, attacks and murders of journalist are becoming all too common in Sri Lanka. Wickrematunge knew the dangers well, but courageously continued reporting," he said.

The British Secretary of State for Foreign and Commonwealth Affairs, David Miliband in a statement said that it was the duty of the authorities to take prompt action on the attacks on the media.

"We condemn such brazen attacks. Of particular concern was the murder, on January 8, of the Chief Editor of *The Sunday Leader* newspaper, Lasantha Wickrematunge. The Sri Lankan authorities have a duty to take prompt action to ensure that a thorough and independent investigation is carried out," Miliband said.

UN Secretary General Ban Ki-moon in a statement called on the government of Sri Lanka to ensure that those responsible for Lasantha Wickrematunge's murder were brought to book and prosecuted.

It was also fitting that in his inaugural speech in the same month as Lasantha's murder, President Obama, whose election campaign Lasantha had followed with such unbridled enthusiasm and devotion, said, "To those who cling to power through corruption and deceit and the silencing of dissent, know that you are on the wrong side of history."

In Vienna, renowned architect and artist Peter Sandbichler, inspired by Lasantha's story of sheer spunk and fortitude, erected an 8-metre monument in the form of concrete grids with abstract messages which as the day unfolded, evolved into the face of Lasantha.

The sculpture was erected on the Museum Quartier forecourt.

Meanwhile, in a bid to clear the air with the foreign media in relation to the spate of negative publicity the government had been receiving the week of the murder both locally and internationally, the President invited the members of the Foreign Correspondents Association to a dinner at Temple Trees. During the meeting, Rajapakse told the journalists it didn't make sense for the government to carry out such a murder at a time when it was enjoying unprecedented popularity.

Throwing more fuel to the political conflagration, Sri Lanka Freedom Party People's Wing Leader and former Minister Mangala Samaraweera held a joint opposition press conference where he charged that on the morning of his murder, Lasantha had received a copy of a Cabinet paper submitted by the President regarding the procurement of emergency defense and air equipment. The contents of this Cabinet document were suspicious, Samaraweera said, because there was no mention of any relevant facts such as what was to be purchased, from where it was to be purchased and the price of the equipment.

The supplier was mentioned as 'single source supplier,' and the procurement agency named was 'Lanka Logistic Technology Ltd' which

Samaraweera called the 'Rajapakse Brothers Company.' Stating that only the technical details of procured items need to be kept secret, Samaraweera told journalists that large procurements of this nature should not be carried out outside of an open tender process.

Samaraweera said Lasantha was in the process of collecting more information before he was to reveal it in *The Sunday Leader*. Lasantha also was in possession of a file, Samaraweera said, which contained details of killer squads called K-9 Group, Mahasona Group and Singha Mafia run by a US citizen in Sri Lanka. Lasantha was planning to hand this file over to the US State Secretary after President elect Barack Obama assumed duties as President," Samaraweera said.

* * *

In the days following Lasantha's murder, hundreds of tributes and statements came pouring in to media establishments, among which were the following. (Courtesy, *The Sunday Leader*)

Ven. Maduluwawe Sobitha Thero, Chief Incumbent of the Kotte Naga Vihara

The assassination of a prominent journalist has rung the death knell of democracy. Sri Lanka is no more a Dharmadveepa (land of the Dhamma); it has turned into a state of murderers.

Although we have seen continuous attacks on journalists over the past few years, the brutal assassination of Lasantha Wickrematunge in broad daylight is the severest blow the country has ever witnessed.

Those behind this cowardly act have not gunned down Wickrematunge but the country's democracy.

Catholic National Association

As a body of the Catholic laity, we are deeply concerned about the recent attacks on media institutions and media personnel as well as the general breakdown in the rule of law. Many have, even by now, expressed grave concern, disgust and anxiety about the most recent incidents such as the wanton destruction of the MTV transmission station and the brutal killing of the Editor of *The Sunday Leader*. These have sent shock-waves not only locally, but also internationally . . . .

We condemn these dastardly acts of murder, violence and intimidation in the strongest possible terms. We consider this not only as an insult to the long-standing honour and dignity of our nation that prides in a two-thousand year history, but also as a tragedy in a country that is often praised as an oasis of four of the world's greatest living religions.

It is a matter of grave urgency for the authorities to take the necessary steps to mete out justice. We reiterate that all those responsible for these despicable and inhuman acts as well as all those who are guilty of aiding and abetting such criminal activities be forthwith brought to justice irrespective of their status and position.

Duleep de Chickera, Anglican Bishop

The assassination of the Editor of *The Sunday Leader*, Lasantha Wickrematunge, in broad daylight on a public road in Colombo last morning, sent shock waves of anger, fear and desperation throughout the country. This deliberate and senseless act must be condemned by all Sri Lankans who value life and media freedom. It is part of a wider and worsening strategy to suppress and silence the media . . . .

Mr. Wickrematunge was a leading media personality, committed to investigative journalism. His assassination, in times like these when truth is deliberately distorted, is a severe blow to the responsible role the media is called upon to play in our journey towards a just, democratic culture. It is also an indication of the worsening crisis in good governance and the fast deteriorating law and order situation.

The Asian Human Rights Commission

The AHRC once more calls on the local and international community to take note of the escalation of violence in Sri Lanka and to do all it can to intervene for the purpose of saving lives.

Mr. Wickrematunge was a primary target of the Rajapakse regime and particularly the Secretary of the Ministry of Defence, Gotabaya Rajapakse. An unsuccessful attempt was made to arrest Mr. Wickrematunge which was prevented by some senior police officers who refused to arrest him and also due to strong intervention on the part of journalists who gathered at his premises . . . .

Thereafter the printing press of *The Sunday Leader*, which was situated close to a security zone was attacked and burned by a group of unidentified persons who were never arrested. It is widely believed that the group was sent by the ruling party.

Just two days earlier, about 20 unidentified attackers raided the premises of Sirasa TV and caused damage amounting to Rs. 200 million to the communications equipment. The group assaulted the staff and left a claymore mine said to weigh eight and half kilogrammes. Sirasa TV is the most important centre for the independent media in Sri Lanka. The opposition leader said that the government is responsible for the attack and that members of a military unit carried it out.

International Federation of Journalists

This brutal attack and murder of a great fighter for press freedom strikes at the heart of democracy. We welcome the President's concern, but given the history of personal attacks that Lasantha and his newspaper group have suffered at the hands of the authorities it is impossible to ignore the fact that the government bears some responsibility for creating the climate that led to this outrage.

In October last year Lasantha met with an international mission of IFJ members. At the time he was in combative action successfully mobilising public support against Sri Lankan government attempts to grab sweeping powers of cancelling broadcast licences and censorship over the content of news channels.

Lasantha was a steadfast opponent of every threat to press freedom. Even when other media kept silent, he would speak out, often as a lone voice. He showed inspiring courage and conviction to all.

Reporters Without Borders

Sri Lanka has lost one of its most talented, courageous and iconoclastic journalists. President Mahinda Rajapakse, his associates and the government media are directly to blame because they incited hatred against him and allowed an outrageous level of impunity to develop as regards violence against the press. Sri Lanka's image is badly sullied by this murder, which is an absolute scandal and must not go unpunished.

The military victories in the north against the Tamil Tiger rebels must not be seen as a green light for death squads to sow terror among government critics, including outspoken journalists. The international community must do everything possible to halt such a political vendetta.

The Sunday Leader's outspoken style and coverage of shady business deals meant that Wickrematunge was often the target of intimidation attempts and libel suits. The most recent lawsuit was brought by the President's brother, Gotabaya Rajapakse, who got a court to ban the newspaper from mentioning him for several weeks.

Lasantha Wickrematunge, who was also a lawyer, told Reporters Without Borders in an interview that his aim as a journalist was to "denounce the greed and lies of the powerful."

The Nava Sihala Urumaya

The Nava Sihala Urumaya recognises Lasantha Wickrematunge as a courageous journalist involved in investigative journalism who worked tirelessly to give the truth to the people. The whole country is aware that there have been several attempts on his life on earlier occasions as well. The assassination of veteran journalist Lasantha Wickrematunge is a deadly blow to democracy. We call on the IGP and the police force to bring to justice these hired assassins.

The High Commission of India

We are deeply shocked and saddened to learn of the demise of the well-regarded Editor of Leader Group of Publications.

This deplorable incident comes in the wake of the series of attacks on and intimidation of media organisations and personalities in Sri Lanka including the recent bombing of the studios of Maharaja TV. We hold media freedom as an essential element of any democracy and such attacks are detrimental to the idea of democratic freedom in Sri Lanka.

The Centre for Policy Alternatives

Mr. Wickrematunge was shot and seriously wounded by unknown persons while driving to work in a suburb of Colombo and was pronounced dead at around 2.15 pm by hospital authorities.

Just over 48 hours after a major arson attack against private TV broadcaster MBC / MTV Networks that destroyed its Main Control Room and studios, this rampant violence against independent media demonstrates an alarming deterioration of democracy, the rule of law, the freedom of expression and dissent.

Tellingly, Sri Lanka has been repeatedly identified as one of the world's most dangerous countries for independent journalists. This latest attack on one of Sri Lanka's best known and most senior journalists confirms fears of a planned terror campaign against critical voices, conducted with complete impunity.

The legitimacy of the war against terror rests on government respecting the norms and values of democracy and human rights, of which the tolerance of criticism is a fundamental facet. Those responsible for this egregious violence are enemies of democracy and become terrorists themselves.

Transparency International Sri Lanka

Transparency International Sri Lanka expresses deep sorrow and dismay at the assassination of Lasantha Wickrematunge, the Editor of *The Sunday Leader*. Mr. Wickrematunge was a pioneering journalist who bravely battled corruption through the media, even when his life was under threat.

In 2000 Mr. Wickrematunge's work was appreciated internationally when he was a recipient of the first ever Integrity Award from Transparency International.

The assassination of Mr. Wickrematunge is a terrifying blow against the freedom of expression in the island. Free media is a key component of a democratic state and an absolute prerequisite for good governance. Any attack on journalists and their institutions will only further erode good governance in this country, ultimately resulting in an unsafe environment for all Sri Lankans . . . .

The Editors Guild of Sri Lanka

The Editors Guild of Sri Lanka condemns the assassination of *The Sunday Leader* Editor Lasantha Wickrematunge with the severest possible terms and records its disgust at the trend in which media freedom, or what is left of it in Sri Lanka, is being trampled upon.

This incident, coming in the wake of the arson attack on the MTV/MBC station early on Tuesday morning, clearly displays a complete disregard for democracy and rule of law. We are witnessing an ongoing campaign against the dissemination of information to the citizenry and democratic dissent. An adversarial relationship between any government and the media is good for governance and Lasantha epitomised this.

It is also the inalienable right of the people to be kept informed and to decide on the choice of media. What is most disconcerting is that there is no real attempt to stop or in the least to discourage this violent campaign that has been unleashed.

The finger, therefore, would point in the direction of the government due to the inaction on its part to stem, this slide into authoritarianism that the people of this country abhor.

Sri Lanka Muslim Congress (SLMC) Leader Rauf Hakeem

The assassination of the Editor of *The Sunday Leader* is testimony to the courage and ability he had to expose corruption, bribery and mismanagement within the present regime.

Lasantha did not die in vain but for the cause of fearless reporting. He fought against corruption and bribery within the government and was strong enough to expose many controversial dealings of this government. He also fought for media freedom although he could not achieve it. His death is a great loss to the country and the opposition considers this assassination more serious than the assassination of a politician. Although we are opposition members we still did not have the courage to take on the government as Lasantha did.

Lasantha was the only person who could expose fearlessly the corruption at the highest levels of government.

We urge the Government of Sri Lanka to investigate these attacks fully and bring the perpetrators of these reprehensible attacks to justice."

The British High Commission

We condemn in the strongest possible terms the continuing acts of violence and intimidation against the media in Sri Lanka, including the attack on January 6 on the MTV headquarters and the killing of the Chief Editor of *The Sunday Leader*. We welcome the stated commitment of the government to investigate these incidents. Prompt action to hold those responsible to account is essential in creating an environment in which people from all communities in Sri Lanka can live without fear and in which progress on a political solution to end the conflict will be possible.

Journalists of Nepal

We journalists of Nepal have been rendered speechless by the killing of courageous Sri Lankan Editor Lasantha Wickrematunge on January 8. The Editor of *The Sunday Leader* has always been at the forefront of the struggle for accountability, rule of law, human rights, and healthy, peaceful politics. In the end, Editor Wickrematunge had to pay for his ethics and high principles with his life. At the moment of this cowardly slaying, we extend our condolences to colleagues at the Leader Group as well as all journalists of Sri Lanka.

We believe that they will not let the lamp of free media and democracy die even as forces bent on destruction take recourse to the tools of violence and assassination. Lasantha Wickrematunge was a trailblazer for journalists all over South Asia, and his absence shall forever remind us of the value of free and fearless journalism in the protection of democracy.

V. Anandasangaree, President of the Tamil United Liberation Front, (TULF)

I am shocked and greatly grieved at the brutal killing of Mr. Lasantha Wickrematunge, a very popular and courageous journalist. He had been a long-standing friend of mine. I have attended a number of seminars along with him and his presentations had been very remarkable. On one occasion we spent more than a week together at a workshop on Conflict Resolution held in Austria.

This type of brutal murders are now on the increase. Where are we heading to? Is it not the responsibility of all of us, as citizens of this country, to help to track down the culprits responsible for this cowardly act? It is a shame on all of us, if the culprits are not arrested immediately and brought before the court of law and punished.

The Board of Directors of the Sri Lanka Press Institute

It is well known that the late Wickrematunge had an adversarial relationship with both the incumbent government as well as its predecessor. This killing has taken place just two days after the armed attack on the MTV/MBC television station at Depanama.

Inaction over previous such incidents has created a public perception that both these attacks may have involved a state agency and it is incumbent on the President and the government to dispel such suspicion by a thorough and meticulous investigation. No suspects have been arrested over recent attacks on media personalities including Keith Noyahr, Deputy Editor of *The Nation*, and Namal Perera of the Sri Lanka Press Institute.

The transparent investigation and speedy arrest of suspects is most essential in the interest of all concerned. The directors of the SLPI urge the government to utilise all resources at its command to bring the killers to justice.

Politburo of Janatha Vimukthi Peramuna

This government is trying to introduce Marcos style governance to Sri Lanka and if it is so, all the patriotic movements in the country are ready to defeat it. The brutal assassination of *The Sunday Leader* Editor, Lasantha

Wickrematunge is highly regrettable and although the JVP too is against the stance of some media personalities, we believe in handling the situation in a democratic manner.

Leader of the Democratic People's Front

I do not look at Lasantha Wickrematunge as an individual alone. Apart from being an individual, he is an institution. He was a symbol of free media in the country. The regime has assassinated a person who raised his voice for the benefit of the free media. This cannot be taken as an isolated incident where media persons and institutions have been targeted.

The Asia Media Forum

The brutal attacks on independent media in Sri Lanka, which resulted in the strafing of an independent TV station complex and the execution-style murder of veteran journalist Lasantha Wickrematunge, once more casts doubt on the state of press freedom in this island nation. For years now, the Sri Lankan media have been the victims of threats and other forms of violence and from the looks of it, the situation is at its worst.

The World Bank

Violence against media has a profoundly negative impact on the ability of the media to fulfill its core watchdog function and to carry out its role as a medium of accountability and reflection of the citizen's voice. The World Bank urges the Government of Sri Lanka to hold full and transparent investigations into incidents of violence against the media.

Prayathna People's Movement

This is the second cruel attack on the media within 72 hours. The entire civil society is shocked by this sad news.

This is not the first time *The Sunday Leader* has been attacked. Earlier, Mr. Wickrematunge was threatened and the printing press burnt. Two days ago we pointed out that a fascist shadow is being spread all over the country. With this attack, this has been well proved. It is now clear that a powerful group which does not tolerate any dissenting views operates in the country.

Mr. Wickrematunge is one of the few journalists who revealed corruption and malpractice in the country. He always stood for media freedom. Media freedom is fundamental in any democracy. The attack on Wickrematunge clearly demonstrates that there is a threat to journalists.

Rohantha Athukorala, Director Economic Affairs, Government Peace Secretariat

After having worked for over 15 years in global companies I decided to serve the country whilst reading for the doctorate but, the recent attack on MBC/MTV and now the killing of *The Sunday Leader* Editor de-motivates people like us who want to work for the betterment of the country. The killers/offenders must be brought to justice immediately so that professionals from the private sector will want to voluntarily come and serve the nation and bring peace to this beautiful country of ours.

Robert Wood, Acting Spokesman, The United States State Department

The serious reports of media attacks in Sri Lanka are disturbing indicators of the deteriorating atmosphere for media independence in Sri Lanka.

A free and independent media is vital to ensuring the health and continuation of any democracy. We call on the Government of Sri Lanka to protect all of its citizens by enforcing law and order, preventing intimidation of the media, and by conducting swift, full, and credible investigations into attacks on journalists, and other civilians.

Benita Ferrero-Waldner, European Commissioner for External Relations and European Neighbourhood Policy

I was deeply shocked to learn about today's assassination of Lasantha Wickrematunge, the chief Editor of Sri Lanka's *Sunday Leader* newspaper. This attack comes just two days after a privately-owned television station was attacked and set on fire and follows several incidents of harassment and threats to journalists in Sri Lanka that have occurred over recent months. Our concerns about the freedom of the media, already under severe pressure from assaults and intimidation, have been exacerbated by the killing of Lasantha Wickrematunge.

As in other countries where the safety and independence of people working in the media are under threat, I express my admiration at the willingness of Sri Lankan journalists to continue their work in the face of risks like these.

I call upon the government to put in place protection mechanisms to ensure the safety of journalists in Sri Lanka. It is essential that citizens continue to benefit from media providing free and accurate reporting on national affairs.

I urge the Sri Lankan authorities to take all necessary steps to bring the perpetrators to justice, as there can be no impunity for these terrible crimes.

The National Peace Council

Barely three days after the MTV television station was bombed and razed by an armed group, armed assassins have claimed the life of one of Sri Lanka's foremost journalists, Lasantha Wickrematunge. The killing of this courageous journalist will add to the sense of intimidation and fear in the media, which has already suffered several such attacks and killings of media persons.

As Editor of *The Sunday Leader*, Lasantha Wickrematunge was fearless in exposing political weaknesses and corruption in the government and society in general, and the impunity that accompanies them. He also advocated a negotiated political solution to the ethnic conflict and highlighted the cost of the war which the government is undertaking. Although an individual, he was also the creator and leader of a media institution and his assassination can be construed as a death blow to media freedom to take up the issues he did.

Lasantha Wickrematunge will long be remembered by those who believe in the role of the media to create a politically literate society which alone can protect democracy. The National Peace Council condemns his assassination and mourns his loss. We grieve with his family, colleagues and friends and trust that his sacrifice would mark an end to a culture of impunity that seems to be overtaking us.

Amnesty International

"Amnesty International urges the Government of Sri Lanka to publicly condemn this as well as other attacks on the media and launch an independent investigation. To date, Amnesty International is unaware of any investigation that has led to the arrest and prosecution of those believed responsible for the killing of journalists and other media workers. The lack of any thorough investigations into killings means that these kinds of attacks can continue with impunity.

The Sunday Leader has carried a number of articles exposing political interference and corruption in privatisation deals. *The Sunday Leader* commentators have also drawn attention to human rights abuses in the context of intensified fighting.

This is not the first time that *The Sunday Leader* and its staff have come under attack: in 2007, the printing presses at Leader Group of Publications were attacked by 10 armed men who threatened employees and set fire to some of the equipment and the newspaper that had just been printed. In 2006, Lasantha Wickrematunge was threatened with arrest under anti-terrorist laws over a story criticising the President . . .

Ranjan Wijeratne Foundation

It is with horror and disgust that we learnt of the murder of your Chief Editor Mr. Lasantha Wickrematunge at the hands of a vile assassin. Please accept our deepest sympathies on this sad occasion.

Whilst we do have a different opinion of the attitude towards the war and its operation to the views expressed by your newspaper, in the past he has allowed our critical comments to be published. We know that he encouraged freedom of speech and media rights. It is because of this stance that he paid a heavy price.

We hope that despite this setback you will continue. We fully support media freedom but we will challenge you if it is necessary but we will do so with a pen, NOT with a gun.

World for Humanity

World for Humanity expresses its deepest sympathies on the demise of the fearless Editor-in-Chief of *The Sunday Leader*, Lasantha Wickrematunge who was gunned down for working to preserve democracy in Sri Lanka. We cannot believe this. Is this how democracy and media freedom is practised in Sri Lanka? Whatever is done, democracy cannot be destroyed in Sri Lanka.

* * *

CHAPTER TWELVE
The Murder Inquiry That Isn't

> *"Foolish men imagine that because judgment for an evil thing is delayed, there is no justice; but only accident here below. Judgment for an evil thing is many times delayed some day or two, some century or two, but it is sure as life, it is sure as death."*—Thomas Carlyle, writer, essayist, historian.

DESPITE the government and no less a person than the President of the country himself promising a speedy and thorough investigation into the murder of Lasantha Wickrematunge, it was evident from the outset that there was no hope of a credible investigation ever taking place.

Two weeks into the assassination, despite four teams of police officers, both from the Mirihana and Mt. Lavinia Police Stations having been assigned to the case by the Inspector General of Police, they admitted that no significant leads had been received.

Every small lead that emerged thereafter eventuated into nothing but a damp squib, or at best, a red-herring.

The first 'break' in the case came three weeks after the savage killing. On January 27 President Mahinda Rajapakse told newspaper editors there would be a major breakthrough in the police investigation into the murder. On January 29 police announced that two persons had been arrested in connection with the theft of Lasantha's mobile phone. Both were trishaw drivers; one of them was Sugath Perera, a heroin addict and the man charged with stealing the phone at Kalubowila Hospital on the day Lasantha was attacked, and the other, H. Sanjeewa Pushpakumara, the man who had purchased it from him for a sum of Rs. 4,000.

While Pushpakumara was released, Sugath Perera was further detained. He was later absolved of any involvement in the killing but a fresh case relating to theft and criminal possession of stolen goods was filed against him.

A few days after the arrests, police announced they had found an abandoned motorcycle lying in a ditch which they believed may have been used in the Editor's murder. Nothing further was forthcoming on this development.

According to phone records obtained from the Dialog phone company, 33 calls were recorded on Lasantha's mobile phone between 6.45 am and

10.31 am on January 8—the day of the murder. Of these, Lasantha received 15 calls and made 18.

Police spokesperson SSP Ranjith Gunasekera told journalists they were awaiting court approval to investigate the telephone calls Lasantha had made and received moments before he was attacked and hoped these would lead to some arrests. On Court orders, several telephone companies released the names of the people whose numbers showed up on phone records of Lasantha's mobile on the day of the murder. Acting on this, police interviewed several persons Lasantha had spoken to, hoping he may have passed on to them details of the killers. However no significant leads were made.

On November 29, 2009, Former Army Commander General Sarath Fonseka announced his candidacy in the Presidential Election due to be held on January 26, 2010. General Fonseka was the joint opposition candidate running against President Rajapakse.

When Fonseka emerged as the main opposition contender for the presidency, the Rajapakses fell over themselves in their haste to pin the murder squarely on Fonseka.

Sarath Fonseka responded, "Let them show one shred of evidence that I was involved in or responsible for the killing of Lasantha and I am prepared to face any inquiry."

In November 2009, Fonseka, in his capacity as the opposition's common presidential candidate, addressed lawyers at an event organised by the National Lawyers Association honouring members including Lasantha who had died that year. In his speech, Fonseka said the government was now flinging their dirt on him by trying to implicate him in Lasantha's murder. He insisted that despite some journalists having their own personal perspectives on the war which were at odds with those of the armed forces, he had never entertained an idea of harming a journalist.

Later, Fonseka gave journalists a classic photo opportunity by garlanding a picture of the slain Editor.

A few weeks later *The Sunday Leader* ran a story in its December 13, 2009, issue titled "Gota ordered them to be shot—General Sarath Fonseka." Written by its new Editor Frederica Jansz, the story was based on what General Fonseka told Frederica following an interview he had given a *Leader* journalist. The story in *The Sunday Leader* attributed a statement to General Fonseka that during the final days of the war, Defence Secretary Gotabaya Rajapakse issued an order that LTTE leaders who were surrendering with white flags be shot. The story had massive repercussions and ended with General Fonseka being prosecuted and eventually handed a three year prison sentence after a very public trial.

A few days after the story was published in the *Leader* Lasantha's brother Lal received a call from President Rajapakse. With more than a hint of sarcasm in his voice, the President thanked Lal for running the story. "Now our Army personnel can't even go overseas because they have been labelled as soldiers who shoot people that surrender," the President said.

Rajapakse then made reference to General Fonseka garlanding a picture of Lasantha the previous month. 'It's good that he worshipped Lasantha's picture and atoned for his sins (*pau samadam kala*)," the President said.

* * *

Ten months after investigations had commenced into Lasantha's murder, the case was transferred to the Criminal Investigation Department (CID). From here, it was handed over to the Terrorism Investigation Department (TID).

In February 2010, The TID arrested 17 soldiers from the Army's Military Intelligence Unit headed by a Fonseka loyalist. The 17 were later narrowed down to seven suspects. All were subsequently released. It was whispered at the time that they were released because they could incriminate senior members of the government.

One Brigadier Duminda Keppetivalana, a former aide of Sarath Fonseka who at the time was in charge of security in Colombo, was also arrested on charges of conspiring to overthrow the government and alleged involvement in the assassination of Lasantha. In response to the arrest, in an interview with *The Sunday Leader* General Fonseka said Brigadier Keppetivalana was being forced to say he had planned the murder following his (Fonseka's) orders. The Brigadier was later released on bail.

When police recorded a statement from Lal Wickrematunge, a former CID officer himself, he advised them to check the electronic route that Lasantha's phone had taken on the day of the murder. Police conducted investigations and the numbers of five mobile phones which matched the electronic route of Lasantha's phone on the day he was murdered and traversed the exact distance Lasantha did, emerged. According to police the phones had, on January 8, 2009, passed through 11 cellular phone towers beginning in Nugegoda and ending in Attidiya. The phones had not been used prior to January 8.

One of the phones, police said, had been used to control the entire operation. The five mobile phones were found to have communicated regularly with each other on the day of the murder. One of the five phone numbers indicated on the mobile path showed a call having been made from the very spot Lasantha was attacked in Bakery Junction, Ratmalana. Only one call was made after the assassination and that was a call between two of the phones. The phones were never used thereafter.

Police discovered that the SIM cards used to operate the five telephones were purchased in the name of one Pitchai Jesudasan, a 40-year-old garage owner from Magastota Estate in the hills of Nuwara Eliya. TID sleuths swooped down on his humble home in the dead of night, arrested him and later interrogated him at the Colombo Secretariat Building. He was later transferred to Boossa Camp and thereafter to Welikada Magazine Prison.

Jesudasan in his defence said he had lost his ID card and ventured that someone could have used his ID card to purchase the SIM cards in question. Jesudasan also said he had from time to time joined a soldier from the Army's Sinha Regiment by the name of Kandegedera Priyawansa for a drink. Priyawansa was later arrested by police on suspicion that he had used Jesudasan's ID card to purchase the SIM cards. At the time, Priyawansa was a member of the Army's Military Intelligence Directorate.

Jesudasan had on August 23, 2008, reported the loss of his National ID to the Grama Sevaka of Ruwan Eliya, S. M. P. S. Samarakoon.

According to the report presented to the Magistrate by the Officer-In-Charge of the Terrorism Investigation Division, Chief Inspector Prasanna De Alwis, "During further investigations conducted by this Division in relation to the suspects, information has been received that the suspects were involved in acts that embarrassed the government, conspiring to overthrow the lawfully established government, bringing disrepute to the government and assassinating Editor in Chief of The Sunday Leader newspaper Lasantha Wickrematunge. Further investigations are being conducted in respect to this."

On May 12, 2010, Kandegedara Priyawansa dropped a bombshell when he revealed to the Mount Lavinia Magistrate that he had been instructed by the Officer-in-Charge of the TID to claim that General Sarath Fonseka was involved in the killing of the Editor. Priyawansa charged in open court that in exchange for making the false allegation, he had been promised he would be made a state witness and sent overseas on employment. Priyawansa's lawyer Upul Wickremaratne made a request that the Magistrate record a statement from his client. This was later done in the Magistrate's official chambers in a process which took three hours.

TID Sub Inspector A. E. Adhikari rejected the statement made by Priyawansa who was later enlarged on bail after he made an application in the High Court.

So half-hearted was the entire murder inquiry that two years went by before the Terrorist Investigation Department made an application for a handwriting sample from Priyawansa so it could be matched to the writing on the SIM card application form. The handwriting report is yet to be submitted to court.

In another twist to this convoluted state of affairs, Jesudasan who had been in the Welikada prison, suddenly died while still in custody.

Jesudasan had been taken to the Mt. Lavinia Magistrate court for the Wickrematunge murder trial on October 13, 2011 where he collapsed following a sudden fit. Although the Magistrate instructed the prison guards to have him admitted to hospital without delay, Jesudasan was instead taken back to the prison and later admitted to the prisons hospital. When his condition worsened, he was transferred to the General Hospital.

According to hospital sources, Jesudasan died of a blood clot in the brain. The Coroner returned an open verdict on his death. Despite this, no further investigations were carried out.

Meanwhile, the family of Jesudasan was unaware of what had become of him since he was taken away one night in February 2010. They were in a helpless state, uncertain of where or whom to turn to until a lawyer from Colombo, Kaushalya Wijesinghe, who had read their story in the newspaper, decided to help the family.

Jesudasan's brother Albert told *The Sunday Leader* that the police informed them Jesudasan had bought five SIM cards and given them to Wickrematunge's killers. Albert and the rest of the family were perplexed; to their understanding, Jesudasan was a kind man who would not even harm a fly.

Albert said at first they didn't know who the victim of the murder was because they were not educated people and were not familiar with Wickrematunge's work. He asked *The Sunday Leader* journalist to convey their sympathies to the family of the slain editor and to tell them their brother was not involved in the killing.

Albert also said Jesudasan had lost his National Identity Card and had obtained a letter from the Grama Sevaka to have a new one issued. He had then made several trips to the police station but his statement had not been recorded and so he was unable to apply for a new ID card.

Jesudasan's family lamented that even the Grama Sevaka's letter had been taken away by the police and now they did not have a document to prove that Jesudasan had lost his ID card and had been trying to obtain a new one.

Prior to all this, in March 2009, Lasantha's brother Lal, in a newspaper article, disclosed details of an encounter he had had with a man who claimed to have information on the murder. About a month and a half after the murder, Lal said a small-made, dishevelled man turned up at his office and related an amazing story explaining how Lasantha was killed and who was behind it. The man, who Lal referred to as "Mr. X" said he had been released from Welikada Prison on an amnesty granted to prisoners on Independence Day in 2009. In prison he said, he heard an inmate convicted of murder bragging about how he had been given a contract to kill someone and details of how the operation had been conducted. The "hit," the man said had been on someone called Lasantha and a sharp instrument had been used to carry out the murder.

The stranger told Lal a politician had given the contract to kill Lasantha to one Kalu Thushara who used a prisoner by the name of Lakshman Kumara to carry out the contract even though Lakshman Kumara was in jail. "The weapon used in the murder he said was sourced from Vavuniya and those who transported the weapon stayed with a ruling party provincial councillor at Anuradhapura. A three wheeler was used to transport the weapon concealed in a cavity made for transportation of drugs," Lal said.

Lal wrote, "The three wheel vehicle belonged to an employee at the Transport Board in Ambalantota. The motor cycles used for this operation were sourced by one Indika from Piliyandala.

"It was Thusitha, an ex army person, who rode one bike to commit this murder. Chatura of Kottawa, Ashan from Kaluaggala and Saman also rode bikes while Bernard of Pannipitiya drove the three-wheeler.

"The 'hit' was monitored by Lakshman Kumara from within the prison by using cellular no 07163 . . . which was later confiscated by Jailor Silva on a search conducted within the prison. He also used cellular no 0715727814 and his brother Chaminda used cellular no 0725672771.

"The Minister who master-minded the operation visited Lakshman Kumara in prison that night in a special room and gave him biriyani and Rs. 1.8 million for a job well done."

Lal decided to make a statement on what he was told by this visitor, to one arm investigating the murder case. The story was dismissed.

A year after Lasantha's murder, on January 24, 2010, political analyst, cartoonist—and father of two—Prageeth Ekneligoda disappeared.

In December of that year, Lal received a telephone call from the President's Secretary Gamini Senerath who intimated that the President wished to meet him with *The Sunday Leader* Editor Frederica Jansz. The duo then went to President's House where they were served chicken soup and the President, in a very relaxed mood, showed them around upstairs pointing out pictures hanging on the walls. The President told them how some of these pictures had been stolen. "It wasn't done during Chandrika Kumaratunga's time but before that," he told Lal and Frederica.

Later the President showed the duo his shrine room and remarked in passing that he prayed there every day. He then moved on to the subject of Lasantha's murder and said in Sinhala, "*Sarath Fonseka thamai meka karey.*"(It is Sarath Fonseka that did this). Lal then inquired why if that was the case, Fonseka had not been charged to which the President made some vague reply about a lack of evidence.

Two years after Lasantha's murder, Reporters Without Borders released a statement which said, "Reporters Without Borders is appalled by the fact that the Sri Lankan government is doing nothing to solve this murder and in fact is clearly preventing the truth from coming to light. By blocking the investigation and by fostering a climate of impunity and indifference, the government has become an accomplice."

Four years after the assassination, the Lasantha Wickrematunge murder case is still continuing. Whether justice will ever be done, just like it has not in so many other attacks, killings and disappearances of journalists, is anybody's guess. All we have seen thus far in this case is police hogwash and political game-playing.

One cannot be faulted for believing then that a conspiracy is well in place to hush-up the murder. One cannot also fault those who view the apathy in prosecuting this case as proof of complicity in the murder. To those that follow this line of reasoning, the answer lies in a classic Sinhala adage:

Horagey Ammagen pena ahanawa wagey.

The Big Stories

> *"News is what somebody, somewhere wants to suppress; all the rest is advertising."*—Lord Northcliffe, British newspaper magnate

DURING his 15-year tenure as Editor-In-Chief of *The Sunday Leader* from June 1994 to January 2009, Lasantha published a large number of stories that had a monumental impact on the government and the people of Sri Lanka.

The newspaper bagged dozens of scoops and investigated hundreds of cases of corruption and graft. It delved into dubious tender awards made outside of tender procedure or without cabinet approval, arms procurements steeped in controversy and illegal favours granted to friends and family of those in high places. The stories were always substantiated with relevant documentation, corroborative evidence, letters and photographs.

Among the exhaustive stories that sometimes ran into several weeks was the AirLanka (SriLankan Airlines) deal with Emirates, the extension of the Shell monopoly, the Prima deal, the Colombo Port extension project with Peninsular and Orient Navigation Co. Ltd (P&O), the Southern Expressway project, the importing of 44 super-luxury bullet proof vehicles outside tender and without cabinet approval, stories on kickbacks received on arms procurements and hundreds of other investigations that brought to light corruption in high places. The story on the Evans fiasco where the Sri Lankan government had to fork out 200 million rupees to Evans International as a face-saving measure after Evans, the winning bidder on the Colombo Fort re-building program was prevented from carrying on with the project, won its writer, editor Lasantha Wickrematunge (writing under the pseudonym Suranimala) the Editors Guild award for 'Scoop of The Year.'

The *Leader* also wrote extensively on the Presidential Security Division in the 90s which was allegedly functioning as a political hit squad for the ruling People's Alliance where even underworld thugs were allowed to run amok with impunity.

The newspaper also conducted extensive investigations into the scandalous transactions in several privatisation deals.

Following are details of eight investigations published in *The Sunday Leader* during Lasantha Wickrematunge's stewardship as Editor-in-Chief.

The locomotive deal

In 1997, *The Sunday Leader* published details of how a cabinet-appointed sub-committee awarded the tender for purchasing 10 locomotives for Sri Lanka Railways to a French company, GEC Alsthom, which was among a shortlist of bidders. The French locomotives were fitted with ship engines and had never been tested on rail tracks in a tropical country. The engines could not even be tested in France, as the French had a different gauge of rail track to Sri Lanka. Despite this, and the warnings of the Cabinet Appointed Tender Board and the Technical Evaluation Committee, and the fact that GEC Alsthom quoted Rs. 500 million more than the other bidders, four ministers sitting on the cabinet sub-committee decided GEC Alsthom was the most suitable bidder.

The other two bidders, General Motors and Samsung, insisted their offers fully complied with the operating requirements of the tender specification. They also pointed out that their offers were cheaper and came with a massive saving on spare parts. Tender clause 4.8.3 specified that the wheel base should not be greater than 10 ft 6" and on this basis the Presidential Additional Secretary, going against a decision by the Finance Ministry Secretary and Transport Ministry Secretary recommended GEC Alsthom over Samsung, Korea and General Motors, Canada, both of which had a 3.5" or 2.8% deviation on wheel base.

The story written by Frederica Jansz and published over several weeks in *The Sunday Leader* in 1997 created huge public interest.

After their arrival in 2000, three of the locomotives had to undergo repairs since the fuel tanks were found to be completely corroded. Various modifications were also effected in order to make the engines more compatible to local rail tracks. Sri Lanka Railways also had to replace railway sleepers at various points on the upcountry line to strengthen the tracks.

In 2001, the General Manager for Railways was forced to appoint a special committee to investigate the shortcomings reported by railway engineers who complained that the French locomotives could not be used upcountry beyond Nawalapitiya and were stalling continuously on their runs to Galle and Matara in the southern coast.

The report stated that the wheel base specification of 10 ft 6" stipulated in the original tender document was arrived at without any calculation and was not based on any scientific or technical study.

The Navy Sonar Scandal

In June 2008, *The Sunday Leader* revealed details of a questionable tender procedure with regard to a Sri Lanka Navy tender for the provision and installation of four underwater sonar detection systems in the harbours of Sri Lanka. An official attached to the British High Commission was promoting QinetiQ, a British company that was not a state trading organisation registered with the British government and had been rejected by the Technical Evaluation Committee (TEC) in 2004 for failing to meet the stipulated tender conditions.

The systems on offer by QinetiQ had been rejected by the US Navy after trials in Rhode Island and in Singapore.

In a follow-up to the sonar investigation, *The Sunday Leader* in its issue of August 24, 2008, in a detailed, full-page investigation wrote how months of endless bickering and grandstanding between the Ports Authority and the Sri Lanka Navy had led to the security of Sri Lanka's harbours and ports being jeopardised, and a phenomenal amount of money wasted by the government.

Excerpts of the article: "*The Sunday Leader* first broke the story of the shadiness in the sonar deal after the MV Invincible was sunk in Trincomalee Harbour. It was after this event that we discovered the Navy's move to buy a product more than twice the price of its competitor, without having tested it in its installation environment."

The two bidders were Qinetiq and Oceanscan. Qinetiq failed to install their system out at sea, and was granted permission by the Technical Evaluation Committee (TEC) to perform their trials inside the harbor. Oceanscan initially refused to modify its tests to suit the failings of a competitor. The company cited the specifications given in Annex B of the 'Navy Sonar System Tender (revised)' which did not call for trials inside the harbour.

The exhaustive investigation concluded, "What is ridiculous is that the CID has focused its attention on why the Ports Authority signed a Rs. 1 million rent contract, and not on how the Navy Commander asserted total control over a tender process and lied about the credentials of one bidder in order to award the contract to one party for Rs 200 million.

" . . . . The rest is mostly history. *The Sunday Leader* has already reported on how the first Qinetiq sonar head arrived and was 'operating' in Colombo harbour with a flaw so serious that the Navy Commander himself requested that we do not print details of the flaw out of national security considerations.

"The Navy Commander also lied, misquoting the British Defence Attach, Lt. Col. Anton Gash, as having told him that he has "never heard of Oceanscan," and was advocating Qinetiq on behalf of the British government. Lt. Col. Gash at that time told *The Sunday Leader* that the British government would equally support both parties . . . .

"Instead of running a 'witch hunt' against journalists who supposedly jeopardise national security with their articles revealing bumbling and incompetence within government ranks, the President and two of his brothers now have a perfect opportunity to see for themselves the consequences of letting their puppets and stooges run amok in the military and state institutions, and do something about it, in the name of national security."

Cricket Board saga

In the latter part of 2003, *The Sunday Leader* published details of how the Chairman of the Board of Control for Cricket in Sri Lanka (BCCSL) and Chairman, Sri Lanka Telecom (SLT) allegedly had links to certain underworld elements and allegedly financed, using cricket board funds, one such underworld figure, Dhammika Amarasinghe's visit to England in 1999 under a false identity and passport to see the World Cup Cricket matches.

In the October 5 issue of *The Sunday Leader,* journalist Frederica Jansz wrote that the BCCSL Chairman had done so "while aiding and abetting Dhammika to use a forged passport which Dhammika had secured from the Immigration and Emigration Department by using the name of Bada Mahinda's younger brother, Buddhika Priyashantha Godage.

When the BCCSL Chairman was consequently charged under the Immigration and Emigration Act as a direct result of the *Sunday Leader* revelations, the editor of *The Sunday Leader* Lasantha Wickrematunge was called in as a witness and gave evidence in court.

The case took a dramatic turn when the first accused, Dhammika Amarasinghe, was shot dead while being produced for a non-summary inquiry in Hulftsdorp in January 2004.

Waters Edge

This story revolved around an ambitious Mass Rapid Transit System (MRT) project handed over in an unsolicited proposal to an Indian company – NEB Rapid Infrastructure Projects Pvt Limited of Bangalore, India – by the government of Sri Lanka. The MRT project involved the establishment of a 22 km metro rail system beginning in Battaramulla and extending to Ratmalana via Pettah. According to the exposure in the *Sunday Leader*, the company had also been gifted on June 22, 2007, even before being officially valued, two and a half acres of state land near Water's Edge in Battaramulla, worth more than Rs.900 million, to construct a massive commercial complex.

According to the story, more controversial was the fact that a VVIP's son was allegedly involved in the project through his friends. Soil tests for the MRT project were carried out before even approvals were received from the local authorities.

Mihin Lanka

In a series of investigations into the launch of the controversial airline Mihin Lanka, *The Sunday Leader* exposed how the state-funded budget airline 'was not only an unaffordable extravagance and a political embarrassment but also one that raised serious questions about passenger safety,' and was initiated without cabinet approval or the required approval from the Civil Aviation Authority prior to the launch. *The Sunday Leader* carried a series of damning exposures on the huge drain Mihin inflicted on the public purse and questioned the legality behind the allocation of capital to the airline.

The newspaper published details of how the Treasury doled out to Mihin, Rs. 500 million as partial equity. Lankaputhra Development Bank, at the time headed by the father of Mihin CEO, invested a sum of Rs. 300 million as redeemable preference shares with an annual interest coupon of 15% payable by Mihin.

The total cost of the airline, which according to the *Leader* story had turned into a 'family and friends' airline transporting the Rajapakses and their retinues on overseas trips, amounted to US$ 36.16 billion, double the country's foreign debt at the time.

Despite the unprecedented State assistance, Mihin Lanka, it was reported in *The Sunday Leader*, incurred losses amounting to Rs. 8-9 million per day.

Diyawanna Golf Course Project

A *Sunday Leader* investigation unearthed Urban Development Authority (UDA) documents which revealed that a close friend of a VVIP was involved in the golf course project at Battaramulla. This was despite the fact that he was not a director or shareholder of the investor company.

One full page investigation on the project said, "While we have no objection to state land being alienated in a transparent manner to genuine investors, it is needless to say, a totally unacceptable and corrupt practice to alienate land to personal friends so that they could in turn sell it to genuine investors at a huge premium. As has been in this case."

Evidence later surfaced that this same friend was also involved in the Colombo-Katunayake expressway project.

Colombo-Katunayake Expressway

This 10billion project was steeped in controversy after the tender to build a 25 kilometer expressway from Colombo to Katunayake was awarded to a bidder who was disqualified during the initial tender evaluation stage. The article in *The Sunday Leader* dated November 18, 2001 by Frederica Jansz said, "A mega project, which has been estimated at a cost of Rs. 10 billion has been handed over to a bidder who was disqualified during the initial tender evaluation stage on the basis that the company failed to score a required 50% out of 100 marks for technical and management aspects. Daewoo-Keangnam-Korea-Joint Venture despite having failed to comply with requirements of the tender were later . . . awarded the multi billion rupee tender."

The Sunday Leader carried several in-depth exposes' on how high-powered interference led to this award being made.

Southern Expressway

The story highlighted how a disqualified tender application to construct a section of the Southern Expressway funded by the Asian Development Bank, was made viable after 'commissions' amounting to millions of rupees allegedly passed hands.

"Despite failing to score an overall minimum of 60 points in order to pre-qualify and make a bid for the project, Kumagai Gumi Co. Ltd, which scored only 54 points, was allowed to make the bid together with two other contenders who had passed and secured the necessary points to make a bid. Not only were Kumagai allowed to make a bid – their price was accepted and they were passed for recommendation to a Cabinet Appointed Tender Board by the Technical Evaluation Committee.

"The Technical Evaluation Committee discovered that the last balance sheet dated March 31, 2000 showed the company had a negative financial liability which exceeded the company's current assets. Despite all concerns however, Kumagai was allowed to make a bid, which was accepted.

"*The Sunday Leader* investigation revealed that Kumagai was allowed to make an alternative bid as well in order to make sure that on the surface of the matter at least, it would appear that their bid was the lowest.

"This is how they fixed their bid in connivance with government officials including members of the Road Development Authority (RDA). They made two financial offers. One is for Rs. 12,545,531,250. The second is for Rs. 12,491,206,137.90. Of these two offers, Kumagai have further offered a discount of Rs. 1,899,000,250 on the first offer and a discount of Rs. 1,900,661,137.90 on the second offer.

"The other two shortlisted tenderers have made the following bids. Hyundai Engineering and Construction Co. Ltd., has proposed a bid of Rs. 13,360,342,516.69. China State Nopawong-Civil Joint Venture has in fact made the lowest bid of Rs. 11,669,111,660 with a discounted offer from this amount, amounting to Rs. 10,881,401,660.

"It does not take a mathematician to subtract the second discounted offer (of Rs. 1,900,661,137.90) made by Kumagai against the company's second bid for Rs. 12, 491,206,137.90. After making the necessary subtraction, Kumagai's second offer is Rs. 291 million cheaper than China State Nopawong.

"This is because both China State Nopawong and Hyundai Engineering and Construction Ltd., were not 'in' on the 'deal' as it were, and made only one bid with a discounted offer unlike Kumagai who was allowed to make two bids.

"Meanwhile, in this instance too, Daewoo Consortium in a joint venture with Hanjung was among the four shortlisted bidders who were evaluated at the pre-qualification stage by TEC. The joint venture had to later opt out of the process when Daewoo had been forced to admit that the company was facing a financial crisis and was unable to provide a credible allowance of accounts for 1999-2000.

"It is this group of companies that previously together with a joint venture of Keangnam had already been awarded a multi billion rupee tender by the government to construct the Colombo-Katunayake expressway.

"During the evaluation process of the above tender, *The Sunday Leader* has proof that Daewoo-Keangnam were on that occasion too disqualified by TEC, on conditions of bankruptcy and inadequate technical capabilities. However, the joint venture company was later asked to re-bid when a VVIP stepped in and insisted they be allowed to re-negotiate their proposal. The final result was that TEC was forced to recommend Daewoo-Keangnam to the CATB and the award was duly made."

* * *

Awards

UNESCO/Guillermo Cano World Press Freedom Prize 2009

On April 7, 2009, Lasantha Wickrematunge was posthumously awarded the UNESCO/Guillermo World Press Freedom prize on behalf of the Southeast Asian Press Alliance (SEAPA).

"In a country where journalists are routinely assassinated by various vested interests, Lasantha always knew that his life was in danger. And though a trained lawyer, he chose to be a journalist above all, finding in its daily struggles, the nobility and need of being one with Sri Lanka's people," SEAPA said.

Joe Thloloe, President of the Jury and Press Ombudsman of the Press Council of South Africa said, "Jury members were moved to an almost unanimous choice by a man who was clearly conscious of the dangers he faced but nevertheless chose to speak out, even beyond his grave. Lasantha Wickrematunge continues to inspire journalists around the world."

The Director-General of UNESCO, Koïchiro Matsuura, stated, "In awarding the 2009 World Press Freedom Prize to a committed journalist who opposed war, UNESCO, along with media professionals from all over the world, recognises the important role that freedom of expression can play in fostering mutual understanding and reconciliation, the theme of this year's World Press Freedom Day celebration."

Harvard award

On 17 November 2009, Lasantha Wickrematunge was posthumously awarded the Nieman Foundation for Journalism at Harvard presented by the Louis M. Lyons Award for Conscience and Integrity in Journalism. The award was shared with journalists of Afghanistan.

National Press Club Press Freedom Award

Lasantha Wickrematunge and David S. Rohde were awarded the National Press Club's 2009 John Aubuchon Press Freedom Awards. The awards are bestowed on one international journalist and one American journalist who embody the principles of a free press.

James Cameron Award

Lasantha Wickrematunge was posthumously honoured with a special James Cameron Award in 2009. The James Cameron award is bestowed in memory of the renowned foreign correspondent and author, James Cameron, who died in 1985. In 2009 the *Guardian*'s Gary Younge won the James Cameron prize for his on-the-ground reporting during the run-up to and aftermath of the election of Barack Obama. That year, a special posthumous award was made to Wickrematunge in recognition of his work.

Guardian Award

In April 2009 Lasantha Wickrematunge was conferred the Guardian Award at the 2009 Freedom of Expression Journalism Awards held in London.

Speaking at the event, British presenter of current affairs, political commentator and writer, Jonathan Dimbleby said, 'Freedom of expression helps to define our essence as human beings and citizens. Everywhere this right is under growing threat. The Index on Censorship Freedom of Expression Awards are a chance to celebrate those who, against all odds, have made distinguished contributions to this vital cause – to protect and enhance liberty in Britain and around the world.'

Asia Media Forum Award

Lasantha Wickrematunge was conferred the first Asia Media Forum Award for Press Freedom at a ceremony held in Bangkok, Thailand in March 2009. The award read: "Mr. Lasantha Wickrematunge, a brave Asian journalist from Sri Lanka, for sacrificing his life for the freedom of the press."

The Sepala Gunasena Award for Defending Press Freedom of Sri Lanka

In 2009, the Sri Lanka Press Institute and the Editors Guild of Sri Lanka posthumously awarded Lasantha Wickrematunge with the Sepala Gunasena Award for Defending Press Freedom in Sri Lanka.

IPI World Press Freedom Hero Award

In February 2010 Lasantha Wickrematunge was posthumously declared the International Press Institute's 53rd World Press Freedom Hero.

Transparency International Award

In 2000, the global anti-corruption community recognised Lasantha Wickrematunge's fearless pursuit of the truth and the years he spent exposing corruption in Sri Lankan politics by granting him Transparency International's very first Integrity Award.

"As Editor of *The Sunday Leader* newspaper, Lasantha Wickrematunge has earned a reputation for courageous investigative journalism that has been dedicated to exposing corruption in all its forms.

"His exposes' have dealt with issues ranging from petty to grand corruption in areas such as privatisations and arms deals. Lasantha Wickrematunge has demonstrated perseverance in his mission to uncover the truth despite repression from the authorities and physical threats which have included assault and being fired at with automatic weapons.

"When government authorities shut down his newspaper in May 2000, he fought back and succeeded in resuming publication.

"In presenting this Integrity Award, Transparency International wishes to recognise the fundamental role of a free and independent press in fostering accountability and transparency and to acknowledge the great courage of Lasantha Wickrematunge in pursuing this goal regardless of the dangers and hardships he was made to endure."

Lightning Source UK Ltd.
Milton Keynes UK
UKOW04f1901251114

242177UK00001B/25/P